POISONED PENS

POISONED PENS

Literary invective from
Amis to Zola

edited by
Gary Dexter

POISONED PENS

Frances Lincoln Limited
4 Torriano Mews
Torriano Avenue
London NW5 2RZ
www.franceslincoln.com

First paperback edition 2010

British Library Cataloguing in Publication Data
A catalogue record for this book is available from the British Library

ISBN 978-0-7112-3162-7

Printed in the UK by CPI Bookmarque, Croydon, CR0 4TD

9 8 7 6 5 4 3 2 1

CONTENTS

INTRODUCTION

Given the choice, which of the following two quotes by George Bernard Shaw is the more amusing?

> I pity the man who cannot enjoy Shakespear. He has outlasted thousands of abler thinkers, and will outlast a thousand more.

Or:

> With the single exception of Homer, there is no eminent writer, not even Sir Walter Scott, whom I can despise so entirely as I despise Shakespear when I measure my mind against his. The intensity of my impatience with him occasionally reaches such a pitch, that it would positively be a relief to me to dig him up and throw stones at him, knowing as I do how incapable he and his worshippers are of understanding any less obvious form of indignity.

Very little contest. The nasty Shaw contains infinitely more Shaw than the nice Shaw. Here is genuine passion and indignation. Shaw knew that posterity would never bestow the same garlands on *Caesar and Cleopatra* as it had on *Antony and Cleopatra*, and found it difficult to bear.

When writers write negatively about other writers there are three reasons (that I can think of) for giving them consideration.

Firstly, attacks by writers on other writers confirm our reasonable suspicions that some of the canonized masters have occasionally been over-rated by timid critics and snobs. After having struggled through Browning's denser works – *Sordello* or *The Ring and the Book* – how interesting to read the following anecdote:

> Lord Tennyson manfully tackled *Sordello*, but is reported to have admitted in bitterness of spirit: 'There were only two lines in it that I understood, and they were both lies: "Who will may hear Sordello's story told" and "Who would has heard Sordello's story told."'

So not only are we *not* idiots but we concur with Tennyson!

Secondly, what is negative is, if nothing else, generally sincere. Good reports of fellow writers can easily be flattery or log-rolling: just think of the ways book-reviewers operate. It is only in the negative and the scabrous that we can be sure of a writer's true feelings.

Thirdly, writers often do their best work when they are attacking other writers. Sometimes writers are remembered more for their attacks than for anything else they ever wrote. Edmund Gosse gave the following warning to ambitious critics: 'Never mind whom you praise, but be very careful whom you blame.' He went on:

> Who recollects the admirable treatises of John Dennis, acute, learned, sympathetic? To us he is merely the sore old bear, who was too stupid to perceive the genius of Pope. The grace and discrimination lavished by Francis Jeffrey over a thousand pages, weigh like a feather beside one sentence about Wordsworth's *Excursion*, and one tasteless sneer at Charles Lamb. Even the mighty figure of Sainte-Beuve totters at the whisper of the name Balzac. Even Matthew Arnold would have been wiser to have taken counsel with himself before he laughed at Shelley.

Their outbursts of petulance were destined to outshine their most fulsome encomia, and we, the reading public, egged them on.

A few words on the choice of quotes for inclusion here: this book deals, except in a very few cases, with writers on writers; not critics, reviewers or journalists on writers. After fifty years no one cares about what paid hacks might have thought; but what Byron thought of Keats will endure for ever.

Denunciations at length are favoured over one-line waspish barbs. It seems impossible nowadays to have much to say against that colossus, Laurence Sterne: but Walter Scott, given the space, does a great job, comparing him unfavourably to Rabelais and accusing him convincingly of plagiarism and inanity (see page 45). Likewise Forster's lengthy evisceration of Scott carries conviction (see page 61), and Woolf's of Forster (see page 169).

Because this book deals with the abusive and the mocking, there is not always room for the balancing quote (though there has been no editing to take out the balancing if it exists: lacunae do not hide something positive amid the negativity). But if the remark catches the writer on a bad day and he has nice things to say elsewhere, those nice things are occasionally given in a footnote.

The book is ordered chronologically, in five sections, so that 'friends' from the Classical, Augustan, Romantic, Victorian and Modern periods are grouped together and their opinions of one another can be more readily studied. Although this book does include many barbs directed at writers who wrote in languages other than English – at Dostoevsky, Zola, Flaubert, Hugo, Tolstoy, Sand, Goethe, Schiller, Eco, Cervantes, Dante and others – the emphasis is generally on the writers most familiar to English-speaking readers.

Gary Dexter

1 CONTEMPT FOR THE CLASSICS

Where there are writers there are rivalries: this has always been true and presumably always will be. Literature is a competitive sport. Even at the dawn of literature we find Aristophanes attacking Euripides (he felt him to be too modern) and Socrates (whom he considered merely a paid Sophist). Homer, Cicero, Chaucer, Dante – all came in for similar treatment. The splenetic colleagues who attacked them rendered us, the readers, an important service. They removed from our shoulders the burden of respect for the founts of European culture.

Of all such burdens, possibly the greatest, for the English-speaking reader, is respect for Shakespeare. He is worshipped everywhere – 'on this side idolatry', as Ben Jonson put it. But it was not always so. In fact, not so long ago, Shakespeare was just an also-ran, hardly more esteemed than Beaumont, Fletcher, Rowley or Middleton. In the seventeenth century, the marvel of the previous hundred years was not Shakespeare but Sir Philip Sidney (whose works, though doubtless influential, are now hardly ever read). 'Sidney the Lawrell wore, Spenser and Shakespeare did in art excel,' wrote John Taylor (the 'Water-poet') – putting Shakespeare third – and it seems to have been a popular view. Others set Jonson above Shakespeare, or even Fletcher above Shakespeare. In 1647 William Cartwright addressed these lines to Fletcher:

> Shakespeare to thee was dull, whose best jest lyes
> I'th Ladies questions, and the Fooles replyes;
> Old fashion'd wit, which walkt from town to town
> In turn'd Hose, which our fathers call'd the Clown;
> Whose wit our nice times would obsceannesse call,
> And which made Bawdry passe for Comicall:
> Nature was all his Art, thy veine was free
> As his, but without his scurility.

This, for a century or so, was the common charge against Shakespeare: he was egregious. We find it in Dryden, Johnson, Pepys and Voltaire, and it survived almost to the modern era in such notable exponents of Shakespeare-hatred as Tolstoy ('the unquestionable glory of a great genius which Shakespeare enjoys [...] is a great evil, as is

every untruth') and Shaw. Why is there no modern celebrated
Shakespeare-hater? Why do we not have a Shakespeare-hating Salman
Rushdie, or a Shakespeare-hating Doris Lessing?

This initial selection ends with Milton. There are of course many
reasons to dislike Milton, not least that given by William Blake ('he was
of the Devils party without knowing it'). One opinion not given here
is that of Kingsley Amis, writing in 1947 about Dylan Thomas, but
worth quoting because of the way his anger transfers itself to Milton:

> I have got to the stage now with mr toss that I have only
> reached with Chaucer and Dryden, not even with Milton, that
> of VIOLENTLY WISHING that the man WERE IN FRONT OF ME, SO
> that I could be DEMONIACALLY RUDE to him about his
> GONORRHEIC RUBBISH, and end up by WALKING ON HIS FACE and
> PUNCHING HIS PRIVY PARTS.

HOMER c.9TH CENTURY BC

Thomas De Quincey (1785–1859) on Homer

There is no moral, little or big, foul or fair, to the *Iliad* [. . .] If you
insist on *my* telling *you* what is the moral of the *Iliad*, I insist upon *your*
telling *me* what is the moral of a rattlesnake, or the moral of a Niagara.
I suppose the moral is – that you must get out of their way, if you
mean to moralise much longer. The going-up (or anabasis) of the
Greeks against Troy, was a *fact*, and a pretty dense fact; and, by accident,
the very first in which all Greece had a common interest. It was a
joint-stock concern – a representative expedition [. . .] There was no
state-cabin; everybody, demigods and all, pigged in the steerage,
amongst beans and bacon. Greece was naturally proud of having
crossed the herring-pond, small as it was, in search of an entrenched
enemy; proud also of having licked him 'into almighty smash'; this was
sufficient; or if an impertinent moralist sought for something more,
doubtless the moral must have lain in the booty. A peach is the moral
of a peach, and moral enough; but if a man *will* have something better
– a moral within a moral – why, there is the peach-stone, and its
kernel, out of which he may make ratafia, which seems to be the

ultimate morality that *can* be extracted from a peach.

'Milton *versus* Southey and Landor', in *Tait's Edinburgh Magazine*, 1847, in
De Quincey as Critic, ed. J.E. Jordan (1973)

EURIPIDES *c.*480 BC–406 BC

Aristophanes[1] (*c.*446 BC–386 BC) on Euripides

EURIPIDES: Don't talk to me; I won't give up the chair, I say
 I am better in the art than he.

DIONYSUS: You hear him, Aeschylus: why don't you speak?

EURIPIDES: He'll do the grand at first, the juggling trick
 He used to play in all his tragedies.

DIONYSUS: Come, my fine fellow, pray don't talk too big.

EURIPIDES: I know the man, I've scanned him through and
 through,
 A savage-creating stubborn-pulling fellow,
 Uncurbed, unfettered, uncontrolled of speech,
 Unperiphrastic, bombastiloquent.

AESCHYLUS: Hah! sayest thou so, child of the garden quean!
 And this to ME, thou chattery-babble-collector,
 Thou pauper-creating rags-and-patches-stitcher?
 Thou shalt abye it dearly!

DIONYSUS: Pray, be still; nor heat thy soul to fury, Aeschylus.

AESCHYLUS: Not till I've made you see the sort of man
 This cripple-maker is who crows so loudly.

DIONYSUS: Bring out a ewe, a black-fleeced ewe, my boys
 Here's a typhoon about to burst upon us.

AESCHYLUS: Thou picker-up of Cretan monodies,
 Foisting thy tales of incest on the stage—

DIONYSUS: Forbear, forbear, most honoured Aeschylus;
 And you, my poor Euripides, begone
 If you are wise, out of this pitiless hail,

---

[1] From *The Frogs*, the play in which Aristophanes mounts his most concerted attack
on Euripides. The scene is a verbal contest between Aeschylus and Euripides in Hades,
which Aeschylus wins. Euripides had died the year before the play was first produced.

Lest with some heady word he crack your skull
And batter out your brain-less Telephus.
And not with passion, Aeschylus, but calmly
Test and be tested. 'Tis not meet for poets
To scold each other, like two baking-girls.
But you go roaring like an oak on fire.

EURIPIDES: I'm ready, I! I don't draw back one bit.
I'll lash or, if he will, let him lash first
The talk, the lays, the sinews of a play:
Aye and my Peleus, aye and Aeolus,
And Meleager, aye and Telephus.

DIONYSUS: And what do *you* propose? Speak, Aeschylus.

AESCHYLUS: I could have wished to meet him otherwhere.
We fight not here on equal terms.

DIONYSUS: Why not?

AESCHYLUS: My poetry survived me: his died with him:
He's got it here, all handy to recite.
Howbeit, if so you wish it, so we'll have it.

DIONYSUS: O bring me fire, and bring me frankincense.
I'll pray, or e'er the clash of wits begin,
To judge the strife with high poetic skill.
Meanwhile (*to the Chorus*) invoke the Muses with a song.

The Frogs, in *Nine Greek Dramas by Aeschylus, Sophocles, Euripides and Aristophanes*, trans. E.D.A. Morshead et al. (1909)

SOCRATES c.469 BC–399 BC

Aristophanes[2] (c.446 BC–386 BC) on Socrates

PHEIDIPPIDES: But what if, having the worst Cause, I shall

---

[2]   These are the final few lines of Aristophanes' play *The Clouds*: the entire play is an extended attack on Socrates, whom Aristophanes knew personally. Aristophanes presents Socrates as a Sophist, a hired gun who can defend even the most absurd of propositions, advancing weak arguments by using specious reasoning. In *The Clouds* Socrates' school is called the Thinking Shop (or the 'Thinkery'), and among its discoveries are that Jove, chief of the gods, does not exist; and that a gnat hums through its anus. The plot revolves around a father and son, Strepsiades and Pheidippides, who have issues around inter-genera-tional respect. The scene above begins with Pheidippides arguing in favour of

	conquer you in arguing, proving that it is right to beat one's mother?
STREPSIADES:	Most assuredly, if you do this, nothing will hinder you from casting yourself and your Worse Cause into the pit along with Socrates. These evils have I suffered through you, O Clouds! Having entrusted all my affairs to you.
CHORUS:	Nay, rather, you are yourself the cause of these things, having turned yourself to wicked courses.
STREPSIADES:	Why, pray, did you not tell me this, then, but excited with hopes a rustic and aged man?
CHORUS:	We always do this to him whom we perceive to be a lover of wicked courses, until we precipitate him into misfortune, so that he may learn to fear the gods.
STREPSIADES:	Ah me! It is severe, O Clouds! But it is just; for I ought not to have withheld the money which I borrowed. Now, therefore, come with me, my dearest son, that you may destroy the blackguard Chaerephon and Socrates, who deceived you and me.
PHEIDIPPIDES:	I will not injure my teachers.
STREPSIADES:	Yes, yes, reverence Paternal Jove.
PHEIDIPPIDES:	'Paternal Jove' quoth'a! How antiquated you are! Why, is there any Jove?
STREPSIADES:	There is.
PHEIDIPPIDES:	There is not, no; for Vortex reigns having expelled Jupiter.
STREPSIADES:	He has not expelled him; but I fancied this, on account of this Vortex here. Ah me, unhappy man! When I even took you who are of earthenware for a god.
PHEIDIPPIDES:	Here rave and babble to yourself.

[Exit PHEIDIPPIDES]

---

beating his own mother: Strepsiades, in his fury, turns on Socrates and burns down the Thinking Shop. The play has been taken as Aristophanes' attempt to claim the superiority of Poetry over Philosophy, though many scholars argue that Aristophanes was attacking the younger Socrates rather than the mature Socrates, and that the satire was essentially good-natured.

STREPSIADES: Ah me, what madness! How mad, then, I was when I ejected the gods on account of Socrates! But O dear Hermes, by no means be wroth with me, nor destroy me; but pardon me, since I have gone crazy through prating. And become my adviser, whether I shall bring an action and prosecute them, or whatever you think. You advise me rightly, not permitting me to get up a lawsuit, but as soon as possible to set fire to the house of the prating fellows. Come hither, come hither, Xanthias! Come forth with a ladder and with a mattock and then mount upon the Thinking Shop and dig down the roof, if you love your master, until you tumble the house upon them.

[XANTHIAS mounts upon the roof]

But let some one bring me a lighted torch and I'll make some of them this day suffer punishment, even if they be ever so much impostors.

FIRST DISCIPLE (from within): Hollo! Hollo!

STREPSIADES: It is your business, O torch, to send forth abundant flame.

[Mounts upon the roof]

FIRST DISCIPLE: What are you doing, fellow?

STREPSIADES: What am I doing? Why, what else, than chopping logic with the beams of your house?

[Sets the house on fire]

SECOND DISCIPLE (from within): You will destroy us! You will destroy us!

STREPSIADES: For I also wish this very thing; unless my mattock deceive my hopes, or I should somehow fall first and break my neck.

SOCRATES (from within): Hollo you! What are you doing, pray, you fellow on the roof?

STREPSIADES: I am walking on air, and speculating about the sun.

SOCRATES: Ah me, unhappy! I shall be suffocated, wretched man!

CHAEREPHON: And I, miserable man, shall be burnt to death!

STREPSIADES: For what has come into your heads that you acted insolently toward the gods, and pried into the seat of

                    the moon? Chase, pelt, smite them, for many reasons,
                    but especially because you know that they offended
                    against the gods!
[The Thinking Shop is burned down]
CHORUS: Lead the way out; for we have sufficiently acted as
                    chorus for today.

The Clouds, in *The Comedies of Aristophanes*, trans. W.J. Hickie (1853)

Thomas Babington Macaulay (1800–1859) on Socrates

The more I read about him, the less I wonder that they poisoned him.
If he had treated me as he is said to have treated Protagoras, Hippias,
and Gorgias, I could never have forgiven him.

Letter to Thomas Ellis, 29 May 1835, in George Otto Trevelyan,
The Life and Letters of Lord Macaulay (1876)

Bertrand Russell (1872–1970) on Socrates

He is dishonest and sophistical in argument, and in his private thinking
he uses intellect to prove conclusions that are to him agreeable, rather
than in a disinterested search for knowledge. There is something smug
and unctuous about him, which reminds one of a bad type of cleric.
His courage in the face of death would have been more remarkable if
he had not believed that he was going to enjoy eternal bliss in the
company of the gods. Unlike some of his predecessors, he was not
scientific in his thinking, but was determined to prove the universe
agreeable to his ethical standards. This is treachery to truth, and the
worst of philosophic sins. As a man, we may believe him admitted to
the communion of saints; but as a philosopher he needs a long
residence in a scientific purgatory.

A History of Western Philosophy (1945)

ARISTOTLE 384 BC–322 BC

Martin Luther (1483–1546) on Aristotle

Aristotle, that histrionic mountebank, who from behind a Greek mask
has so long bewitched the Church of Christ, that most cunning juggler
of souls, whom, if he had not been accredited as human blood and bone,

we should have been justified in maintaining to be the veritable devil.[3]

Letter, 1516, in John Stuart Blackie, Four Phases of Morals (1871)

Bertrand Russell (1872–1970) on Aristotle

Aristotle could have avoided the mistake of thinking that women have fewer teeth than men, by the simple device of asking Mrs Aristotle to keep her mouth open while he counted.

Unpopular Essays (1950)

MARCUS TULLIUS CICERO 106 BC–43 BC

Michel de Montaigne (1533–1592) on Cicero

But to confess the truth boldly (for once you have crossed over the barriers of impudence there is no more curb), his way of writing, and every other similar way, seems to me boring. For his prefaces, definitions, partitions, etymologies, consume the greater part of his work; what life and marrow there is, is smothered by his long-winded preparations. If I have spent an hour in reading him, which is a lot for me, and I remember what juice and substance I have derived, most of the time I find nothing but wind; for he has not yet come to the arguments that serve his purpose and the reasons that properly touch on the crux, which I am looking for.[4]

'Of Books', 1580, in The Complete Essays of Montaigne,
ed. D. Frame (1958)

---

[3] This is not an isolated remark by Luther. Elsewhere he said: 'What will they not believe who have credited that ridiculous and injurious blasphemer Aristotle? His propositions are so absurd that an ass or a stone would cry out at them' and 'It is my advice that the books of Aristotle – Physics, Metaphysics, The Soul, and Ethics – which have hitherto been esteemed the best, be entirely removed [from the curriculum].' His enmity was due to his perception of Aristotle as the chief prop of Catholic and Scholastic theology.

[4] Montaigne's estimation of Cicero was mixed: he found Cicero too smooth, remarking that 'there was not much excellence in his soul', yet also said that 'Cicero's eloquence will never be matched' and that he was 'a good citizen, of an affable nature'.

GEOFFREY CHAUCER c.1343–1400

George Gordon, Lord Byron (1788–1824) on Chaucer

Chaucer notwithstanding the praises bestowed on him, I think obscene, and contemptible, he owes his celebrity, merely to his antiquity, which he does not deserve so well as Pierce Plowman, or Thomas of Ercildoune.[5]

> Memorandum book dated 30 November 1807, in *Life, Letters, and Journals of Lord Byron*, ed. T. Moore (1839)

DANTE ALIGHIERI c.1265–1321

Saverio Bettinelli[6] (1718–1808) on Dante

On the front I read *The Divine Comedy of Dante*, and it seemed a strange title to everyone, since we were convinced that this had to be an epic poem, which the whole of Italy was praising on a par with the *Iliad* and the *Aeneid*, nor could we understand why it was entitled *Comedy*. And it seemed even stranger when we found this *Divine Comedy* to be divided into three parts, as though it were a scientific treatise, and these parts were to be entitled *Hell, Purgatory* and *Paradise*. It occurred to everyone that Dante meant to jest, and indeed to make a comedy, but to us such tremendous and venerable names did not seem too suitable for this.

[…] But very soon I was seized with boredom as I continued to read. Why then, I asked, has Dante made a poem of Hell, Purgatory and Paradise, if he has actually read the *Aeneid*? I certainly have not taught him to begin with a dream, a wolf and a lion, or with dividing the poem into parts which are mutually repellent and distant one from

---

[5]   aka Thomas the Rhymer, known chiefly for the ballad named after him.

[6]   Bettinelli, a Jesuit polemicist and critic, is writing here in the persona of Virgil (Dante's guide in the *Divine Comedy*). Virgil is depicted lounging with his fellow antique poets Lucretius, Ovid, Homer and others, and discussing the parlous state of modern Italian poetry. Bettinelli is thus not to be taken entirely seriously; but from other remarks elsewhere in his own voice (Dante is 'hard and barbarous in taste and language') it is clear that this attack is not too far from representing his own feelings.

the other. […] Has he perchance learnt it from me, to make Beatrice come and look for me, Beatrice who had been called by Lucia, by Lucia who sat I know not where, together with ancient Rachel, and other such nonsense? What could I know of Can della Scala, or of the 'chosen vessel', which he links with Aeneas, or with a hundred such matters? The more one read, the less one understood, even though to each word there was a note, and to each note a commentary more obscure than the text, but yet equally long, so that the volume was in folio. […] Lucretius himself yawned, the Greeks were disgusted, no one saw what was being talked about, and, among them all, Ovid burst out laughing, declaring the poem to be a chaos of confusion greater than anything he had described.

Lettere virgiliane, 1757, ed. V.E. Alfieri (1930)

MIGUEL CERVANTES 1547–1616

Martin Amis (1949–) on Cervantes

While clearly an impregnable masterpiece, *Don Quixote* suffers from one fairly serious flaw – that of outright unreadability. This reviewer should know, because he has just read it. The book bristles with beauties, charm, sublime comedy; it is also, for long stretches (approaching about 75 per cent of the whole), inhumanly dull. Looming like one of the Don's chimerical adversaries, it is a giant 'with legs like lofty steeples, and arms resembling the masts of vast and warlike ships; while each eye, as large as a millwheel, beams and burns like a glass furnace'. But the giant has a giant weight problem, and is elderly, and soft-brained. Reading *Don Quixote* can be compared to an indefinite visit from your most impossible senior relative, with all his pranks, dirty habits, unstoppable reminiscences, and terrible cronies. When the experience is over, and the old boy checks out at last (on page 846 – the prose wedged tight, with no breaks for dialogue), you will shed tears all right: not tears of relief or regret but tears of pride. You made it, despite all that *Don Quixote* could do.

Written in the days before novel-reviewing – indeed, in the days before novels – *Don Quixote* was probably never intended to be read in the modern manner: that is, straight through. Group or family recitations of a chapter a night were, in all likelihood, the most that Cervantes expected anyone to manage. His epic is epic in length only; it has no pace, no drive. An anthology, an agglomeration, it simply accrues. The question 'What happens next?' has no meaning, because there is no next in *Don Quixote*'s world: there is only more.

> Review of *Don Quixote* in *Atlantic Monthly*, March 1986,
> in *The War Against Cliché* (2001)

EDMUND SPENSER 1552–1599

John Dryden (1631–1700) on Spenser

The English have only to boast of Spenser and Milton, who neither of them wanted either genius or learning to have been perfect poets; and yet both of them are liable to many censures. For there is no uniformity in the design of Spenser; he aims at the accomplishment of no one action; he raises up a hero for every one of his adventures, and endows each of them with some particular moral virtue, which renders them all equal, without subordination or preference: every one is most valiant in his own legend: only we must do him that justice to observe that magnanimity, which is the character of Prince Arthur, shines throughout the whole poem, and succours the rest when they are in distress. The original of every knight was then living in the court of Queen Elizabeth, and he attributed to each of them that virtue which he thought was most conspicuous in them – an ingenious piece of flattery, though it turned not much to his account. Had he lived to finish his poem in the six remaining legends, it had certainly been more of a piece; but could not have been perfect, because the model was not true. But Prince Arthur, or his chief patron Sir Philip Sidney, whom he intended to make happy by the marriage of his Gloriana, dying before him, deprived the poet both of means and spirit to accomplish his design.

> *A Discourse Concerning the Original and Progress of Satire* (1693)

James Russell Lowell (1819–1891) on Spenser

As a narrative [*The Faerie Queene*] has, I think, every fault of which that kind of writing is capable. The characters are vague, and, even were they not, they drop out of the story so often and remain out of it so long, that we have forgotten who they are when we meet them again; the episodes hinder the advance of the action instead of relieving it with variety of incident or novelty of situation; the plot, if plot it may be called,

> That shape has none
> Distinguishable in member, joint, or limb[7]

recalls drearily our ancient enemy, the Metrical Romance; while the fighting, which, in those old poems, was tediously sincere, is between shadow and shadow, where we know that neither can harm the other, though are tempted to wish he might. Hazlitt bids us not mind the allegory, and says that it won't bite us nor meddle with us if we do not meddle with it. But how if it bore us, which after all is the fatal question? The truth is that it is too often forced upon us against our will, as people were formerly driven to church till they began to look on a day of rest as a penal institution, and to transfer to the Scriptures that suspicion of defective inspiration which was awakened in them by the preaching. The true type of the allegory is the Odyssey, which we read without suspicion as pure poem, and then find a new pleasure in divining its double meaning, as if we somehow got a better bargain of our author than he meant to give us. But this complex feeling must not be so exacting as to prevent our lapsing into the old Arabian Nights simplicity of interest again. The moral of a poem should be suggested, as when in some mediaeval church we cast down our eyes to muse over a fresco of Giotto, and are reminded of the transitoriness of life by the mortuary tablets under our feet. The vast superiority of Bunyan over Spenser lies in the fact that we help make his allegory out of our own experience. Instead of striving to embody abstract passions and temptations, he has given us his own in all their pathetic simplicity. He is the Ulysses of his own prose-epic. This is the secret of his power and his charm, that, while the representation of what may happen to all men comes home to none of us in particular, the story of any one man's real experience finds its startling parallel in that of every one of us. The very homeliness of Bunyan's names and the everydayness of his

---

[7]   From Milton's *Paradise Lost*, Bk II.

scenery, too, put us off our guard, and we soon find ourselves on as easy a footing with his allegorical beings as we might be with Adam or Socrates in a dream. Indeed, he has prepared us for such incongruities by telling us at setting out that the story was of a dream. The long nights of Bedford jail had so intensified his imagination, and made the figures with which it peopled his solitude so real to him, that the creatures of his mind become *things*, as clear to the memory as if we had seen them. But Spenser's are too often mere names, with no bodies to back them, entered on the Muses' musterroll by the specious trick of personification. [. . .] As Bunyan rises not seldom to a natural poetry, so Spenser sinks now and then, through the fault of his topics, to unmistakable prose. Take his description of the House of Alma, for instance: –

> The master cook was cald Concoctioen,
> A careful man, and full of comely guise;
> The kitchen-clerk, that hight Digestion,
> Did order all the achates in seemly wise.

And so on through all the organs of the body.[8] [. . .] This, I admit, is the worst failure of Spenser in this kind; though, even here, when he gets on to the organs of the mind, the enchantments of his fancy and style come to the rescue and put us in good-humor again, hard as it is to conceive of armed knights entering the chamber of the mind, and talking with such visionary damsels as Ambition and Shamefastness.

Spenser (1875)

WILLIAM SHAKESPEARE 1564–1616

John Dryden (1631–1700) on Shakespeare

Shakspeare, who many times has written better than any poet in any language, is yet so far from writing wit always, or expressing that wit

---

[8]   C.S. Lewis agreed, saying '[Spenser] can be as prosaic as Wordsworth: he can be clumsy, unmusical and flat.' Most critics who deprecate Spenser, however, admit to their partiality for him; Lowell was no exception. Elsewhere he says: 'There is much in Spenser that is contemporary and evanescent; but the substance of him is durable, and his work was the deliberate result of intelligent purpose and ample culture.'

according to the dignity of the subject, that he writes in many places below the dullest writers of ours or of any precedent age. Never did any author precipitate himself from such heights of thought to so low expressions, as he often does. He is the very Janus of poets; he wears almost every where two faces; and you have scarce begun to admire the one, ere you despise the other.

'Defence of the Epilogue', 1672, in *The Critical and Miscellaneous Prose Works of John Dryden*, ed. E. Malone (1800)

Samuel Johnson (1709–1784) on Shakespeare

He [i.e. Johnson] again talked of the passage in Congreve with high commendation, and said, 'Shakspeare never has six lines together without a fault. Perhaps you may find seven, but this does not refute my general assertion. If I come to an orchard, and say there's no fruit here, and then comes a poring man, who finds two apples and three pears, and tells me, "Sir, you are mistaken, I have found both apples and pears," I should laugh at him: what would that be to the purpose?'

In James Boswell, *Life of Johnson* (1791)

Ben Jonson (1572–1637) on Shakespeare

I remember the players have often mentioned it as an honour to Shakspeare, that in his writing (whatsoever he penned) he never blotted out a line. My answer hath been, 'Would he had blotted a thousand,' which they thought a malevolent speech. I had not told posterity this but for their ignorance who chose that circumstance to commend their friend by wherein he most faulted; and to justify mine own candour, for I loved the man, and do honour his memory on this side idolatry as much as any. He was, indeed, honest, and of an open and free nature, had an excellent phantasy, brave notions, and gentle expressions, wherein he flowed with that facility that sometimes it was necessary he should be stopped. *Sufflaminandus erat,*[9] as Augustus said of Haterius. His wit was in his own power; would the rule of it had been so, too. Many times he fell into those things, could not escape laughter, as when he said in the person of Cæsar, one speaking to him, 'Cæsar, thou dost me wrong.' He replied, 'Cæsar did never wrong but with just cause;' and

---

[9]   'He had to be suppressed.'

such like, which were ridiculous. But he redeemed his vices with his virtues. There was ever more in him to be praised than to be pardoned.

Timber, Or Discoveries (1640)

Samuel Pepys (1633–1703) on Shakespeare

I sent for some dinner and there dined, Mrs. Margaret Pen being by, to whom I had spoke to go along with us to a play this afternoon, and then to the King's Theatre, where we saw 'Midsummer's Night's Dream', which I had never seen before, nor shall ever again, for it is the most insipid ridiculous play that ever I saw in my life.

Diary for 29 September 1662

George Bernard Shaw (1856–1950) on Shakespeare

There are moments when one asks despairingly why our stage should ever have been cursed with this 'immortal' pilferer of other men's stories and ideas, with his monstrous rhetorical fustian, his unbearable platitudes, his pretentious reduction of the subtlest problems of life to commonplaces against which a Polytechnic debating club would revolt, his incredible unsuggestiveness, his sententious combination of ready reflection with complete intellectual sterility, and his consequent incapacity for getting out of the depth of even the most ignorant audience, except when he solemnly says something so transcendently platitudinous that his more humble-minded hearers cannot bring themselves to believe that so great a man really meant to talk like their grandmothers. With the single exception of Homer, there is no eminent writer, not even Sir Walter Scott, whom I can despise so entirely as I despise Shakespear when I measure my mind against his. The intensity of my impatience with him occasionally reaches such a pitch, that it would positively be a relief to me to dig him up and throw stones at him, knowing as I do how incapable he and his worshippers are of understanding any less obvious form of indignity. To read Cymbeline and to think of Goethe, of Wagner, of Ibsen, is, for me, to imperil the habit of studied moderation of statement which years of public responsibility as a journalist have made almost second nature to me.[10]

The Saturday Review, 22 September 1896

---

[10] In the same piece he adds, however: 'I am bound to add that I pity the man who cannot enjoy Shakspear. He has outlasted thousands of abler thinkers and will outlast a thousand more.'

Voltaire (1694–1778) on Shakespeare

Englishmen believe in ghosts no more than the Romans did, yet they take pleasure in the tragedy of *Hamlet*, in which the ghost of a king appears on the stage. Far be it from me to justify everything in that tragedy; it is a vulgar and barbarous drama, which would not be tolerated by the vilest populace of France, or Italy. Hamlet becomes crazy in the second act, and his mistress becomes crazy in the third; the prince slays the father of his mistress under the pretence of killing a rat, and the heroine throws herself into the river; a grave is dug on the stage, and the grave-diggers talk quodlibets worthy of themselves, while holding skulls in their hands; Hamlet responds to their nasty vulgarities in sillinesses no less disgusting. In the meanwhile another of the actors conquers Poland. Hamlet, his mother, and his father-in-law carouse on the stage; songs are sung at table; there is quarrelling, fighting, killing – one would imagine this piece to be the work of a drunken savage. But amidst all these vulgar irregularities, which to this day make the English drama so absurd and so barbarous, there are to be found in *Hamlet*, by a *bizarrerie* still greater, some sublime passages, worthy of the greatest genius. It seems as though nature had mingled in the brain of Shakespeare the greatest conceivable strength and grandeur with whatsoever witless vulgarity can devise that is lowest and most detestable.

Théâtre Complet, 1768, in *A New Variorum Edition of Shakespeare*,
ed. H.H. Furness (1877)

JOHN DONNE 1572–1631

Thomas De Quincey (1785–1859) on Donne

I have heard it said, by the way, that Donne's intolerable defect of ear grew out of his own baptismal name, when harnessed to his own surname – John Donne. No man, it was said, who had listened to this hideous jingle from childish years, could fail to have his genius for discord, and the abominable in sound, improved to the utmost.

Literary Reminiscences: From The Autobiography of an English Opium-eater (1851)

Edmund Gosse (1849–1928) on Donne

His writings, like his actions, were faulty, violent, a little morbid even, and abnormal. He was not, and did not attempt to be, an average man.

But actions and writings alike, in their strangeness and aloofness, were unadulterated by a tinge of affectation.

The Life and Letters of John Donne (1899)

Henry Hallam[11] (1777–1859) on Donne

Donne is the most inharmonious of our versifiers, if he can be said to have deserved such a name by lines too rugged to seem metre. Of his earlier poems many are very licentious; the later are chiefly devout. Few are good for much; the conceits have not even the merit of being intelligible; it would perhaps be difficult to select three passages that we should care to read again.

Introduction to the Literature of Europe (1864)

BEN JONSON 1572–1637

William Hazlitt (1778–1830) on Jonson

There are people who cannot taste olives – and I cannot much relish Ben Jonson, though I have taken some pains to do it, and went to the task with every sort of good will. I do not deny his power or his merit; far from it: but it is to me of a repulsive and unamiable kind. He was a great man in himself, but one cannot readily sympathize with him. His works, as the characteristic productions of an individual mind, or as records of the manners of a particular age, cannot be valued too highly; but they have little charm for the mere general reader. Schlegel observes, that whereas Shakspeare gives the springs of human nature, which are always the same, or sufficiently so to be interesting and intelligible; Jonson chiefly gives the *humours* of men, as connected with certain arbitrary or conventional modes of dress, action, and expression, which are intelligible only while they last, and not very interesting at any time. Shakspeare's characters are men; Ben Jonson's are more like machines, governed by mere routine, or by the convenience of the poet, whose property they are. In reading the one, we are let into the minds of his characters, we see the play of their thoughts, how their humours flow and work: the author takes a range over nature, and has

---

[11] Historian and critic: father of Arthur Henry Hallam, the dedicatee of Tennyson's 'In Memoriam A.H.H.'.

an eye to every object or occasion that presents itself to set off and heighten the ludicrous character he is describing. His humour (so to speak) bubbles, sparkles, and finds its way in all directions, like a natural spring. In Ben Jonson it is, as it were, confined in a leaden cistern, where it stagnates and corrupts; or directed only through certain artificial pipes and conduits, to answer a given purpose. The comedy of this author is far from being 'lively, audible, and full of vent':[12] it is for the most part obtuse, obscure, forced, and tedious. He wears out a jest to the last shred and coarsest grain. His imagination fastens instinctively on some one mark or sign by which he designates the individual, and never lets it go, for fear of not meeting with any other means to express himself by. A cant phrase, an odd gesture, an old-fashioned regimental uniform, a wooden leg, a tobacco-box, or a hacked sword, are the standing topics by which he embodies his characters to the imagination. They are cut and dried comedy; the letter, not the spirit of wit and humour. Each of his characters has a particular cue, a professional badge which he wears and is known by, and by nothing else. [. . .] There is almost a total want of variety, fancy, relief, and of those delightful transitions which abound, for instance, in Shakspeare's tragi-comedy. In Ben Jonson, we find ourselves generally in low company, and we see no hope of getting out of it. He is like a person who fastens upon a disagreeable subject, and cannot be persuaded to leave it.

Lectures on the English Comic Writers (1819)

JOHN MILTON 1608–1674

Walter Bagehot (1826–1877) on Milton

Of a court, a poet can make but little; of a heaven, he can make very little; but of a courtly heaven, such as Milton conceived, he can make nothing at all. The idea of a court and the idea of a heaven are so radically different, that a distinct combination of them is always grotesque and often ludicrous. *Paradise Lost*, as a whole, is radically tainted by a vicious principle. It professes to justify the ways of God to

---

[12]   From *Coriolanus*: 'Let me have war, say I; it exceeds peace as far as day does night; it's spritely, waking, audible, and full of vent.'

man, to account for sin and death, and it tells you that the whole originated in a *political event*; in a court squabble as to a particular act of patronage and the due or undue promotion of an eldest son. Satan may have been wrong, but on Milton's theory he had an *arguable* case at least. There was something arbitrary in the promotion; there were little symptoms of a job; in *Paradise Lost* it is always clear that the devils are the weaker, but it is never clear that the angels are the better. Milton's sympathy and his imagination slip back to the Puritan rebels whom he loved, and desert the courtly angels whom he could not love, although he praised them. There is no wonder that Milton's hell is better than his heaven, for he hated officials and he loved rebels, for he employs his genius below, and accumulates his pedantry above.

Art in English Poetry (1864)

William Blake (1757–1827) on Milton
The reason Milton wrote in fetters when he wrote of Angels & God, and at liberty when of Devils and Hell, is because he was a true Poet and of the Devils party without knowing it.

The Marriage of Heaven and Hell (1827)

Samuel Johnson (1709–1784) on Milton
The want of human interest is always felt. *Paradise Lost* is one of the books which the reader admires and lays down, and forgets to take up again. None ever wished it longer than it is. Its perusal is a duty rather than a pleasure. We read Milton for instruction, retire harassed and overburdened, and look elsewhere for recreation; we desert our master, and seek for companions.

Lives of the Poets (1779–81)

One of his objections to academical education, as it was then conducted, is, that men designed for orders in the church were permitted to act plays, writhing and unboning their clergy limbs to all the antic and dishonest gestures of trincalos, buffoons, and bawds, prostituting the shame of that ministry which they had, or were near having, to the eyes of courtiers and court ladies, their grooms and mademoiselles.

This is sufficiently peevish in a man, who, when he mentions his exile from the college, relates, with great luxurance, the compensation which the pleasures of the theatre afford him. Plays were therefore only criminal when they were acted by academics.

Lives of the Poets (1779–81)

Claudius Salmasius (1588–1653) on Milton
[A] puppy, once my pretty little man, now blear-eyed, or rather a blindling; having never had any mental vision, he has now lost his bodily sight; a silly coxcomb, fancying himself a beauty; an unclean beast, with nothing more human about him than his guttering eyelids; the fittest doom for him would be to hang him on the highest gallows, and set his head on the Tower of London.[13]

Ad Ioannem Miltonum Responsio, 1660, in Mark Pattison, *Milton* (1926)

William Winstanley (d. 1698) on Milton
John Milton was one whose natural parts might deservedly give him a place amongst the principal of our English Poets, having written two Heroick Poems and a Tragedy, namely *Paradice Lost, Paradice Regain'd*, and *Sampson Agonista*. But his Fame is gone out like a Candle in a Snuff, and his Memory will always stink, which might have ever lived in honourable Repute, had not he been a notorious Traytor, and most impiously and villanously bely'd that blessed Martyr, King *Charles* the First.[14]

Lives of the Most Famous English Poets, 1687, in Edmund Gosse,

Gossip in a Library (1913)

---

[13]   Salmasius's attack was in response to Milton's hostile comments on Salmasius's *Defensio regio Carolo I* (1649).

[14]   Edmund Gosse adds: 'Mr. Winstanley does not leave us in any doubt of his own political bias, and his mode is simply infamous. It is the roughest and most unpardonable expression now extant of the prejudice generally felt against Milton in London, after the Restoration – a prejudice which even Dryden, who in his heart knew better, could not wholly resist. This one sentence is all that most readers of seventeenth-century literature know about Winstanley, and it is not surprising that it has created an objection to him. I forget who it was, among the critics of the beginning of this century, who was accustomed to buy copies of the *Lives of the English Poets* wherever he could pick them up, and burn them, in piety to the angry spirit of Milton. This was certainly more sensible conduct than that of the Italian nobleman, who used to build MSS. of Martial into little pyres, and consume them with spices, to express his admiration of Catullus. But no one can wonder that the world has not forgiven Winstanley for that atrocious phrase about Milton's fame having "gone out

2 DISGUST FOR THE AUGUSTANS

Dryden is commonly held to have ushered in the Augustan Age in English literature (so called because George I referred to himself as a 'second Augustus': George's reign began in August, and he was certainly buried in August). Dryden is therefore seen as a sort of John-the-Baptist-figure to the brilliance of Pope, with whom the Age really got going. Dryden has often been criticized less for being merely second-rate and more for being a sort of literary tart. Macaulay, an unfailingly entertaining critic (he had sharp words, as will be seen, for Johnson, Byron and others, and mounted his most savage attack on Boswell) – described Dryden as exhibiting 'the sluttish magnificence of a Russian noble, all vermin and diamonds, dirty linen and inestimable sables'. Johnson too deprecated Dryden as vain and sloppy.

Pope dominated the Augustan Age almost from the cradle. He wrote the well-known 'Ode on Solitude' ('Happy the man, whose wish and care/A few paternal acres bound') aged twelve. He owed a lot to Dryden: his *Dunciad* drew on Dryden's own score-settling epic, *MacFlecknoe* (directed against Thomas Shadwell, who got the last laugh by becoming poet laureate). Because of Pope's scintillatingly poisonous efforts, the Augustan era was perhaps the most quarrelsome period ever in English letters. Pope's enemies, at various times, included John Dennis, Ambrose Philips, John Hervey, Lady Mary Wortley Montagu, John Ozell and Colley Cibber, to name only the most prominent; he carried pistols to defend himself against people who had strong opinions about pastoral poetry; he walked out, moreover, with a Great Dane almost as tall as he was; and his Scriblerus faction, which set itself up to mock the Whig (Robert Walpole-supporting) literary establishment, mustered some of the greatest literary figures of the period, among them Henry Fielding, John Gay and Jonathan Swift (though perhaps not everyone thought that Swift was quite that great; Johnson thought that *A Tale of a Tub* was too good to have come from the pen of the Dean, and was probably written by his cousin Thomas).

---

like a candle in a snuff, so that his memory will always stink." No, Mr. William Winstanley, it is your own name that – smells so very unpleasantly.' Gosse goes on to doubt whether Winstanley even wrote the words, speculating that they may have been an interpolation by another hand at a later date.

In previous centuries we find much literary criticism but little personal anecdote. In the Augustan era we are blessed with much literary anecdote – on Pope by Cibber, on Richardson by Boswell, on Johnson by Walpole. Much, happily, is negative.

One of the strangest figures of this era was Oliver Goldsmith. He worked as an apothecary's assistant to make ends meet, and was dubbed by Horace Walpole 'the inspired idiot'. Johnson said of him: 'He left scarcely any style of writing untouched, and touched nothing that he did not adorn.' This was an epitaph composed for Goldsmith's tombstone, however. In life, Johnson said of Goldsmith: 'It is amazing how little Goldsmith knows. He seldom comes where he is not more ignorant than any one else.'

JOHN DRYDEN 1631–1700

Samuel Johnson (1709–1784) on Dryden

He had a vanity, unworthy of his abilities, to show, as may be suspected, the rank of the company with whom he lived, by the use of French words, which had then crept into conversation; such as *fraicheur* for *coolness*, *fougue* for *turbulence* and a few more, none of which the language has incorporated or retained. They continue only where they stood first, perpetual warnings to future innovators.

These are his faults of affectation; his faults of negligence are beyond recital. Such is the unevenness of his compositions, that ten lines are seldom found together without something of which the reader is ashamed. Dryden was no rigid judge of his own pages; he seldom struggled after supreme excellence, but snatched in haste what was within his reach; and when he could content others, was himself contented. He did not keep present to his mind an idea of pure perfection; nor compare his works, such as they were, with what they might be made.[15]

Life of Dryden (1779)

---

[15]   It is striking the correspondence between Johnson's opinion here, and that of Macaulay – the later writer – in the passage that follows.

Thomas Babington Macaulay (1800–1859) on Dryden

His critical works are, beyond all comparison, superior to any which had, till then, appeared in England. They were generally intended as apologies for his own poems, rather than as expositions of general principles; he therefore often attempts to deceive the reader by sophistry which could scarcely have deceived himself. His dicta are the dicta, not of a judge, but of an advocate; often of an advocate in an unsound cause. Yet, in the very act of misrepresenting the laws of composition, he shows how well he understands them. But he was perpetually acting against his better knowledge. His sins were sins against light. He trusted that what was bad would be pardoned for the sake of what was good. What was good, he took no pains to make better. He was not, like most persons who rise to eminence, dissatisfied even with his best productions. He had set up no unattainable standard of perfection, the contemplation of which might at once improve and mortify him. His path was not attended by an unapproachable mirage of excellence, for ever receding and for ever pursued. He was not disgusted by the negligence of others, and he extended the same toleration to himself. His mind was of a slovenly character – fond of splendour, but indifferent to neatness. Hence most of his writings exhibit the sluttish magnificence of a Russian noble, all vermin and diamonds, dirty linen and inestimable sables. Those faults which spring from affectation, time and thought in a great measure removed from his poems. But his carelessness he retained to the last. If towards the close of his life he less frequently went wrong from negligence, it was only because long habits of composition rendered it more easy to go right. In his best pieces, we find false rhymes – triplets, in which the third line appears to be a mere intruder, and, while it breaks the music, adds nothing to the meaning – gigantic Alexandrines of fourteen and sixteen syllables, and truncated verses for which he never troubled himself to find a termination or a partner.

Critical and Miscellaneous Essays (1854)

DANIEL DEFOE c.1659–1731

Walter Scott (1771–1832) on Defoe

In general the language is loose and inaccurate, often tame and creeping, and almost always that of the lower classes in society. Neither does the charm depend upon the character of the incidents; for although in *Robinson Crusoe* the incidents are very fine, yet in the *History of the Plague* the events are disgusting, and scarce less in these works where the scene lies in low life. Yet, like Pistol eating his leek, we go on growling and reading to the end of the volume, while we nod over many a more elegant subject, treated by authors who exhibit a far greater command of language. Neither can it be the artful conducting of the story, by which we are so much interested. De Foe seems to have written too rapidly to pay the least attention to this circumstance; the incidents are huddled together like paving-stones discharged from a cart, and have as little connexion between the one and the other. The scenes merely follow, without at all depending on each other. They are not like those of the regular drama, connected together by a regular commencement, continuation, and conclusion, but rather resemble the pictures in a showman's box, which have no relation further than as being enclosed within the same box, and subjected to the action of the same string.

'Daniel De Foe', in *The Complete Works of Sir Walter Scott* (1847)

Anthony Trollope (1815–1882) on Defoe

Robinson Crusoe did not deal with love. Defoe's other stories, which are happily forgotten, are bad in their very essence. *Roxana* is an accurate example of what a bad book may be. It relates the adventures of a woman thoroughly depraved, and yet for the most part successful, – is intended to attract by its licentiousness, and puts off till the end the stale scrap of morality which is brought in as a salve to the conscience of the writer. Putting aside *Robinson Crusoe,* which has been truly described as an accident, Defoe's teaching as a novelist has been altogether bad.

'Novel-Reading', *The Nineteenth Century*, January 1879,
in David Dowling, *Novelists on Novelists* (1983)

JONATHAN SWIFT 1667–1745

Samuel Johnson (1709–1784) on Swift

Swift has a higher reputation than he deserves. His excellence is strong sense; for his humour, though very well, is not remarkably good. I doubt whether The Tale of a Tub be his; for he never owned it, and it is much above his usual manner.[16]

In James Boswell, *Life Of Johnson* (1791)

William Makepeace Thackeray (1811–1863) on Swift

[. . .] giant and great as this Dean is, I say we should hoot him. Some of this audience mayn't have read the last part of Gulliver, and to such I would recall the advice of the venerable Mr. Punch to persons about to marry, and say, 'Don't'. When Gulliver first lands among the Yahoos, the naked howling wretches clamber up trees and assault him, and he describes himself as 'almost stifled with the filth which fell about him.' The reader of the fourth part of 'Gulliver's Travels' is like the hero himself in this instance. It is Yahoo language: a monster gibbering shrieks, and gnashing imprecations against mankind – tearing down all shreds of modesty, past all sense of manliness and shame; filthy in word, filthy in thought, furious, raging, obscene.[17]

The English Humourists of the Eighteenth Century (1853)

ALEXANDER POPE 1688–1744

Colley Cibber (1671–1757) on Pope

As Mr. Pope has so particularly picked me out of the number of sinners to make an example of, why may I not take the same liberty,

---

[16] There was controversy during Swift's life and after – though not generally today – over the authorship of *A Tale of a Tub*. It originally appeared (in 1704) anonymously, and Swift's cousin Thomas Swift claimed it as his own. Jonathan Swift disputed the claim.

[17] Thackeray's fastidiousness did not obscure insight into or appreciation of Swift: elsewhere in the same essay he writes: 'As fierce a beak and talon as ever struck – as strong a wing as ever beat, belonged to Swift. [. . .] One can gaze, and not without awe and pity, at the lonely eagle chained behind the bars [. . .] An immense genius: an awful downfall and ruin. So great a man he seems to me, that thinking of him is like thinking of an empire falling.'

and even single him out for another, to keep me in countenance? He must excuse me, then, if, in what I am going to relate, I am induced to make bold with a little private conversation: but as he has shewn no mercy to Colley, why should so unprovoked an aggressor expect any for himself? and if truth hurts him, I cannot help it. He may remember, then (or if he will not, I will) when Button's coffee house was in vogue, and so long ago as when he had not translated above two or three books of *Homer*, there was a late young nobleman (as much his *Lord* as mine) who had a good deal of wicked humour; and who, though he was fond of having wits in his company, was not so restrained by his conscience, but that he loved to laugh at any merry mischief he could do them. This noble wag, I say, in his usual *gayete de coeur*, with another gentleman still in being, one evening slily seduced the celebrated Mr. Pope as a wit, and myself as a laugher, to a certain house of carnal recreation, near the Haymarket; where his lordship's frolick proposed was, to *slip his little Homer*, as he called him, at a girl of the game, that he might see what sort of figure a man of his size, sobriety, and vigour (in verse) would make, when the frail fit of love had got into him; in which he so far succeeded, that the smirking damsel, who served us with tea, happened to have charms sufficient to tempt the little tiny manhood of Mr. Pope into the next room with her: at which, you may imagine, his lordship was in as much joy, at what might happen within, as our small friend could probably be in possession of it: but I (forgive me all ye mortified mortals whom his fell satire has since fallen upon) observing he had staid as long as without hazard of his health he might, I, 'pricked to it by foolish honesty and love', as Shakespere says, without ceremony, threw open the door upon him, where I found this little hasty hero, like a terrible *tom tit*, pertly perched upon the mount of love! But such was my surprise, that I fairly laid hold of his heels, and actually drew him down safe and sound from his danger. My Lord, who staid tittering without, in hopes the sweet mischief he came for would have been completed, upon my giving an account of the action within, began to curse and call me a hundred silly puppies, for my impertinently spoiling the sport; to which with great gravity, I replied, Pray, my lord, consider what I have done was in regard to the honour of our nation! for would you have had so glorious a work as that of making *Homer* speak elegant

English cut short, by laying up our little gentleman of a malady, of which his thin body might never have been cured? no, my lord, *Homer* would have been too serious a sacrifice to our evening's merriment. Now, as his *Homer* has since been so happily completed, who can say that the world may not have been obliged to the kindly care of Colley that so great a work ever came to perfection?[18]

'A Letter from Mr Cibber to Mr Pope', 1742, in Anon., *Eccentric Biography, or, Memoirs of Remarkable Characters* (1804)

Thomas De Quincey (1785–1859) on Pope

The indignation of Juvenal was not always very noble in its origin, or pure in its purpose: it was sometimes mean in its quality, false in its direction, extravagant in its expression: but it was tremendous in the roll of its thunders, and as withering as the scowl of a Mephistopheles. Pope having no such internal principle of wrath boiling in his breast, being really (if one must speak the truth) in the most pacific and charitable frame of mind towards all scoundrels whatever, except such as might take it into their heads to injure a particular Twickenham grotto, was unavoidably a hypocrite of the first magnitude when he affected (or sometimes really conceited himself) to be in a dreadful passion with offenders as a body. It provokes fits of laughter, in a man who knows Pope's real nature, to watch him in the process of brewing the storm that spontaneously will not come; whistling, like a mariner, for a wind to fill his satiric sails; and pumping up into his face hideous grimaces in order to appear convulsed with histrionic rage. Pope should have been counselled never to write satire, except on those evenings when he was suffering horribly from indigestion. By this means the indignation would have been ready-made. The rancour

---

[18] At the time of the publication of this letter the famous feud between Cibber and Pope was at its height. The anonymous author of the *Eccentric Biography* notes: 'This ludicrous story occasioned several whimsical pamphlets, in which the actor and poet had each their advocates; the chief of these were "A Letter to Mr. Cibber on his Letter to Mr. Pope," "Homer Preserved by Colley's Brazen Face; or, the Twickenham Squire Laid by the Heels," "A Blast upon Bays; or, A New Lick at the Laureat," "Blast upon Blast; or, A New Lesson for Mr. P.", "The Cudgel; or, A Crab Tree Lecture to the Author of the Dunciad," &c. &c.' It also occasioned a new 1743 edition of the *Dunciad* in which Cibber was enshrined as the 'prince of Dulness', and thereby found immortality.

against all mankind would have been sincere; and there would have needed to be no extra expense in getting up the steam. As it is, the short puffs of anger, the uneasy snorts of fury in Pope's satires, give one painfully the feeling of a locomotive engine with unsound lungs. Passion of any kind may become in some degree ludicrous, when disproportioned to its exciting occasions. But it is never entirely ludicrous, until it is self-betrayed as counterfeit. Sudden collapses of the manufactured wrath, sudden oblivion of the criminal, announce Pope's as *always* counterfeit.

'The Poetry of Pope' in the *North British Review*,
1848, in *De Quincey as Critic*, ed. J.E. Jordan (1973)

John Hervey (1696–1743) on Pope

Prone, *where he ne'er received, to give offence*,
But most averse to merit and to sense;
Base to his foe, but baser to his friend;
Lying to blame, and sneering to commend:
Then let him boast that honourable crime
Of making *those who fear not God, fear* HIM,–
When the great honour of that boast is such,
That hornets and mad dogs may boast as much.
Such is th' injustice of his daily theme.
And such the lust that breaks his nightly dream,
That vestal fire of undecaying hate,
Which time's cold tide itself can ne'er abate.[19]

'The Difference between Verbal and Practical Virtue, Exemplified in Some
Instances Both Ancient and Modern', 1742, in *Memoirs of the
Reign of George the Second*, ed. J.W. Croker (1848)

---

[19] Pope's ladlefuls of boiling oil heaped on the second Baron Hervey – he ridiculed him as 'Sporus' and 'Lord Fanny', and mocked his appearance in lines such as 'This painted child of dirt, who stinks and sings' (a reference to Hervey's habit of wearing make-up) – are much better known than this reply by Hervey. The sixth line here is a reference to Pope's famous couplet: 'Yes, I am proud, and must be proud to see/Those not afraid of God afraid of me.'

Lady Mary Wortley Montagu (1689–1762) on Pope

Nor think thy weakness shall be thy defence,
The female scold's protection in offence.
Sure 'tis as fair to beat who cannot fight,
As 'tis to libel those who cannot write.
And if thou draw'st thy pen to aid the law,
Others a cudgel, or rod, may draw.
If none with vengeance yet thy crimes pursue,
Or give thy manifold affronts their due;
If limbs unbroken, skin without a stain,
Unwhipped, unblanketed, unkicked, unslain,
That wretched little carcase you retain,
The reason is, not that the world wants eyes,
But thou'rt so mean, they see, and they despise:
When fretful porcupine, with rancorous will,
From mounted back shoots forth a harmless quill,
Cool the spectators stand; and all the while
Upon the angry little monster smile.
Thus 'tis with thee:— whilst impotently safe,
You strike unwounding, we unhurt can laugh.
'Who but must laugh, this bully when he sees,
A puny insect shivering at a breeze?'
Is this the thing to keep mankind in awe,
'To make those tremble who escape the law?'
Is this the ridicule to live so long,
'The deathless satire and immortal song?'
No: like thy self-blown praise, thy scandal flies;
And, as we're told of wasps, it stings and dies.
If none do yet return th'intended blow,
You all your safety to your dullness owe [. . .][20]

Verses Addressed to the Imitator of the First Satire
of the Second Book of Horace (1733)

---

[20] Pope, who was at first friends with Lady Mary, and may have been in love with her, finally fell out with her in spectacular fashion. The cause may have been that when he declared his love for her she burst out laughing – or may have been due to her friendship with John Hervey, who collaborated with her in writing this poem. The repeated slights on Pope's personal appearance and stature (he was less than five foot tall) are clinched by the accusation of 'dullness', Pope's own polemical stock-in-trade.

Robert Southey (1774–1843) on Pope

The age of Pope was the golden age of poets – but it was the
pinchbeck age of poetry. They flourished in the sunshine of public and
private patronage; the art meantime was debased, and it continued to
be so as long as Pope continued lord of the ascendant. More injury was
not done to the taste of his countrymen by Marino in Italy, nor by
Gongora in Spain, than by Pope in England. The mischief was effected
not by his satirical and moral pieces, for these entitle him to the
highest place among poets of his class; it was by his Homer. There have
been other versions as unfaithful; but none were ever so well executed
in as bad a style; and no other work in the language so greatly vitiated
the diction of English poetry. Common readers (and the majority must
always be such) will always be taken by glittering faults, as larks are
caught by bits of looking-glass; and in this meretricious translation, the
passages that were most unlike the original, which were most untrue
to nature, and therefore most false in taste, were precisely those which
were most applauded, and on which critic after critic dwelt with one
cuckoo note of admiration.

The Works of William Cowper, ed. R. Southey (1853)

Lytton Strachey (1880–1932) on Pope

The verses, when they were written, resembled nothing so much as
spoonfuls of boiling oil, ladled out by a fiendish monkey at an upstairs
window upon such passers-by whom the wretch had a grudge against.

Pope: The Leslie Stephen Lecture for 1925 (pamphlet, 1925)

SAMUEL RICHARDSON 1689–1761

James Boswell (1740–1795) on Richardson

One day at his country-house at Northend, where a large company
was assembled at dinner, a gentleman who was just returned from
Paris, willing to please Mr. Richardson, mentioned to him a very
flattering circumstance – that he had seen his *Clarissa* lying on the
King's brother's table. Richardson observing that part of the company
were engaged in talking to each other, affected then not to attend to it.
But by and by, when there was a general silence, and he thought that

the flattery might be fully heard, he addressed himself to the gentleman, 'I think, Sir, you were saying something about—', pausing in a high flutter of expectation. The gentleman, provoked at his inordinate vanity, resolved not to indulge it, and with an exquisitely sly air of indifference answered, 'A mere trifle, Sir, not worth repeating.' The mortification of Richardson was visible, and he did not speak ten words more the whole day. Dr. Johnson was present, and appeared to enjoy it much.

In James Boswell, *Life of Johnson* (1791)

George Gordon, Lord Byron (1788–1824) on Richardson

I was out of spirits – read the papers – thought what fame was, on reading, in a case of murder, that Mr. Wych, grocer, at Tunbridge, sold some bacon, flour, cheese, and, it is believed, some plums, to some gipsy woman accused. He had on his counter (I quote faithfully) 'a *book*, the Life of *Pamela*, which he was *tearing* for *waste paper*, etc. etc. In the cheese was found, etc., and a *leaf* of *Pamela wrapt round the bacon.*' What would Richardson, the vainest and luckiest of *living* authors (i.e. while alive) – he who, with Aaron Hill, used to prophesy and chuckle over the presumed fall of Fielding (the *prose* Homer of human nature) and of Pope (the most beautiful of poets) – what would he have said, could he have traced his pages from their place on the French prince's toilets (see Boswell's *Johnson*) to the grocer's counter and the gipsy-murderess's bacon!!!

Diary for 4 January 1821, in *Byron, A Self Portrait*, ed. P. Quennell (1950)

VOLTAIRE 1694–1778

Charles Baudelaire (1821–67) on Voltaire

I grow bored in France – and the main reason is that everybody here resembles Voltaire.

When Emerson wrote his *Representatives of Humanity,* he forgot Voltaire. He could have written an attractive chapter entitled: 'Voltaire, or the anti-poet' – the king of nincompoops, the prince of the superficial, the anti-artist, the spokesman of janitresses, the Father Gigogne of the editors of *Siècle.*

In his *Lord Chesterfield's Ears,* Voltaire pokes fun at that immortal soul who for nine months dwelt amidst excrement and urine. Like all idlers, Voltaire hated mystery. He might at least have detected, in this choice of dwelling-place, a grudge or satire directed by Providence against love – and thus, in the method of procreation, a sign of Original Sin. After all, we can make love only with the organs of excretion.[21]

> *My Heart Laid Bare*, 1864–66, trans. N. Cameron (1975)

HENRY FIELDING 1707–1754

Arnold Bennett (1867–1931) on Fielding

There is no dull chapter. But he makes the hero too good. He seems to think that so long as Tom goes in for a little miscellaneous fornication he will be saved from priggishness. I doubt if this is so, especially at the end, where Tom's angelicalness upon the misfortunes of Blifil is really a bit thick.

> Journal for 19 August 1911, in *The Journals of Arnold Bennett*,
> ed. F. Swinnerton (1954)

Samuel Richardson (1689–1761) on Fielding

I must confess, that I have been prejudiced by the Opinion of Several judicious Friends against the truly coarse-titled Tom Jones; and so have been discouraged from reading it. – I was told, that it was a rambling Collection of Waking Dreams, in which Probability was not observed: And that it had a very bad Tendency. And I had Reason to think that the Author intended for his Second View (His *first*, to fill his Pocket, by accommodating it to the reigning Taste) in writing it, to whiten a vicious Character, and to make Morality bend to his Practices. What Reason had he to make his Tom illegitimate, in an Age where Keeping is become a Fashion? Why did he make him a common – What shall I call it? And a Kept Fellow, the Lowest of all Fellows, yet in Love with a Young Creature who was trapsing after him, a Fugitive from her Father's House? – Why did he draw his

---

[21]   Not an original observation. As Havelock Ellis wrote: '*Inter fæces et urinam nascimur* is an ancient text which has served the ascetic preachers of old for many discourses on the littleness of man and the meanness of that reproductive power which plays so large a part in man's life.'

Heroine so fond, so foolish, and so insipid? – Indeed he has one
Excuse – He knows not how to draw a delicate Woman – He has not
been accustomed to such Company, – And is too prescribing, too
impetuous, too immoral, I will venture to say, to take any other Byass
than that a perverse and crooked Nature has given him; or Evil
Habits, at least, have confirm'd in him. Do Men expect Grapes of
Thorns, or Figs of Thistles? But, perhaps, I think the worse of the
Piece because I know the Writer, and dislike his Principles both
Public and Private, tho' I wish well to the *Man*, and Love Four worthy
Sisters of his, with whom I am well acquainted. And indeed should
admire him, did he make the Use of his Talents which I wish him to
make, For the Vein of Humour, and Ridicule, which he is Master of,
might, if properly turned do great Service to ye Cause of Virtue.[22]

> Letter to Astraea and Minerva Hill, 4 August 1749, in *Henry Fielding: The*
> *Critical Heritage*, ed. R. Paulson and T. Lockwood (1995)

I have not been able to read any more than the first volume of Amelia.
Poor Fielding! I could not help telling his sister, that I was equally
surprised at, and concerned for, his continued lowness. Had your
brother, said I, been born in a stable, or been a runner at a sponging-
house, we should have thought him a genius, and wished he had had
the advantage of a liberal education, and of being admitted into good
company; but it is beyond my conception, that a man of family, and
who had some learning, and who really is a writer, should descend so
excessively low in all his pieces. Who can care for any of his people? A
person of honour asked me, the other day, what he could mean, by
saying, in his Covent Garden Journal, that he had followed Homer and
Virgil in his Amelia? I answered, that he was justified in saying so,
because he must mean Cotton's Virgil Travestied, where the women are
drabs, and the men scoundrels.[23]

> Letter to Lady Dorothy Bradshaigh, 23 February 1752, in *Henry Fielding:*
> *The Critical Heritage*, ed. R. Paulson and T. Lockwood (1995)

---

[22] Fielding had rubbished Richardson's *Pamela* in his squib *Shamela* (1741) and
then went on almost to build his career on the characters he had invented for
the purpose, making Shamela's brother Joseph the hero of his next novel, *Joseph
Andrews*. In the light of this Richardson seems quite restrained.

[23] Charles Cotton's mock-heroic poem *Scarronides, or Virgile Travestie* (1664).

SAMUEL JOHNSON 1709–1784

Thomas De Quincey (1785–1859) on Johnson

Dr. Johnson tampered with medical studies, and fancied himself
learned enough in such studies to prescribe for his female
correspondents. The affectionateness with which he sometimes did
this is interesting; but his ignorance of the subject is not the less
apparent. In his own case he had the merit of one heroic self-
conquest: he weaned himself from wine, once having become
convinced that it was injurious. But he never brought himself to take
regular exercise. He ate too much at all times of his life. And in
another point, he betrayed a thoughtlessness which (though really
common at laughter) is yet extravagantly childish. Everybody knows
that Dr. Johnson was all his life reproaching himself with lying too
long in bed. Always he was sinning (for he thought it a sin); always he
was repenting; always he was vainly endeavouring to reform. But why
vainly? Cannot a resolute man in six weeks bring himself to rise at
any hour of the twenty-four? Certainly he can; but not without
appropriate means. Now, the doctor rose about eleven A.M. This, he
fancied, was shocking; he was determined to rise at eight, or at seven.
Very well; why not? But will it be credited that the one sole change
occurring to the doctor's mind was to take a flying leap backwards
from eleven to eight, without any corresponding leap at the other
terminus of his sleep. To rise at eight instead of eleven, presupposes
that a man goes off to bed at twelve instead of three. Yet this recondite
truth never to his dying day dawned on Dr. Johnson's mind. The
conscientious man continued to offend; continued to repent;
continued to pave a disagreeable place with good intentions, and daily
resolutions of amendment; but at length died full of years, without
having once seen the sun rise, except in some Homeric description,
written (as Mr. Fynes Clinton makes it probable) thirty centuries
before. The fact of the sun's rising at all the doctor adopted as a point
of faith, and by no means of personal knowledge, from an insinuation
to that effect in the most ancient of Greek books.

Review in *Tait's Edinburgh Magazine*, 1845/6, in *De Quincey as Critic*,
ed. J.E. Jordan (1973)

Horace Walpole (1717–1797) on Johnson

Often, indeed, Johnson made the most brutal speeches to living persons; for though he was good-natured at bottom, he was very ill-natured at top. He loved to dispute, to show his superiority. If his opponents were weak, he told them they were fools; if they vanquished him, he was scurrilous – to nobody more than to Boswell himself, who was contemptible for flattering him so grossly, and for enduring the coarse things he was continually vomiting on Boswell's own country, Scotland. [. . .] Johnson's blind Toryism and known brutality kept me aloof; nor did I ever exchange a syllable with him: nay, I do not think I ever was in a room with him six times in my days. Boswell came to me, said Dr. Johnson was writing the 'Lives of the Poets,' and wished I would give him anecdotes of Mr. Gray. I said, very coldly, I had given what I knew to Mr. Mason. Boswell hummed and hawed, and then dropped, 'I suppose you know Dr. Johnson does not admire Mr. Gray.'[24] Putting as much contempt as I could into my look and tone, I said, 'Dr. Johnson don't! – humph !' – and with that monosyllable ended our interview. After the Doctor's death, Burke, Sir Joshua Reynolds, and Boswell sent an ambling circular-letter to me, begging subscriptions for a Monument for him – the two last, I think, impertinently; as they could not but know my opinion, and could not suppose I would contribute to a Monument for one who had endeavoured, poor soul! to degrade my friend's superlative poetry. I would not deign to write an answer; but sent down word by my footman, as I would have done to parish officers with a brief, that I would not subscribe. In the two new volumes Johnson says, and very probably did, or is made to say, that Gray's poetry is dull, and that he was a dull man! The same oracle dislikes Prior, Swift, and Fielding. If an elephant could write a book, perhaps one that had read a great deal would say, that an Arabian horse is a very clumsy ungraceful animal. Pass to a better chapter!

Letter to Miss Berry, 26 May 1791, in *The Letters of Horace Walpole*,
ed. P. Cunningham (1861)

---

[24] See Johnson on Gray, page 49.

A clergyman told Sir John very lately, that being with Johnson, he said to him, 'Doctor, you have such command of your pen you can do anything: I wish you would write me a sermon.' 'No, sir,' said the Mercenary, 'I cannot write but for money; since I have dealt with the heathens (the booksellers), I have no other inspiration. I knew they could not do without me, and I made them pay five guineas a sheet for my "Rasselas"; you must pay me if I write for you.' And the five guineas per sheet, no doubt, was the price; but I do not know why he called the booksellers *heathens*, unless for their worshipping such an uncouth idol as he is: yet, he has other motives than lucre, – prejudice, and bigotry, and pride, and presumption, and arrogance, and pedantry, are the hags that brew his ink, though wages alone supply him with paper.

Letter to the Rev. William Mason, 7 February 1782,
in The Letters of Horace Walpole, ed. P. Cunningham (1861)

LAURENCE STERNE 1713–1768

Samuel Taylor Coleridge (1772–1834) on Sterne

With regard to Sterne, and the charge of licentiousness which presses so seriously upon his character as a writer, I would remark that there is a sort of knowingness, the wit of which depends, 1st, on the modesty it gives pain to; or, 2ndly, on the innocence and innocent ignorance over which it triumphs; or, 3rdly, on a certain oscillation in the individual's own mind between the remaining good and the encroaching evil of his nature – a sort of dallying with the devil – a fluxionary art of combining courage and cowardice, as when a man snuffs a candle with his fingers for the first time, or better still, perhaps, like that trembling daring with which a child touches a hot tea-urn, because it has been forbidden; so that the mind has its own white and black angel; the same or similar amusement as may be supposed to take place between an old debauchee and a prude, – the feeling resentment, on the one hand, from a prudential anxiety to preserve appearances and have a character; and, on the other, an inward sympathy with the enemy. We have only to suppose society innocent, and then nine-tenths of this sort of wit would be like a stone that falls in snow, making no sound, because exciting no resistance; the remainder rests on its being an offence against the good manners of human nature itself.

This source, unworthy as it is, may doubtless be combined with wit, drollery, fancy, and even humour; and we have only to regret the misalliance; but that the latter are quite distinct from the former, may be made evident by abstracting in our imagination the morality of the characters of Mr. Shandy, my Uncle Toby, and Trim, which are all antagonists to this spurious sort of wit, from the rest of 'Tristram Shandy,' and by supposing, instead of them, the presence of two or three callous debauchees. The result will be pure disgust. Sterne cannot be too severely censured for thus using the best dispositions of our nature as the panders and condiments for the basest.

Literary Remains, 1836, in William Makepeace Thackeray,
The English Humourists of the Eighteenth Century (1853)

Samuel Richardson (1689–1761) on Sterne

Who is this Yorick? you are pleased to ask me. You cannot, I imagine, have looked into his books: execrable I cannot but call them; for I am told that the third and fourth volumes are worse, if possible, than the two first, which, only, I have had the patience to run through. One extenuating circumstance attends his works, that they are too gross to be inflaming.

Letter to Mark Hildesley, January-February 1761, in *Selected Letters of Samuel Richardson*, ed. J. Carroll (1964)

Walter Scott (1771–1832) on Sterne

[T]he greatest admirers of Sterne must own, that his style is affected, eminently, and in a degree which even his wit and pathos are inadequate to support. The style of Rabelais, which he assumed for his model, is to the highest excess rambling, excursive, and intermingled with the greatest absurdities. But Rabelais was in some measure compelled to adopt this harlequin's habit, in order that, like licensed jesters, he might, under the cover of his folly, have permission to vent his satire against church and state. Sterne assumed the manner of his master, only as a mode of attracting attention, and of making the public stare; and, therefore, his extravagancies, like those of a feigned madman, are cold and forced, even in the midst of his most irregular flights. A man may, in the present day, be, with perfect impunity, as wise or as witty as he can, without assuming the cap and bells of the ancient jester as an apology; and that Sterne chose voluntarily to appear under such a disguise, must be set down as mere affectation, and ranked with the tricks of black or marbled pages, as used merely *ad captandum vulgus*.[25] All popularity thus founded, carries in it the seeds of decay; for eccentricity in composition, like fantastic modes of dress, however attractive when first introduced, is sure to be caricatured by stupid imitators, to become soon unfashionable, and of course to be neglected.

If we proceed to look more closely into the manner of composition which Sterne thought proper to adopt, we find a sure guide in the ingenious Dr Ferriar, of Manchester, who, with most singular patience, has traced our author through the hidden sources whence he borrowed most of his learning, and many of his more striking and peculiar expressions. Rabelais (much less read than spoken of), the lively but licentious miscellany called *Moyen de parvenir*,[26] and D'Aubigné's *Baron de Foeneste*, with many other forgotten authors of the sixteenth century, were successively laid under contribution. Burton's celebrated work on Melancholy (which Dr Ferriar's Essay instantly raised to double price in the book-market) afforded Sterne an endless mass of quotations, with which he unscrupulously garnished his pages, as if they had been collected in the course of his own extensive reading. The style of the same author, together with that of Bishop Hall, furnished the author of *Tristram* with many of those whimsical expressions, similes, and illustrations, which were long believed the genuine effusions of his own eccentric wit. For proofs of this sweeping charge we must refer the readers to Dr Ferriar's well-known Essay and Illustrations, as he delicately terms them, of Sterne's Writings, in which it is clearly shown, that he, whose manner and style were so long thought original, was, in fact, the most unhesitating plagiarist who ever cribbed from his predecessors in order to garnish his own pages. It must be owned, at the same time, that Sterne selects the materials of his mosaic work with so much art, places them so well, and polishes them so highly, that in most cases we are disposed to pardon the want of originality, in consideration of the exquisite talent with which the borrowed materials are wrought up into the new form.

One of Sterne's most singular thefts, considering the tenor of the passage stolen, is his declamation against literary depredators of his own

---

25 'To win over the crowd'.

26 By Béroalde de Verville (1556–1626).

class: 'Shall we,' says Sterne, 'for ever make new books, as apothecaries make new medicines, by pouring only out of one vessel into another? Are we for ever to be twisting and untwisting the same rope – for ever in the same track – for ever at the same pace?' The words of Burton are, 'As apothecaries, we make new mixtures, every day pour out of one vessel into another; and as the Romans robbed all the cities in the world to set out their bad-sited Rome, we skim the cream of other men's wits, pick the choice flowers of their tilled gardens, to set out our own sterile plots. We weave the same web, still twist the same rope again and again.' We cannot help wondering at the coolness with which Sterne could transfer to his own work so eloquent a tirade against the very arts which he was practising.

Much has been said about the right of an author to avail himself of his predecessors' labours; and, certainly, in a general sense, he that revives the wit and learning of a former age, and puts it into the form likely to captivate his own, confers a benefit on his contemporaries. But to plume himself with the very language and phrases of former writers, and to pass their wit and learning for his own, was the more unworthy in Sterne, as he had enough of original talent, had he chosen to exert it, to have dispensed with all such acts of literary petty larceny.

Lives of the Novelists (1825)

William Makepeace Thackeray (1811–1863) on Sterne

A perilous trade, indeed, is that of a man who has to bring his tears and laughter, his recollections, his personal griefs and joys, his private thoughts and feelings to market, to write them on paper, and sell them for money. Does he exaggerate his grief, so as to get his reader's pity for a false sensibility – feign indignation, so as to establish a character for virtue? elaborate repartees, so that he may pass for a wit? steal from other authors, and put down the theft to the credit side of his own reputation for ingenuity and learning? feign originality? affect benevolence or misanthropy? appeal to the gallery gods with claptraps and vulgar baits to catch applause? How much of the paint and emphasis is necessary for the fair business of the stage, and how much of the rant and rouge is put on for the vanity of the actor. His audience trusts him: can he trust himself? How much was deliberate calculation and imposture – how much was false sensibility – and how much true feeling? Where did the lie begin, and did he know where? and where did the truth end in the art and scheme of this man of genius, this actor, this quack? Some time since I was in the company of a French actor, who began after dinner, and at his own request, to sing French songs of the sort called *des chansons grivoises*, and which he performed admirably, and to the dissatisfaction of most persons present. Having finished these, he commenced a sentimental ballad – it was so charmingly sung that it touched all persons present, and especially the singer himself, whose voice trembled, whose eyes filled with emotion, and who was snivelling and weeping quite genuine tears by the time his own ditty was over. I suppose Sterne had this artistical sensibility; he used to blubber perpetually in his study, and finding his tears infectious, and that they brought him a great popularity, he exercised the lucrative gift of weeping, he utilised it, and cried on every occasion. I own that I do not value or respect much the cheap dribble of those fountains. He fatigues me with his perpetual disquiet and his uneasy appeals to my risible or sentimental faculties. He is always looking in my face, watching his effect, uncertain whether I think him an impostor or not; posture-making, coaxing, imploring me. 'See what sensibility I have – own now that I'm very clever – do cry now, you can't resist this.' The humour of Swift and Rabelais, whom he pretended to succeed, poured from them as naturally as song does from a bird; they lose no manly dignity with it, but laugh their hearty great laugh out of their broad chests as nature bade them. But this man – who can make you laugh, who can make you cry too – never lets his reader alone, or will permit his audience repose; when you are quiet, he fancies he must rouse you, and turns head over heels, or sidles up and whispers a nasty story. The man is a great jester, not a great humourist. He goes to work systematically and of cold blood; paints his face, puts on his ruff and motley clothes, and lays down his carpet and tumbles on it. [. . .]

There is not a page in Sterne's writing but has something that were better away, a latent corruption – a hint, as of an impure presence. Some of that dreary *double entendre* may be attributed to freer times and manners than ours, but not all. The foul Satyr's eyes leer out of the leaves constantly: the last words the famous author wrote were bad and wicked – the last lines the poor stricken wretch penned were for pity and pardon. I think of these past writers and of one who lives amongst us now, and am grateful for the innocent laughter and the sweet and

unsullied page which the author of 'David Copperfield' gives to
my children.[27]

The English Humourists of the Eighteenth Century (1853)

THOMAS GRAY 1716–1771

Samuel Johnson (1709–1784) on Gray

Next day I dined with Johnson at Mr. Thrale's. He attacked Gray,
calling him 'a dull fellow.' BOSWELL. 'I understand he was reserved,
and might appear dull in company; but surely he was not dull in poetry.'
JOHNSON. 'Sir, he was dull in company, dull in his closet, dull every
where. He was dull in a new way, and that made many people think him
GREAT. He was a mechanical poet.' He then repeated some ludicrous
lines, which have escaped my memory, and said, 'Is not that GREAT, like
his Odes?'[28]

In James Boswell, *Life of Johnson* (1791)

Christopher Smart (1722–1771) on Gray

[The editor of *Facetiae Cantabrigienses*, Richard Gooch, writes:] Those
who remember Mr. Gray when at the University of Cambridge, where
he resided the greater part of his life, will recollect that he was a little
prim fastidious man, distinguished by a short shuffling step. He commonly
held up his gown behind with one of his hands, at the same time cocking
up his chin, and perking up his nose. Christopher Smart, who was
contemporary with him at Pembroke Hall, used to say that Gray walked
'as if he had fouled his small-clothes, and looked as if he smelt it.'

Facetiae Cantabrigienses: Consisting of Anecdotes, Smart Sayings, Satirics, Retorts, &c,
&c, by or Relating to Celebrated Cantabs, ed. R. Gooch (1825)

---

[27] Virginia Woolf detected some of the same masquerading, particularly in *A
Sentimental Journey*, saying the mood was 'too uniformly kind, tender, and compas-
sionate to be quite natural', but also took issue with Thackeray, saying, 'Was not
Thackeray's coward [i.e. Sterne] – the man who trifled so immorally with so many
women and wrote love-letters on gilt-edged paper when he should have been lying
on a sick-bed writing sermons – was he not a stoic in his own way and a moralist,
and a teacher?'

[28] Johnson was famous for his contrarianism over Gray, who was almost universally admired. However, Johnson did have praise for the *Elegy in a Country
Churchyard*, saying 'it abounds with images which find a mirror in every mind'.

ADAM SMITH 1723-1790

Walter Scott (1771–1832) on Smith

Mr. Boswell has chosen to omit, for reasons which will be presently obvious, that Johnson and Adam Smith met at Glasgow; but I have been assured by Professor John Miller that they did so, and that Smith, leaving the party in which he had met Johnson, happened to come to another company where Miller was. Knowing that Smith had been in Johnson's society, they were anxious to know what had passed, and the more so as Dr. Smith's temper seemed much ruffled. At first Smith would only answer, 'He's a brute – he's a brute;' but on closer examination, it appeared that Johnson no sooner saw Smith than he attacked him for some point of his famous letter on the death of Hume.[29] Smith vindicated the truth of his statement. 'What did Johnson say?' was the universal inquiry. 'Why, he said,' replied Smith, with the deepest impression of resentment, 'he said, *you lie!*' 'And what did you reply?' 'I said, *you* are the son of a –.' On such terms did these two great moralists meet and part, and such was the classical dialogue between two great teachers of philosophy.

Note to J.W. Croker's edition of Boswell's Life of Johnson (1831)

OLIVER GOLDSMITH c.1730–1784

Joshua Reynolds (1723–1792) on Goldsmith

Goldsmith had no wit in conversation, but to do him justice, he did not much attempt it. When in company with ladies he was always endeavouring after humour, and as continually failed; but his ill success was equally diverting to the company as if he had succeeded. If they laughed, he was happy and did not seem to care whether it was with him or at him. But when he was in company with the philosophers, he was grave, wise and very inclinable to dispute established opinions. This immediately produced a general cry. Every man had arguments of

---

[29]   Smith eulogized Hume thus: 'Upon the whole, I have always considered him, both in his lifetime and since his death, as approaching as nearly to the idea of a perfectly wise and virtuous man, as perhaps the nature of human frailty will permit.' Johnson considered the atheistic Hume to be a dangerous radical.

confutation ready, and he himself was at once placed in the situation he so much loved, of being the object of attention of the whole company. [. . .]

What Goldsmith intended for humour was purposely repeated as serious. However, to do justice to the world, a man seldom acquires the character of absurd without deserving it. As the *bons mots* of other wits are handed about the town, the Doctor's blunders and absurdities, circulated with equal success, helped to increase his fame and give everybody a desire of seeing the man, and this perhaps not without some mixture of self-congratulation to find a person whom they were obliged to look up to for superior talent sink below their level when in conversation.

Goldsmith's mind was entirely unfurnished. When he was engaged in a work, he had all his knowledge to find, which when he found, he knew how to use, but forgot it immediately after he had used it.[30]

Portraits by Sir Joshua Reynolds, ed. F.W. Hilles (1952)

Mark Twain (1835–1910) on Goldsmith

Also, to be fair, there is another word of praise due to this ship's library: it contains no copy of *The Vicar of Wakefield*, that strange menagerie of complacent hypocrites and idiots, of theatrical cheap-john heroes and heroines, who are always showing off, of bad people who are not interesting, and good people who are fatiguing. A singular book. Not a sincere line in it, and not a character that invites respect; a book which is one long waste-pipe discharge of goody-goody puerilities and dreary moralities; a book which is full of pathos which revolts, and humor which grieves the heart. There are few things in literature that are more piteous, more pathetic, than the celebrated 'humorous' incident of Moses and the spectacles.

Following the Equator (1897)

---

[30] Goldsmith and Reynolds met in 1762 and both became members of Samuel Johnson's literary club. This sketch was published around 1776. It is above all the affectionate description of an extraordinary character, and begins: 'If anyone thinks that Dr. Goldsmith was a man not worth the investigation, we must refer him to the public advertisements, where he will find the booksellers have lived upon his reputation, as his friends have lived upon his character, ever since his death.' Reynolds's comments on Goldsmith in the second paragraph are strikingly similar to Johnson's remarks in Boswell's *Life*, where the following conversation is reported:

EDWARD GIBBON 1737–1794

James Boswell (1740–1795) on Gibbon

I don't know but you have spoken too highly of Gibbon's book; the Dean of Derry, who is of our Club as well as Gibbon, talks of answering it. I think it is right that as fast as infidel wasps or venomous insects, whether creeping or flying, are hatched, they should be crushed. [. . .] He is an ugly, affected, disgusting fellow, and poisons our literary Club to me.

Letters of James Boswell, Addressed to the Rev. W.J. Temple (1857)

Samuel Taylor Coleridge (1772–1834) on Gibbon

Gibbon's style is detestable, but his style is not the worst thing about him. His history has proved an effectual bar to all real familiarity with the temper and habits of imperial Rome. Few persons read the original authorities, even those which are classical; and certainly no distinct knowledge of the actual state of the empire can be obtained from Gibbon's rhetorical sketches. He takes notice of nothing but what may produce an effect; he skips on from eminence to eminence, without ever taking you through the valleys between: in fact, his work is little else but a disguised collection of all the splendid anecdotes which he could find in any book concerning any persons or nations from the Antonines to the capture of Constantinople. When I read a chapter in Gibbon, I seem to be looking through a luminous haze or fog: – figures come and go, I know not how or why, all larger than life, or distorted or discoloured; nothing is real, vivid, true; all is scenical, and, as it were, exhibited by candlelight. And then to call it a History of the Decline and Fall of the Roman Empire! Was there ever a greater misnomer? I protest I do not remember a single philosophical attempt made

---

JOHNSON: 'It is amazing how little Goldsmith knows. He seldom comes where he is not more ignorant than any one else.'

SIR JOSHUA REYNOLDS: 'Yet there is no man whose company is more liked.'

JOHNSON: 'To be sure, Sir. When people find a man of the most distinguished abilities as a writer, their inferiour while he is with them, it must be highly gratifying to them. What Goldsmith comically says of himself is very true, – he always gets the better when he argues alone; meaning, that he is master of a subject in his study, and can write well upon it; but when he comes into company, grows confused, and unable to talk.'

throughout the work to fathom the ultimate causes of the decline or fall of that empire. How miserably deficient is the narrative of the important reign of Justinian! And that poor scepticism, which Gibbon mistook for Socratic philosophy, has led him to misstate and mistake the character and influence of Christianity in a way which even an avowed infidel or atheist would not and could not have done. Gibbon was a man of immense reading; but he had no philosophy; and he never fully understood the principle upon which the best of the old historians wrote. He attempted to imitate their artificial construction of the whole work – their dramatic ordonnance of the parts – without seeing that their histories were intended more as documents illustrative of the truths of political philosophy than as mere chronicles of events. The true key to the declension of the Roman empire – which is not to be found in all Gibbon's immense work – may be stated in two words: – the imperial character overlaying, and finally destroying, the national character. Rome under Trajan was an empire without a nation.

Specimens of the Table Talk of the Late Samuel Taylor Coleridge,
ed. H.N. Coleridge (1835)

JAMES BOSWELL 1740–1795

Samuel Johnson (1709–1784) on Boswell
Sir, you have but two topicks, yourself and me. I am sick of both.

In James Boswell, *Life of Johnson* (1791)

Thomas Babington Macaulay (1800–1859) on Boswell
We are not sure that there is in the whole history of the human intellect so strange a phaenomenon as this book. Many of the greatest men that ever lived have written biography. Boswell was one of the smallest men that ever lived, and he has beaten them all. He was, if we are to give any credit to his own account or to the united testimony of all who knew him, a man of the meanest and feeblest intellect. Johnson described him as a fellow who had missed his only chance of immortality by not having been alive when the Dunciad was written. Beauclerk used his name as a proverbial expression for a bore. He was the laughing-stock of the whole of that brilliant society which has

owed to him the greater part of its fame. He was always laying himself at the feet of some eminent man, and begging to be spit upon and trampled upon. [. . .] Servile and impertinent, shallow and pedantic, a bigot and a sot, bloated with family pride, and eternally blustering about the dignity of a born gentleman, yet stooping to be a talebearer, an eavesdropper, a common butt in the taverns of London [. . .] such was this man, and such he was content and proud to be. Everything which another man would have hidden, everything the publication of which would have made another man hang himself, was matter of gay and clamorous exultation to his weak and diseased mind. [. . .] All the caprices of his temper, all the illusions of his vanity, all his hypochondriac whimsies, all his castles in the air, he displayed with a cool self-complacency, a perfect unconsciousness that he was making a fool of himself, to which it is impossible to find a parallel in the whole history of mankind. He has used many people ill; but assuredly he has used nobody so ill as himself. [. . .]

Of the talents which ordinarily raise men to eminence as writers, Boswell had absolutely none. There is not in all his books a single remark of his own on literature, politics, religion, or society, which is not either commonplace or absurd. His dissertations on hereditary gentility, on the slave-trade, and on the entailing of landed estates, may serve as examples. To say that these passages are sophistical would be to pay them an extravagant compliment. They have no pretence to argument, or even to meaning. He has reported innumerable observations made by himself in the course of conversation. Of those observations we do not remember one which is above the intellectual capacity of a boy of fifteen. He has printed many of his own letters, and in these letters he is always ranting or twaddling. Logic, eloquence, wit, taste, all those things which are generally considered as making a book valuable, were utterly wanting to him. He had, indeed, a quick observation and a retentive memory. These qualities, if he had been a man of sense and virtue would scarcely of themselves have sufficed to make him conspicuous; but because he was a dunce, a parasite, and a coxcomb, they have made him immortal.

Critical and Historical Essays, vol II (1843)

3 RANCOUR FOR THE ROMANTICS

The eighteenth century is generally thought to be a time of plain speaking and foul language, the era of Hogarth and Fielding, when life was nasty, brutish and short, but rather enjoyable in places – such as the Turk's Head Inn in Gerrard Street. Then the nineteenth century got its hands on literature and began cleaning out the Augustan stables. The sensual was displaced by the sensitive, masculine virtues by feminine, the pleasures of the flesh by the recollection of emotions in tranquillity. This is of course a simplification (if not a travesty). The Augustan period, as we have seen, was itself marked by a desire to move on from the rusticity of Renaissance literature and to embrace 'correctness' (the key word for Pope) and a greater literary sophistication. And the Romantic period was by no means free of plain speaking. In the following pages we learn, for example (and usually from close friends), that Wordsworth was witless, Coleridge was catatonic, Byron was bulimic, Southey was soporific, Shelley squeaked and Keats . . . well, best to leave it to Byron to say what Keats was.

Through the Romantic period move two rather odd figures, figures of the age and yet not of the age: Thomas De Quincey and William Hazlitt. Neither was primarily an artist of the imagination, and yet it is hard to imagine the age without them and their interpretation of it. In their role as observers rather than creators they were trenchant critics. De Quincey – translator, essayist and author of the *Confessions of an English Opium Eater*, a man always poor, often sick, and addicted to opium (though not loth to criticize Coleridge for the same failing) – battened on to Wordsworth and Coleridge in Grasmere, finally falling out with them in spectacular fashion ('A man who can set such an example, I hold to be a pest in society,' wrote Wordsworth). De Quincey had a unique invective talent, dispensing praise with his right hand and then delivering a roundhouse blow of insult with his left; by his death in 1859 he had outlived, and fallen foul of, all the other major figures of the movement. Hazlitt pursued a similar career as an outsider, also battened on to Wordsworth and Coleridge, and also fell out with them, after a sexual escapade with one of the poets' rural neighbours (Wordworth wrote that Hazlitt was 'the most perverse and malevolent Creature that ill luck has ever thrown in my way').

Between the two of them they give some of the best first-hand accounts of the major figures of the period, often negative.

Perhaps what comes across most strikingly in the Romantic period is that, at first at least, the major figures were no longer divided into armed camps along political lines: post-1789, all feeling it bliss to be alive, everyone was on the same side (with the exception of Byron, who, looking back to Pope stylistically, struck a defiant anti-Romantic pose). Then age and caution took a hold, Napoleon began his ascent, and Wordsworth and Coleridge in particular began revising their political opinions, which the likes of Hazlitt and Shelley felt to be a betrayal. The Romantics started off in bed with one another; when they quarrelled they did so with a rancour that only former bedfellows can achieve.

JOHANN WOLFGANG VON GOETHE 1749–1832

Samuel Butler (1835–1902) on Goethe

I have been reading a translation of Goethe's *Wilhelm Meister*. Is it good? To me it seems perhaps the very worst book I ever read. No Englishman could have written such a book. I cannot remember a single good page or idea, and the priggishness is the finest of its kin that I can call to mind. Is it all a practical joke? If it really is Goethe's *Wilhelm Meister* that I have been reading, I am glad I have never taken the trouble to learn German.

Letter to Eliza Savage, 6 November 1874, in *Letters between Samuel Butler and E.M.A. Savage, 1871–1885* (1935)

FRIEDRICH SCHILLER 1759–1805

Samuel Taylor Coleridge (1772–1834) on Schiller

Schiller's blank verse is bad. He moves in it as a fly in a glue bottle. His thoughts have their connection and variety, it is true, but there is no sufficiently corresponding movement in the verse.

Specimens of the Table Talk of the Late Samuel Taylor Coleridge, ed. H.N. Coleridge (1835)

WILLIAM WORDSWORTH 1770–1850

George Gordon, Lord Byron (1788–1824) on Wordsworth

> Next comes the dull disciple of thy school,
> That mild apostate from poetic rule,
> The simple Wordsworth, framer of a lay
> As soft as evening in his favourite May,
> Who warns his friend 'to shake off toil and trouble,
> And quit his books, for fear of growing double';
> Who, both by precept and example, shows
> That prose is verse, and verse is merely prose;
> Convincing all, by demonstration plain,
> Poetic souls delight in prose insane;
> And Christmas stories tortur'd into rhyme
> Contain the essence of the true sublime.
> Thus, when he tells the tale of Betty Foy,
> The idiot mother of 'an idiot boy';
> A moon-struck, silly lad, who lost his way,
> And, like his bard, confounded night with day;
> So close on each pathetic part he dwells,
> And each adventure so sublimely tells,
> That all who view the 'idiot in his glory'
> Conceive the bard the hero of the story.

English Bards, and Scotch Reviewers: A Satire (1809)

Thomas Carlyle (1795–1881) on Wordsworth

The languid way in which he gives you a handful of numb unresponsive fingers is very significant. It seems also rather to grieve him that you have any admiration for anybody but him. No man that I ever met has given me less, has disappointed me less. My peace be with him, and a happy evening to his, on the whole, respectable life.[31]

In J.A. Froude, *Thomas Carlyle: A History of his Life in London 1834–1881* (1884)

---

[31] Carlyle met Wordsworth in 1843.

Thomas De Quincey (1785–1859) on Wordsworth

To begin with his figure: – Wordsworth was, upon the whole, not a
well-made man. His legs were pointedly condemned by all the female
connoisseurs in legs that ever I heard lecture upon that topic; not that
they were bad in any way which would force itself upon your notice
– there was no absolute deformity about them; and undoubtedly they
had been serviceable legs beyond the average standard of human
requisition; for I calculate, upon good data, that with these identical
legs Wordsworth must have traversed a distance of 175 to 180,000
English miles – a mode of exertion which, to him, stood in the stead
of wine, spirits, and all other stimulants whatsoever to the animal
spirits; to which he has been indebted for a life of unclouded
happiness, and we for much of what is most excellent in his writings.
But, useful as they have proved themselves, the Wordsworthian legs
were certainly not ornamental; and it was really a pity, as I agreed
with a lady in thinking, that he had not another pair for evening dress
parties – when no boots lend their friendly aid to masque our
imperfections from the eyes of female rigorists – the *elegantes formarum
spectatrices*. A sculptor would certainly have disapproved of their
contour. But the worst part of Wordsworth's person was the bust:
there was a narrowness and a droop about the shoulders which
became striking, and had an effect of meanness when brought into
close juxtaposition with a figure of a most statuesque order. Once on
a summer morning, walking in the vale of Langdale with Wordsworth,
his sister, and Mr J –, a native Westmoreland clergyman, I remember
that Miss Wordsworth was positively mortified by the peculiar
illustration which settled upon this defective conformation. Mr J–, a
fine towering figure, six feet high, massy and columnar in his
proportions, happened to be walking, a little in advance, with
Wordsworth; Miss Wordsworth and myself being in the rear; and from
the nature of the conversation which then prevailed in our front rank,
something or other about money, devises, buying and selling, we of
the rear-guard thought it requisite to preserve this arrangement for a
space of three miles or more; during which time, at intervals, Miss
W– would exclaim, in a tone of vexation, 'Is it possible? – can that be
William? How very mean he looks!' and could not conceal a

mortification that seemed really painful, until I, for my part, could not forbear laughing outright [. . .].[32]

'William Wordsworth', in *Tait's Edinburgh Magazine*, 1839, in *Recollections of the Lakes and Lake Poets*, ed. D. Wright (1970)

Thomas Powell[33] (1809–1887) on Wordsworth

At a friend's house, after dinner the conversation turned upon wit and humour. The author of *Lalla Rookh*,[34] who was present, gave some illustrations from Sheridan's 'sayings, doings, and writings'. Starting from his reverie, Wordsworth said that he did not consider himself to be a witty poet. 'Indeed,' continued he, 'I do not think I was ever witty but once in my life.' A great desire was naturally expressed by all to know what this special drollery was. After some hesitation the old poet said – 'Well, well, I will tell you. I was standing some time ago at the entrance of my cottage at Rydal Mount. A man accosted me with the question – 'Pray, sir, have you seen my wife pass by?'; whereupon I said, 'Why, my good friend, I didn't know till this moment that you had a wife!' The company stared, and finding that the old bard had discharged his entire stock, burst into a roar of laughter, which the facetious Wordsworth, in his simplicity, accepted as a genuine compliment to the brilliancy of his wit.

The Living Authors of England (1849)

---

[32] De Quincey was even less flattering in his descriptions of Wordsworth's wife and sister. Wordsworth's wife, Mary, he described as 'neither handsome, nor even comely' and with a squint 'much beyond that slight obliquity which is often supposed to be an attractive foible of the countenance'. Dorothy Wordsworth, the poet's sister, he described as 'ungraceful' and 'unsexual', with a 'stooping attitude while walking', adding: 'rarely, in a woman of English birth, had I seen a more determinate gypsy tan.' No wonder then that when these opinions were published – in *Tait's* magazine in 1839 – Wordsworth commented: 'A man who can set such an example, I hold to be a pest in society, and one of the most worthless of mankind.'

[33] Powell was a colourful character, a journalist and hack-writer who fled to America in 1849 to escape prosecution for forgery.

[34] Thomas Moore (1779–1852)

Bertrand Russell (1872–1970) on Wordsworth

In his youth Wordsworth sympathized with the French Revolution, went to France, wrote good poetry, and had a natural daughter. At this period he was called a 'bad' man. Then he became 'good,' abandoned his daughter, adopted correct principles, and wrote bad poetry.[35]

'The Harm That Good Men Do', in *Sceptical Essays* (1928)

Percy Bysshe Shelley (1792–1822) on Wordsworth

What a beastly and pitiful wretch that Wordsworth! That such a man should be such a poet! I can compare him with no one but Simonides, that flatterer of Sicilian tyrants, and at the same time the most natural and tender of lyric poets.[36]

Letter to Thomas Love Peacock, 25 July 1818, in *Fraser's Magazine*, 1860

J.K. Stephen (1859–92) on Wordsworth

Two voices are there: one is of the deep;
It learns the storm-cloud's thunderous melody,
Now roars, now murmurs with the changing sea,
Now bird-like pipes, now closes soft in sleep:
And one is of an old half-witted sheep
Which bleats articulate monotony,
And indicates that two and one are three,
That grass is green, lakes damp, and mountains steep:
And, Wordsworth, both are thine: at certain times
Forth from the heart of thy melodious rhymes,
The form and pressure of high thoughts will burst:
At other times – good Lord! I'd rather be
Quite unacquainted with the ABC
Than write such hopeless rubbish as thy worst.

'Sonnet', in *The Granta* (1891)

---

[35] Russell went on: 'Coleridge went through a similar change: when he was wicked he wrote *Kubla Khan*, and when he was good he wrote theology.'

[36] Shelley admired Wordsworth's early poetry but was infuriated by his later political sympathies and the stodgy quality of later productions such as *The Excursion*. In his sonnet 'To Wordsworth' (1816) he made the bone of contention

WALTER SCOTT 1771–1832

George Gordon, Lord Byron (1788–1824) on Scott

> And think'st thou, Scott! by vain conceit perchance,
> On public taste to foist thy stale romance,
> Though Murray with his Miller may combine
> To yield thy muse just half-a-crown per line?
> No! when the sons of song descend to trade,
> Their bays are sear, their former laurels fade.
> Let such forego the poet's sacred name,
> Who rack their brains for lucre, not for fame:
> Still for stern Mammon may they toil in vain!
> And sadly gaze on gold they cannot gain!
> Such be their meed, such still the just reward
> Of prostituted muse and hireling bard!
> For this we spurn Apollo's venal son,
> And bid a long 'good night to Marmion'.

English Bards, and Scotch Reviewers: A Satire (1809)

E.M. Forster (1879–1970) on Scott

Who shall tell us a story?

Sir Walter Scott of course.

Scott is a novelist over whom we shall violently divide. For my own part I do not care for him, and find it difficult to understand his continued reputation. His reputation in his day – that is easy to understand. There are important historical reasons for it, which we should discuss if our scheme was chronological. But when we fish him out of the river of time, and set him to write in that circular room with the other novelists, he presents a less impressive figure. He is seen to have a trivial mind and a heavy style. He cannot construct. He has neither artistic detachment nor passion, and how can a writer who is devoid of both create characters who will move us deeply? Artistic detachment – perhaps it is priggish to ask for that. But passion – surely

---

clear: 'In honoured poverty thy voice did weave/Song consecrate to truth and liberty –/Deserting these, thou leavest me to grieve/Thus having been, that thou should cease to be.'

passion is lowbrow enough, and think how all Scott's laborious mountains and scooped-out glens and carefully ruined abbeys call out for passion, passion, and how it is never there! If he had passion he would be a great writer – no amount of clumsiness or artificiality would matter then. But he only has a temperate heart and gentlemanly feelings, and an intelligent affection for the countryside; and this is not basis enough for great novels. And his integrity – that is worse than nothing, for it was a purely moral and commercial integrity. It satisfied his highest needs and he never dreamt that another sort of loyalty exists.

Aspects of the Novel (1927)

Anthony Trollope (1815–1882) on Scott

[Of *The Bride of Lammermoor*] I cannot call this a good novel, though the plot has been so well chosen and the incidents are so pathetic that it has attained enduring popularity, and as a rule is known as widely as any by the author. But the telling of it is often dull and always tedious and the characters are not life-like. The Master is a wooden Hamlet, – Lucy Ashton a galvanized Ophelia. We know that they love simply because we are told so. We see nothing of it and only believe it because such belief is necessary to our interest. Lady Ashton would not have endured Bucklaw as a son-in-law or Craigengelt as a companion. Henry, the boy, is childish. Alice is magniloquent and mysterious we known [sic] not why. And the other old women are unnaturally fiendish. Caleb has been very successful. The character has the same claims upon us as have those of Dugald Dalgetty and Dandie Dinmont (by far the greater of the three) [. . .]

We have been told of late that Scott wrote bad English. He did not do so frequently, – but very frequently, very constantly, he wrote awkward English; – as when he says that Miss Ashton's 'manners grew mopish'. This is manifestly the case in the Bride of Lammermoor, and seems to come from quick working, which was subjected to correction by an ear not accurate in ascertaining such faults.

The chief merit of this novel is that it is really pathetic; – its chief fault is that it is unusually tedious.[37]

---

[37] Trollope was a critic but also a lover of Scott: whenever he writes about

Comment written in Trollope's copy of *The Bride of Lammermoor*,
1 January 1871, in Bradford A. Booth, 'Trollope on Scott:
Some Unpublished Notes', *Nineteenth-Century Fiction*, vol. 5, no. 3 (1950)

Mark Twain (1835–1910) on Scott

Then comes Sir Walter Scott with his enchantments, and by his single
might checks this wave of progress,[38] and even turns it back; sets the
world in love with dreams and phantoms; with decayed and swinish
forms of religion; with decayed and degraded systems of government;
with the sillinesses and emptinesses, sham grandeurs, sham gauds, and
sham chivalries of a brainless and worthless long-vanished society. He
did measureless harm; more real and lasting harm, perhaps, than any
other individual that ever wrote. Most of the world has now out lived
a good part of these harms, though by no means all of them; but in our
South they flourish pretty forcefully still. Not so forcefully as half a
generation ago, perhaps, but still forcefully. There, the genuine and
wholesome civilization of the nineteenth century is curiously confused
and commingled with the Walter Scott Middle-Age sham civilization;
and so you have practical, common-sense, progressive ideas, and
progressive works; mixed up with the duel, the inflated speech, and the
jejune romanticism of an absurd past that is dead, and out of charity
ought to be buried. But for the Sir Walter disease, the character of the
Southerner – or Southron, according to Sir Walter's starchier way of
phrasing it – would be wholly modern, in place of modern and
mediaeval mixed, and the South would be fully a generation further
advanced than it is. It was Sir Walter that made every gentleman in the
South a Major or a Colonel, or a General or a Judge, before the war;
and it was he, also, that made these gentlemen value these bogus
decorations. For it was he that created rank and caste down there, and
also reverence for rank and caste, and pride and pleasure in them.
Enough is laid on slavery, without fathering upon it these creations and
contributions of Sir Walter.

---

him he exhibits this schizophrenic tendency. Elsewhere he says: 'I read Scott's
novels also from time to time and marvel at the power of story-telling, at the
infinite imagination, and twenty-horse-power vivacity. But there is an infinity
of padding, and a very great amount of very lax work.'

[38] Twain has been speaking of the progress brought about by the French
Revolution, though he recognizes its excesses and those of Bonapartism.

Sir Walter had so large a hand in making Southern character, as it existed before the war, that he is in great measure responsible for the war. It seems a little harsh toward a dead man to say that we never should have had any war but for Sir Walter; and yet something of a plausible argument might, perhaps, be made in support of that wild proposition. The Southerner of the American Revolution owned slaves; so did the Southerner of the Civil War: but the former resembles the latter as an Englishman resembles a Frenchman. The change of character can be traced rather more easily to Sir Walter's influence than to that of any other thing or person.[39]

Life on the Mississippi (1883)

William Wordsworth (1770–1850) on Scott
Someone having observed that the next Waverley novel was to be 'Rob Roy', Wordsworth took down his volume of Ballads, and read to the company 'Rob Roy's Grave'; then, returning it to the shelf, observed, 'I do not know what more Mr. Scott can have to say upon the subject.'

In Charles Cowden Clarke, *Recollections of Writers* (1878)

SAMUEL TAYLOR COLERIDGE 1772–1834

Thomas Carlyle (1795–1881) on Coleridge
Figure a fat flabby incurvated personage, at once short, rotund and relaxed, with a watery mouth, a snuffy nose, a pair of strange brown timid yet earnest looking eyes, a high tapering brow, and a great bush of grey hair – you will have some faint idea of Coleridge. He is a kind, good soul, full of religion and affection, and poetry and animal magnetism. His cardinal sin is that he wants *will*; he has no resolution, he shrinks from pain or labour in any of its shapes. His very attitude bespeaks this: he never straightens his knee joints, he stoops with his fat ill shapen shoulders, and in walking he does not tread but shovel and slide – my father would call it *skluiffing*. He is also always busied to

---

39 This extraordinary charge relates above all to one book, *Ivanhoe*. Twain satirized the 'Sir Walter disease' in *A Connecticut Yankee in King Arthur's Court*.

keep by strong and frequent inhalations the water of his mouth from overflowing; and his eyes have a look of anxious impotence; he would do with all his heart, but he knows he dare not.[40]

In J.A. Froude, *Thomas Carlyle: A History of His Life in London, 1834–1881*

(1884)

To sit as a passive bucket and be pumped into, whether you consent or not, can in the long-run be exhilarating to no creature; how eloquent soever the flood of utterance that is descending. But if it be withal a confused unintelligible flood of utterance, threatening to submerge all known landmarks of thought, and drown the world and you! – I have heard Coleridge talk, with eager musical energy, two stricken hours, his face radiant and moist, and communicate no meaning whatsoever to any individual of his hearers, – certain of whom, I for one, still kept eagerly listening in hope; the most had long before given up, and formed (if the room were large enough) secondary humming groups of their own. He began anywhere: you put some question to him, made some suggestive observation: instead of answering this, or decidedly setting out towards answer of it, he would accumulate formidable apparatus, logical swim-bladders, transcendental life-preservers and other precautionary and vehiculatory gear, for setting out; perhaps did at last get under way, – but was swiftly solicited, turned aside by the glance of some radiant new game on this hand or that, into new courses; and ever into new; and before long into all the Universe, where it was uncertain what game you would catch, or whether any.

The Life of John Sterling (1851)

Thomas De Quincey (1785–1859) on Coleridge

And we that were more constant, too often found reason to be disappointed with the quality of his lecture.[41] His appearance was

---

[40]   This was Carlyle's first meeting with Coleridge, in 1824, when Carlyle was 29 and Coleridge 52. Carlyle had the highest expectations of Coleridge. In the second quote Coleridge has advanced in years, is now 'towards sixty' and is staying at Highgate with his friends the Gilmans.

[41]   Coleridge was booked for a series of lectures at the Royal Institution on Poetry and the Fine Arts in the spring of 1808, but failed to appear at many of them

generally that of a person struggling with pain and overmastering illness. His lips were baked with feverish heat, and often black in colour; and in spite of the water which he continued drinking through the whole course of his lecture, he often seemed to labour under an almost paralytic inability to raise the upper jaw from the lower. In such a state it is clear that nothing could save the lecture itself from reflecting his own feebleness and exhaustion, except the advantage of having been precomposed in some happier mood. But that never happened: most unfortunately he relied upon his extempore ability to carry him through. Now, had he been in spirits, or had he gathered animation and kindled by his own motion, no written lecture could have been more effectual than one of his unpremeditated colloquial harangues. But either he was depressed originally below the point from which any re-ascent was possible, or else this re-action was intercepted by continual disgust, from looking back upon his own ill success; for assuredly he never once recovered that free and eloquent movement of thought which he could command at any time in a private company. The passages he read, moreover, in illustrating his doctrines, were generally unhappily chosen, because chosen at hap-hazard, from the difficulty of finding, at a moment's summons, those passages which he had in his eye. Nor do I remember any that produced much effect, except two or three, which I myself put ready marked into his hands, among the Metrical Romances edited by Ritson.

Generally speaking, the selections were as injudicious and as inappropriate, as they were ill delivered; for amongst Coleridge's accomplishments good reading was not one; he had neither voice, nor management of voice. [. . .] However this defect chiefly concerned the immediate impression; the most afflicting to a friend of Coleridge's was the entire absence of his own peculiar and majestic intellect; no heart, no soul, was in anything he said; no strength of feeling in recalling universal truths; no power of originality or compass of moral relations in his novelties – all was a poor faint reflection from jewels

---

because of illness and opium abuse. According to Alethea Hayter in *Opium and the Romantic Imagination* Coleridge was at this point imbibing about 20,000 drops of opium per day. De Quincey too, of course, was in thrall to the same substance, which was available over the counter, and cheaply, at any chemist's shop.

once scattered in the highway by himself, in the prodigality of his early opulence – a mendicant dependance on the alms dropped from his own overflowing treasury of happier times. Such a collapse, such a quenching of the eagle's talons, never was seen before. And as I returned from one of the most afflicting of these disappointments, I could not but repeat to myself parts of that divine chorus, –

> 'Oh! dark, dark, dark!
> Amid the blaze of noon
> Irrecoverably dark, total eclipse.' &c. &c.
>> 'Samuel Taylor Coleridge', in *Tait's Edinburgh Magazine*, 1834/5, in
>> *Recollections of the Lakes and Lake Poets*, ed. D. Wright (1970)

Rheumatism, he says, drove him to opium. Very well; but with proper medical treatment the rheumatism would soon have ceased; or even, without medical treatment, under the ordinary oscillations of natural causes. And when the pain ceased, then the opium should have ceased. Why did it not? [. . .] Coleridge, professing to believe (without reason assigned) that opium-eating is criminal, and in some mysterious sense more criminal than wine-drinking or porter-drinking, having, therefore, the strongest *moral* motive for abstaining from it, yet suffers himself to fall into a captivity to this same wicked opium, deadlier than was ever heard of, and under no coercion whatever that he has anywhere explained to us. A slave he was to this potent drug not less abject than Caliban to Prospero – his detested and yet despotic master. [. . .] It is notorious that in Bristol (to *that* I can speak myself, but probably in many other places) he went so far as to hire men – porters, hackney-coachmen, and others – to oppose by force his entrance into any druggist's shop. But, as the authority for stopping him was derived simply from himself, naturally these poor men found themselves in a metaphysical fix, not provided for even by Thomas Aquinas or by the prince of Jesuitical casuists. And in this excruciating dilemma would occur such scenes as the following:

'Oh, sir,' would plead the suppliant porter – suppliant, yet semi-imperative (for equally if he *did*, and if he did not, show fight, the poor man's daily 5s. seemed endangered) – 'really you must not; consider, sir, your wife and—'

Transcendental Philosopher – 'Wife! what wife? I have no wife.'[42]

Porter – 'But, really now, you must not, sir. Didn't you say no longer ago than yesterday—'

Transcend. Philos. – 'Pooh, pooh! yesterday is a long time ago. Are you aware, my man, that people are known to have dropped down dead for timely want of opium?'

Porter – 'Ay, but you tell't me not to hearken—'

Transcend. Philos. – 'Oh, nonsense. An emergency, a shocking emergency, has arisen – quite unlooked for. No matter what I told you in times long past. That which I now tell you, is – that, if you don't remove that arm of yours from the doorway of this most respectable druggist, I shall have a good ground of action against you for assault and battery.'

Confessions of an English Opium Eater, 1821, ed. A. Hayter (1971)

Leigh Hunt (1784–1859) on Coleridge

Coleridge was one evening running before the wind. He had talked about everything, from Moses downwards. At last he came to his own doings at Shrewsbury, and was swinging on, nineteen knots to the hour. 'At this place, at Shrewsbury (which is not only remarkable for its celebrated cakes, and for having been the point of rendezvous for Falstaff's regiment of foot, but also, if I may presume to speak of it, for the first development of the imaginative faculty in myself, by which faculty I would be understood to mean, etc. etc.) – at Shrewsbury I was accustomed to preach. – I believe, Charles Lamb, that you have heard me preach?' pursued he, turning round to his fatigued friend, who rapidly retorted – 'I – I – never heard you do anything else.'[43]

Leigh Hunt's London Journal, 17 October 1835, in Edmund Blunden, *Charles Lamb: His Life Recorded by his Contemporaries* (1934)

ROBERT SOUTHEY 1774–1843

George Gordon, Lord Byron (1788–1824) on Southey

> He said – (I only give the heads) – he said,
> He meant no harm in scribbling; 'twas his way
> Upon all topics; 'twas, besides, his bread,

---

[42] De Quincey inserts as a footnote here: 'Vide *Othello*.'

[43] Lamb had a stutter.

Of which he buttered both sides; 'twould delay
Too long the assembly (he was pleased to dread),
And take up rather more time than a day,
To name his works – he would but cite a few—
'Wat Tyler' – 'Rhymes on Blenheim' – 'Waterloo.'

He had written praises of a Regicide;
He had written praises of all kings whatever;
He had written for republics far and wide,
And then against them bitterer than ever;
For pantisocracy he once had cried
Aloud, a scheme less moral than 'twas clever;
Then grew a hearty anti-jacobin –
Had turned his coat – and would have turned his skin.

He had sung against all battles, and again
In their high praise and glory; he had called
Reviewing 'the ungentle craft,' and then
Became as base a critic as e'er crawled –
Fed, paid, and pampered by the very men
By whom his muse and morals had been mauled:
He had written much blank verse, and blanker prose,
And more of both than anybody knows. [44]

'The Vision of Judgment' (1822)

---

[44]   Byron's 'Vision of Judgment' was a response to Southey's 'Vision of Judgement' of 1821, in which Southey, as poet laureate, imagined the reception of George III into heaven. In the preface Southey had referred to the 'Satanic school' of Byron, and it was this, rather than the unctuousness of the Vision, that incensed Byron. In his own parodic preface Byron wrote: 'If Mr. Southey had not rushed in where he had no business, and where he never was before, and never will be again, the following poem would not have been written. It is not impossible that it may be as good as his own, seeing that it cannot, by any species of stupidity, natural or acquired, be worse. The gross flattery, the dull impudence, the renegado intolerance, and impious cant, of the poem by the author of "Wat Tyler," are something so stupendous as to form the sublime of himself – containing the quintessence of his own attributes. So much for his poem – a word on his preface. In this preface it has pleased the magnanimous Laureate to draw the picture of a supposed "Satanic School," the which he doth recommend to the notice of the legislature; thereby adding to his other laurels the ambition of those of an informer. If there exists anywhere, except in his imagination, such a School, is he not sufficiently armed against it by his own intense vanity?'

William Hazlitt (1778–1830) on Southey

He is ever in extremes, and ever in the wrong! The reason is, that not truth, but self-opinion is the ruling principle of Mr. Southey's mind. The charm of novelty, the applause of the multitude, the sanction of power, the venerableness of antiquity, pique, resentment, the spirit of contradiction have a good deal to do with his preferences. His inquiries are partial and hasty: his conclusions raw and unconcocted, and with a considerable infusion of whim and humour and a monkish spleen. His opinions are like certain wines, warm and generous when new; but they will not keep, and soon turn flat or sour, for want of a stronger spirit of the understanding to give a body to them. He wooed Liberty as a youthful lover, but it was perhaps more as a mistress than a bride; and he has since wedded with an elderly and not very reputable lady, called Legitimacy.[45]

Spirit of the Age: Or Contemporary Portraits (1846)

JANE AUSTEN 1775–1817

Charlotte Brontë (1816–1855) on Austen

Why do you like Miss Austen so very much? I am puzzled on that point. What induced you to say that you would rather have written 'Pride and Prejudice' or 'Tom Jones' than any of the Waverley novels? I had not seen 'Pride and Prejudice' till I read that sentence of yours, and then I got the book. And what did I find? An accurate, daguerreotyped portrait of a commonplace face; a carefully-fenced, high-cultivated garden, with neat borders and delicate flowers; but no glance of a bright, vivid physiognomy, no open country, no fresh air, no blue hill, no bonny beck. I should hardly like to live with her ladies and gentlemen, in their elegant but confined houses. These observations will probably irritate you, but I shall run the risk.

Letter to G.H. Lewes, 12 January 1848, in Elizabeth Gaskell,
The Life of Charlotte Brontë (1858)

[A]nything like warmth or enthusiasm, anything energetic, poignant, heartfelt, is utterly out of place in commending these works: all such

---

[45]   i.e. political legitimacy, or the powers-that-be, in his role as poet laureate.

demonstration the authoress would have met with a well-bred sneer, would have calmly scorned as *outré* and extravagant. She does her business of delineating the surface of the lives of genteel English people curiously well; there is a Chinese fidelity, a miniature delicacy, in the painting: she ruffles her reader by nothing vehement, disturbs him with nothing profound: the passions are perfectly unknown to her; she rejects even a speaking acquaintance with that stormy Sisterhood; even to the Feelings she vouchsafes no more than an occasional graceful but distant recognition; too frequent converse with them would ruffle the smooth elegance of her progress. Her business is not half so much with the human heart as with the human eyes, mouth, hands, and feet; what sees keenly, speaks aptly, moves flexibly, it suits her to study, but what throbs fast and full, though hidden, what the blood rushes through, what is the unseen seat of life and the sentient target of death – this Miss Austen ignores. She no more, with her mind's eye, beholds the heart of her race than each man, with bodily vision, sees the heart in his heaving breast. Jane Austen was a complete and most sensible lady, but a very incomplete and rather insensible (not *senseless*) woman.

> Letter to W.S. Williams, 12 April 1850, in *Jane Austen: Critical Assessments*,
> ed. I. Littlewood (1998)

Ralph Waldo Emerson (1803–1882) on Austen

I am at a loss to understand why people hold Miss Austen's novels at so high a rate, which seem to me vulgar in tone, sterile in artistic invention, imprisoned in their wretched conventions of English society, without genius, wit, or knowledge of the world. Never was life so pinched and narrow. The one problem in the mind of the writer in both the stories I have read, Persuasion, and Pride and Prejudice, is marriageableness. All that interests in any character is still this one: has he or [she] the money to marry with, and conditions conforming? 'Tis the 'nympholepsy of a fond despair',[46] say, rather, of an English boarding-house. Suicide is more respectable.

> Journal for August–September 1861, in *Jane Austen: The Critical Heritage*,
> ed. B.C. Southam (1995)

---

[46]   A quotation from Byron's 'Childe Harold's Pilgrimage'.

D.H. Lawrence (1885–1930) on Austen

This, again, is the tragedy of social life today. In the old England, the curious blood-connection held the classes together. The squires might be arrogant, violent, bullying and unjust, yet in some way they were *at one* with the people, part of the same blood-stream. We feel it in Defoe or Fielding. And then, in the mean Jane Austen, it is gone. Already this old maid typifies 'personality' instead of character, the sharp knowing in apartness instead of togetherness, and she is, to my feeling, thoroughly unpleasant, English in the bad, mean snobbish sense of the word, just as Fielding is English in the good, generous sense.

A Propos of Lady Chatterley's Lover (1930)

Mark Twain (1835–1910) on Austen

I haven't any right to criticize books, and I don't do it except when I hate them. I often want to criticize Jane Austen, but her books madden me so that I can't conceal my frenzy from the reader; and therefore I have to stop every time I begin. Every time I read 'Pride and Prejudice' I want to dig her up and hit her over the skull with her own shin-bone.

Letter, 13 September 1898, in A.B. Paine, *Mark Twain: A Biography* (1912)

Virginia Woolf (1882–1941) on Austen

Whatever 'Bloomsbury' may think of Jane Austen, she is not by any means one of my favourites. I'd give all she ever wrote for half what the Brontës wrote – if my reason did not compel me to see that she is a magnificent artist. What I shall proceed to find out, from her letters, when I've time, is why she failed to be much better than she was. Something to do with sex, I expect; the letters are full of hints already that she suppressed half of her in her novels.[47]

Letter to Ethel Smythe, 20 November 1932, in David Dowling,
Novelists on Novelists (1983)

---

[47] Elsewhere Virginia Woolf spoke of Austen with unqualified praise: 'The wit of Jane Austen has for partner the perfection of her taste [. . .]. Never did any novelist make more use of an impeccable sense of human values.'

CHARLES LAMB 1775–1834

Thomas De Quincey (1785–1859) on Lamb

It is not by chance, or without a deep ground in his nature, *common* to all his qualities, both affirmative and negative, that Lamb had an insensibility to music more absolute than can have been often shared by any human creature, or perhaps than was ever before acknowledged so candidly. The sense of music – as a pleasurable sense, or as any sense at all other than of certain unmeaning and impertinent differences in respect to high and low, sharp or flat – was utterly obliterated as with a sponge by nature herself from Lamb's organization. It was a corollary, from the same large *substratum* in his nature, that Lamb had no sense of the rhythmical in prose composition. Rhythmus, or pomp of cadence, or sonorous ascent of clauses, in the structure of sentences, were effects of art as much thrown away upon *him* as the voice of the charmer upon the deaf adder. We ourselves, occupying the very station of polar opposition to that of Lamb, being as morbidly, perhaps, in the one excess as he in the other, naturally detected this omission in Lamb's nature at an early stage of our acquaintance. Not the fabled Regulus,[48] with his eyelids torn away, and his uncurtained eye-balls exposed to the noon-tide glare of a Carthaginian sun, could have shrieked with more anguish of recoil from torture than we from certain sentences and periods in which Lamb perceived no fault at all.

'Charles Lamb', in the *North British Review*, 1848, in *De Quincey as Critic*, ed.
J.E. Jordan (1973)

Thomas Carlyle (1795–1881) on Lamb

Charles Lamb I sincerely believe to be in some considerable degree insane. A more pitiful, rickety, gasping, staggering, stammering tomfool I do not know. He is witty by denying truisms and abjuring good manners. His speech wriggles hither and thither with an incessant painful fluctuation; not an opinion in it or a fact or even a phrase that you can thank him for: more like a convulsion fit than natural systole

---

[48] De Quincey adds as a footnote here: 'Marcus Atilius Regulus, Roman general of the third century B.C., was by possibly apocryphal tradition, sent as a captive of the Carthaginians to Rome to arrange a peace, counseled against it, returned to Carthage according to his oath, and was fiendishly tortured.'

and diastole. – Besides he is now a confirmed shameless drunkard; asks vehemently for gin-and-water in strangers' houses; tipples till he is utterly mad, and is only not thrown out of doors because he is too much despised for taking such trouble with him. Poor Lamb! Poor England where such a despicable abortion is named genius![49]

In J.A. Froude, *Thomas Carlyle: A History of his Life in London 1834–1881*

MATTHEW GREGORY (MONK) LEWIS 1775–1818

George Gordon, Lord Byron (1788-1824) on Lewis

Lewis at Oatlands was observed one morning to have his eyes red, and his air sentimental. Being asked why, he replied, 'that when people said anything *kind* to him, it affected him deeply; and just now the Duchess has said something *so* kind to me that . . .' Here tears began to flow again. 'Never mind, Lewis,' said Colonel Armstrong to him, 'never mind, don't cry. *She could not mean it.*'

In *Byron: A Self Portrait*, ed. P. Quennell (1950)

Walter Scott (1771–1832) on Lewis

Lewis was fonder of great people than he ought to have been, either as a man of talent or as a man of fashion. He had always dukes and duchesses in his mouth, and was pathetically fond of any one that had a title. You would have sworn he had been a parvenu of yesterday, yet he had lived all his life in good society. His person was extremely small and boyish – he was indeed the least man I ever saw, to be strictly well and neatly made. I remember a picture of him by Saunders being handed round at Dalkeith House. The artist had ingeniously flung a dark folding-mantle around the form, under which was half-hid a dagger, a dark lantern, or some such cut-throat appurtenance; with all this the features were preserved and ennobled. It passed from hand to hand into that of Henry, Duke of Buccleuch, who, hearing the general voice affirm that it was very like, said aloud, 'Like Mat Lewis! Why that picture's like a MAN!' He looked, and lo, Mat Lewis's head was at his elbow.

Scott's marginal note in Byron's diary, in J.G. Lockhart and W. Scott, *Life of Sir Walter Scott* (1853)

---

[49] Carlyle wrote this in his diary in 1831 after visiting Lamb at Enfield.

WILLIAM HAZLITT 1778–1830

Samuel Taylor Coleridge (1772–1834) on Hazlitt

His manners are to 99 in 100 singularly repulsive –: brow-hanging, shoe-contemplative, *strange*. [. . .] he is, I verily believe, kindly-natured; is very fond of, attentive to, and patient with children; but he is jealous, gloomy, and of an irritable pride – and addicted to women, as objects of sexual indulgence.

> Letter to Thomas Wedgwood, 1803, in *Unpublished Letters of Samuel Taylor Coleridge*, ed. E.L. Griggs (1932)

Thomas De Quincey (1785–1859) on Hazlitt

But Hazlitt smiled upon no man, nor exchanged tokens of peace with the nearest of fraternities. Wieland, in his *Oberon*, says of a benign patriarch –

His eye a smile on all creation beamed.

Travestied as to one word, the line would have described Hazlitt –

His eye a scowl on all creation beamed.

This inveterate misanthropy was constitutional; exasperated it certainly had been by accidents of life, by disappointments, by mortifications, by insults, and still more by having wilfully placed himself in collision from the first with all the interests that were in the sunshine of this world, and with all the persons that were then powerful in England; but my impression was, if I had a right to *have* any impression with regard to one whom I knew so slightly, that no change of position or of fortunes could have brought Hazlitt into reconciliation with the fashion of this world, or of this England, or 'this now.' It seemed to me that he hated those whom hollow custom obliged him to call his 'friends' considerably more than those whom notorious differences of opinion entitled him to rank as his enemies. At least within the ring of politics this was so. Between those particular Whigs whom literature had connected him with, and the whole gang of *us* Conservatives, he showed the same difference in his mode of fencing and parrying, and even in his style of civilities, as between the domestic traitor, hiding a stiletto among his robes of peace, and the bold enemy who sends a trumpet before him, and rides up sword-in-hand against your gates. *Whatever is* – so much I conceive to have been a fundamental lemma for Hazlitt – *is wrong*.[50] So much he thought it safe to postulate. *How* it was wrong might require an impracticable investigation; you might fail for a century to discover; but *that* it was wrong he nailed down as a point of faith, that could stand out against all counter-presumptions from argument, or counter-evidences from experience.

> Review in *Tait's Edinburgh Magazine*, 1845/6,
> in *De Quincey as Critic*, ed. J.E. Jordan (1973)

Henry Crabb Robinson (1775–1867) on Hazlitt

I recollect saying to my sister-in-law, 'Whom do you suppose I hold to be the cleverest person I know?' – 'Capel Lofft, perhaps?' – 'No.' – 'Mrs. Clarkson?' – 'Oh! no.' – 'Miss Maling?' – 'No.' – 'I give it up.' – 'William Hazlitt.' 'Oh, you are joking. Why, we all take him to be just the reverse.' At this time he was excessively shy, especially in the company of young ladies, who on their part were very apt to make fun of him. The prettiest girl of our parties about this time was a Miss Kitchener, and she used to drive him mad by teasing him.

> *Diary, Reminiscences, and Correspondence* (1870)

William Wordsworth (1770–1850) on Hazlitt

The miscreant Hazlitt continues, I have heard, his abuses of Southey, Coleridge and myself, in the Examiner. – I hope that you do not associate with the Fellow, he is not a proper person to be admitted into respectable society, being the most perverse and malevolent Creature that ill luck has ever thrown in my way. Avoid him – hic niger est – And this, I understand, is the general opinion wherever he is known in London.[51]

> Letter to Benjamin Robert Haydon, 7 April 1817, in *Critical Opinions of*
> *William Wordsworth*, ed. M.L. Peacock (1950)

---

[50]   A parody of Pope's formulation in the *Essay on Man*, 'Whatever is, is right.'

[51]   Hazlitt had unfavourably reviewed a poem by Wordsworth, 'Now that all hearts are glad, all faces bright', about the 'regal fortitude' of George III in the face of his increasing mental ill-health. Hazlitt implied that it was unworthy of the author of 'The Female Vagrant', a poem about 'the miseries brought on the lower classes by war', when those miseries were chiefly caused by those exercising 'regal fortitude'.

LEIGH HUNT 1784–1859

George Gordon, Lord Byron (1788-1824) on Hunt

He believes his trash of vulgar phrases tortured into compound barbarisms to be old English; and we may say of it as Aimwell says of Captain Gibbet's regiment, when the Captain calls it an 'old corps.' – 'the *oldest* in Europe, if I may judge by your uniform.' He sent out his 'Foliage' by Percy Shelley –[52] and, of all the ineffable Centaurs that were ever begotten by Selflove upon a Night-mare, I think this monstrous Sagittary the most prodigious. *He* (Leigh H.) is an honest Charlatan, who has persuaded himself into a belief of his own impostures, and talks Punch in pure simplicity of heart, taking himself (as poor Fitzgerald said of *himself* in the Morning Post) for *Vates* in both senses, or nonsenses, of the word. Did you look at the translations of his own which he prefers to Pope and Cowper, and says so?

Letter to Thomas Moore, 1 June 1818, in *Byron's Letters and Journals*, ed. L.A. Marchand and J. Murray (1973–82)

GEORGE GORDON, LORD BYRON 1788–1824

Max Beerbohm (1872-1956) on Byron

Byron! – he would be all forgotten to-day if he had lived to be a florid old gentleman with iron-grey whiskers, writing very long, very able letters to 'The Times' about the Repeal of the Corn Laws. Yes, Byron would have been that. It was indicated in him. He would have been an old gentleman exacerbated by Queen Victoria's invincible prejudice against him, her brusque refusal to 'entertain' Lord John Russell's timid nomination of him for a post in the Government [. . .] Did he know that he was to die in service of the Greeks whom he despised? Byron might not have minded that. But what if the Greeks had told him, in so many words, that they despised HIM? How would he have felt then? Would he have been content with his potations of barley-water?[53]

Zuleika Dobson (1911)

---

[52] The dash represents a deletion made in the text when first published.

[53] This is not strictly Beerbohm *qua* Beerbohm: the passage appears in *Zuleika Dobson*, and the words are those of the Duke of Dorset, Zuleika's suitor.

Charles Lamb (1775–1834) on Byron

So we have lost another Poet. I never much relished his Lordship's
mind, and shall be sorry if the Greeks have cause to miss him. He was
to me offensive, and I never can make out his great *power*, which his
admirers talk of. Why, a line of Wordsworths is a lever to lift the
immortal Spirit! Byron can only move the Spleen. He was at best a
Satyrist, – in any other way he was mean enough. I dare say I do him
injustice; but I cannot love him, nor squeeze a tear to his memory.

Letter to Bernard Barton, 15 May 1824,
in *The Letters of Charles and Mary Lamb*, ed. E.V. Lucas (1935)

Thomas Babington Macaulay (1800–1859) on Byron

Never had any writer so vast a command of the whole eloquence of
scorn, misanthropy and despair. That Marah was never dry. No art
could sweeten, no draughts could exhaust, its perennial waters of
bitterness. Never was there such variety in monotony as that of Byron.
From maniac laughter to piercing lamentation, there was not a single
note of human anguish of which he was not master. Year after year, and
month after month, he continued to repeat that to be wretched is the
destiny of all; that to be eminently wretched is the destiny of the
eminent; that all the desires by which we are cursed lead alike to
misery, if they are not gratified, to the misery of disappointment, if
they are gratified, to the misery of satiety. His heroes are men who
have arrived by different roads at the same goal of despair, who are sick
of life, who are at war with society, who are supported in their anguish
only by an unconquerable pride resembling that of Prometheus on the
rock or of Satan in the burning marl, who can master their agonies by
the force of their will, and who, to the last, defy the whole power of
earth and heaven. He always described himself as a man of the same
kind with his favourite creations, as a man whose heart had been
withered, whose capacity for happiness was gone and could not be
restored, but whose invincible spirit dared the worst that could befall
him here or hereafter. How much of this morbid feeling sprang from
an original disease of the mind, how much from real misfortune, how
much from the nervousness of dissipation, how much was fanciful,
how much was merely affected, it is impossible for us, and would
probably have been impossible for the most intimate friends of Lord

Byron, to decide. Whether there ever existed, or can ever exist, a person answering to the description which he gave of himself may be doubted; but that he was not such a person is beyond all doubt. It is ridiculous to imagine that a man whose mind was really imbued with scorn of his fellow-creatures would have published three or four books every year in order to tell them so [. . .]

Among that large class of young persons whose reading is almost entirely confined to works of imagination, the popularity of Lord Byron was unbounded. They bought pictures of him; they treasured up the smallest relics of him; they learned his poems by heart, and did their best to write like him, and to look like him. Many of them practised at the glass in the hope of catching the curl of the upper lip, and the scowl of the brow, which appear in some of his portraits. A few discarded their neckcloths in imitation of their great leader. For some years the Minerva press sent forth no novel without a mysterious, unhappy, Lara-like peer. The number of hopeful under-graduates and medical students who became things of dark imaginings, on whom the freshness of the heart ceased to fall like dew, whose passions had consumed themselves to dust, and to whom the relief of tears was denied, passes all calculation. This was not the worst. There was created in the minds of many of these enthusiasts a pernicious and absurd association between intellectual power and moral depravity. From the poetry of Lord Byron they drew a system of ethics, compounded of misanthropy and voluptuousness, a system in which the two great commandments were, to hate your neighbour, and to love your neighbour's wife.

'Moore's Life of Byron' (1831), in *Critical and Historical Essays: Contributed to the Edinburgh Review by Thomas Babington Macaulay* (1853)

Samuel Rogers (1763–1855) on Byron

When we sat down to dinner, I asked Byron if he would take soup? 'No; he never took soup.' – 'Would he take some fish?' – 'No; he never took fish.' – Presently I asked if he would eat some mutton? 'No; he never ate mutton.' – I then asked if he would take a glass of wine? 'No; he never tasted wine.' – It was now necessary to inquire what he *did* eat and drink; and the answer was, 'Nothing but hard biscuits and soda-water.' Unfortunately, neither hard biscuits nor soda-water were at hand; and he dined upon potatoes bruised down on his plate and drenched with vinegar. – My guests stayed till very late, discussing the merits of Walter Scott and Joanna Baillie. – Some days after, meeting Hobhouse, I said to him, 'How long will Lord Byron persevere in his present diet?' He replied, 'Just as long as you continue to notice it.' I did not then know, what I now know to be a fact – that Byron, after leaving my house, had gone to a Club in St. James's Street, and eaten a hearty meat supper.[54]

Reminiscences and Table Talk of Samuel Rogers, ed. G.H. Powell (1903)

Percy Bysshe Shelley (1792–1822) on Byron

I entirely agree with what you say about *Childe Harold*. The spirit in which it is written is, if insane, the most wicked and mischievous insanity that ever was given forth. It is a kind of obstinate and self-willed folly, in which he hardens himself. I remonstrated with him in vain on the tone of mind from which such a view of things alone arises. For its real root is very different from its apparent one. Nothing can be less sublime than the true source of these expressions of contempt and desperation. The fact is, that first, the Italian women with whom he associates are perhaps the most contemptible of all who exist under the moon – the most ignorant, the most disgusting, the most bigoted; countesses smell so strongly of garlic, that an ordinary Englishman cannot approach them. Well, L.B. is familiar with the lowest sort of these women, the people his gondolieri pick up in the streets. He associates with wretches who seem almost to have lost the gait and physiology of man, and who do not

---

[54]   In modern parlance, Byron suffered from eating disorders and was obsessed with his own body image. He was at some times obese and at others painfully thin, constantly yo-yo-ing between the two states and using dishes such as mashed potatoes and vinegar to quell the pangs. 'When I do dine, I gorge like an Arab or a Boa snake,' he confided to his diary. He wrote to a friend: 'I have taken every means to accomplish the end, by violent exercise & Fasting, as I found myself too plump. I shall continue my Exertions, having no other amusement, I wear *seven* waistcoats, and a great Coat, run, and play at cricket in this Dress, till quite exhausted by excessive perspiration, use the Hip Bath daily, eat only a quarter of a pound of Butcher's Meat in 24 hours, no Suppers or Breakfast, only one Meal a Day [. . .].' His sister Augusta wrote: 'I am quite convinced that if he would condescend to eat & drink & sleep *like other people* he would feel ye good effects – but you know his way is to fast till he is famished & then *devour* more than his stomach in that *weak* state can bear – & so on.'

scruple to avow practices, which are not only not named, but I believe seldom even conceived in England.

> Letter to Thomas Love Peacock, 22 December 1818, in *Essays, Letters from Abroad, Translations and Fragments*, ed. M. Shelley (1845)

JAMES FENIMORE COOPER 1789–1851

Mark Twain (1835–1910) on Cooper

Cooper's art has some defects. In one place in *Deerslayer*, and in the restricted space of two-thirds of a page, Cooper has scored 114 offences against literary art out of a possible 115. It breaks the record.

There are nineteen rules governing literary art in the domain of romantic fiction – some say twenty-two. In *Deerslayer* Cooper violated eighteen of them. These eighteen require:

1. That a tale shall accomplish something and arrive somewhere. But the *Deerslayer* tale accomplishes nothing and arrives in the air.

2. They require that the episodes of a tale shall be necessary parts of the tale, and shall help to develop it. But as the *Deerslayer* tale is not a tale, and accomplishes nothing and arrives nowhere, the episodes have no rightful place in the work, since there was nothing for them to develop.

3. They require that the personages in a tale shall be alive, except in the case of corpses, and that always the reader shall be able to tell the corpses from the others. But this detail has often been overlooked in the *Deerslayer* tale.

4. They require that the personages in a tale, both dead and alive, shall exhibit a sufficient excuse for being there. But this detail also has been overlooked in the *Deerslayer* tale.

5. They require that when the personages of a tale deal in conversation, the talk shall sound like human talk, and be talk such as human beings would be likely to talk in the given circumstances, and have a discoverable meaning, also a discoverable purpose, and a show of relevancy, and remain in the neighborhood of the subject in hand, and be interesting to the reader, and help out the tale, and stop when the people cannot think of anything more to say. But this requirement has been

ignored from the beginning of the *Deerslayer* tale to the end of it.

6. They require that when the author describes the character of a personage in his tale, the conduct and conversation of that personage shall justify said description. But this law gets little or no attention in the *Deerslayer* tale, as 'Natty Bumppo's' case will amply prove.

7. They require that when a personage talks like an illustrated, gilt-edged, tree-calf, hand-tooled, seven-dollar Friendship's Offering in the beginning of a paragraph, he shall not talk like a negro minstrel in the end of it. But this rule is flung down and danced upon in the *Deerslayer* tale.

8. They require that crass stupidities shall not be played upon the reader as 'the craft of the woodsman, the delicate art of the forest,' by either the author or the people in the tale. But this rule is persistently violated in the *Deerslayer* tale.

9. They require that the personages of a tale shall confine themselves to possibilities and let miracles alone; or, if they venture a miracle, the author must so plausibly set it forth as to make it look possible and reasonable. But these rules are not respected in the *Deerslayer* tale.

10. They require that the author shall make the reader feel a deep interest in the personages of his tale and in their fate; and that he shall make the reader love the good people in the tale and hate the bad ones. But the reader of the *Deerslayer* tale dislikes the good people in it, is indifferent to the others, and wishes they would all get drowned together.

11. They require that the characters in a tale shall be so clearly defined that the reader can tell beforehand what each will do in a given emergency. But in the *Deerslayer* tale this rule is vacated. In addition to these large rules there are some little ones. These require that the author shall:

12. *Say* what he is proposing to say, not merely come near it.

13. Use the right word, not its second cousin.

14. Eschew surplusage.

15. Not omit necessary details.

16. Avoid slovenliness of form.

17. Use good grammar.

18. Employ a simple and straightforward style.

Even these seven are coldly and persistently violated in the *Deerslayer* tale.

Cooper's gift in the way of invention was not a rich endowment; but such as it was he liked to work it, he was pleased with the effects, and indeed he did some quite sweet things with it. In his little box of stage properties he kept six or eight cunning devices, tricks, artifices for his savages and woodsmen to deceive and circumvent each other with, and he was never so happy as when he was working these innocent things and seeing them go. A favorite one was to make a moccasined person tread in the tracks of the moccasined enemy, and thus hide his own trail. Cooper wore out barrels and barrels of moccasins in working that trick. Another stage-property that he pulled out of his box pretty frequently was his broken twig. He prized his broken twig above all the rest of his effects, and worked it the hardest. It is a restful chapter in any book of his when somebody doesn't step on a dry twig and alarm all the reds and whites for two hundred yards around. Every time a Cooper person is in peril, and absolute silence is worth four dollars a minute, he is sure to step on a dry twig. There may be a hundred handier things to step on, but that wouldn't satisfy Cooper. Cooper requires him to turn out and find a dry twig; and if he can't do it, go and borrow one. In fact, the Leather Stocking Series ought to have been called the Broken Twig Series.

'Fenimore Cooper's Literary Offences', 1895,
in *Humorous Stories and Sketches* (1996)

PERCY BYSSHE SHELLEY 1792–1822

Thomas Carlyle (1795–1881) on Shelley
Poor soul, he has always seemed to me an extremely weak creature, and lamentable much more than admirable. Weak in genius, weak in character (for these two always go together); a poor thin, spasmodic, hectic, shrill and pallid being; – one of those unfortunates, of whom I often speak, to whom the 'talent of *silence*', first of all, has been denied. The speech of such is never good for much. Poor Shelley, there is something void and Hades-like in the whole inner world of him; his

universe is all vacant azure, hung with a few frosty mournful if beautiful stars; the very voice of him (his style &c), shrill, shrieky, to my ear has too much of the *ghost!*

> Letter to Robert Browning, 8 March 1852, in *The Collected Letters of Thomas and Jane Welsh Carlyle*, ed. C. de L. Ryals and K.J. Fielding (1999)

William Hazlitt (1778–1830) on Shelley

Mr. Shelley's style is to poetry what astrology is to natural science – a passionate dream, a straining after impossibilities, a record of fond conjectures, a confused embodying of vague abstractions, – a fever of the soul, thirsting and craving after what it cannot have, indulging its love of power and novelty at the expense of truth and nature, associating ideas by contraries, and wasting great powers by their application to unattainable objects.

Poetry, we grant, creates a world of its own; but it creates it out of existing materials. Mr. Shelley is the maker of his own poetry – out of nothing. Not that he is deficient in the true sources of strength and beauty, if he had given himself fair play (the volume before us, as well as his other productions, contains many proofs to the contrary): but in him, fancy, will, caprice, predominated over and absorbed the natural influences of things; and he had no respect for any poetry that did not strain the intellect as well as fire the imagination – and was not sublimed into a high spirit of metaphysical philosophy. Instead of giving a language to thought, or lending the heart a tongue, he utters dark sayings, and deals in allegories and riddles. His Muse offers her services to clothe shadowy doubts and inscrutable difficulties in a robe of glittering words, and to turn nature into a brilliant paradox. We thank him – but we must be excused. Where we see the dazzling beacon lights streaming over the darkness of the abyss, we dread the quicksands and the rocks below. Mr. Shelley's mind was of 'too fiery a quality' to repose (for any continuance) on the probable or the true – it soared 'beyond the visible diurnal sphere,' to the strange, the improbable, and the impossible. He mistook the nature of the poet's calling, which should be guided by involuntary, not by voluntary, impulses. He shook off, as an heroic and praiseworthy act, the trammels of sense, custom, and sympathy, and became the creature of his own will. He was 'all air,' disdaining the bars and lies of mortal mould. He ransacked his brain for incongruities, and believed in whatever was incredible. Almost all is effort, almost all is extravagant, almost all is quaint, incomprehensible, and abortive, from aiming to be more than it is. Epithets are applied, because they do not fit; subjects are chosen, because they are repulsive; the colours of his style, for their gaudy, changeful, startling effect, resemble the display of fire-works in the dark, and, like them, have neither durability, nor keeping, nor discriminate form. Yet Mr. Shelley, with all his faults, was a man of genius; and we lament that uncontrollable violence of temperament which gave it a forced and false direction. He has single thoughts of great depth and force, single images of rare beauty, detached passages of extreme tenderness; and, in his smaller pieces, where he has attempted little, he has done most. If some casual and interesting idea touched his feelings or struck his fancy, he expressed it in pleasing and unaffected verse: but give him a larger subject, and time to reflect, and he was sure to get entangled in a system. The fumes of vanity rolled volumes of smoke, mixed with sparkles of fire, from the cloudy tabernacle of his thought. The success of his writings is therefore in general in the inverse ratio of the extent of his undertakings; inasmuch as his desire to teach, his ambition to excel, as soon as it was brought into play, encroached upon, and outstripped, his powers of execution.

Selections from the Edinburgh Review, ed. Maurice Cross (1835)

Charles Kingsley (1819–75) on Shelley

'Lawless love' is Shelley's expressed ideal of the relation of the sexes; and his justice, his benevolence, his pity, are all equally lawless. 'Follow your instincts,' is his one moral rule, confounding the very lowest animal instincts with those lofty ideas of might, which it was the will of Heaven that he should retain, ay, and love, to the very last, and so reducing them all to the level of sentiments. 'Follow your instincts' – But what if our instincts lead us to eat animal food? 'Then you must follow the instincts of me, Percy Bysshe Shelley. I think it horrible, cruel; it offends my taste.' What if our instincts lead us to tyrannize over our fellow-men? 'Then you must repress those instincts. I, Shelley, think that, too, horrible and cruel.' Whether it be vegetarianism or liberty, the rule is practically the same – sentiment which, in his case, as in the case of all sentimentalists, turns out to mean at last, not the sentiments of mankind in general, but the private sentiments of the writer. This is Shelley; a sentimentalist pure and simple; incapable of anything like inductive reasoning; unable to take cognizance of any facts but those which please his taste, or to draw any conclusion from them but such as also pleases his taste; as, for example, in that eighth stanza of the 'Ode to Liberty,' which, had it been written by any other man but Shelley, possessing the same knowledge as he, one would have called a wicked and deliberate lie – but in his case, is to be simply passed over with a sigh, like a young lady's proofs of table-turning and rapping spirits. She wished to see it so – and therefore so she saw it.

For Shelley's nature is utterly womanish. Not merely his weak points, but his strong ones, are those of a woman. Tender and pitiful as a woman; and yet, when angry, shrieking, railing, hysterical as a woman. The physical distaste for meat and fermented liquors, coupled with the hankering after physical horrors, are especially feminine. The nature of a woman looks out of that wild, beautiful, girlish face – the nature: but not the spirit; not

> The reason firm, the temperate will,
> Endurance, foresight, strength and skill.[55]

The lawlessness of the man, with the sensibility of the woman . . . Alas for him!

Miscellanies (1860)

Charles Lamb (1775–1834) on Shelley

Shelley I saw once. His voice was the most obnoxious squeak I ever was tormented with, ten thousand times worse than the Laureat's,[56] whose voice is the worst part about him, except his Laureatship.

Letter to Bernard Barton, 9 October 1822, in *The Life, Letters and Writings of Charles Lamb* (1897)

---

[55]   From Wordsworth's 'She Was a Phantom of Delight'.

[56]   Robert Southey. Southey seems to have attracted more bile than most poets, and his laureateship from 1813–43 was perhaps the major cause of it.

THOMAS CARLYLE 1795–1881

Samuel Butler (1835–1902) on Carlyle

Yes it was very good of God to let Carlyle and Mrs. Carlyle marry one another and so make only two people miserable instead of four . . . .[57]

Letter to Eliza Savage, 21 November 1884,
in *Letters between Samuel Butler and E.M.A. Savage, 1871–1885* (1935)

Anthony Trollope (1815–1882) on Carlyle

I have read – nay, I have bought! – Carlyle's '*Latter Day Pamphlets*', and look on my eight shillings as very much thrown away. To me it appears that the grain of sense is so smothered up in a sack of the sheerest trash, that the former is valueless. He does not himself know what he wants. He has one idea – a hatred of spoken and acted falsehood; and on that he harps through the whole eight pamphlets. I look on him as a man who was always in danger of going mad in literature and who has now done so.[58]

Letter to Frances Trollope, 1850/51, in *The Letters of Anthony Trollope*,
ed. Bradford Allen Booth (1951)

JOHN KEATS 1795–1821

Matthew Arnold (1822–1888) on Keats

What harm he has done in English Poetry. As Browning is a man with a moderate gift passionately desiring movement and fulness, and obtaining but a confused multitudinousness, so Keats with a very high gift, is yet also consumed by this desire: and cannot produce the truly

---

[57]   Margot Asquith, in her *Autobiography* of 1920, remembered Tennyson saying something identical.

[58]   Trollope went so far as to insert a caricature of Carlyle in *The Warden* of 1855, Dr Pessimist Anticant, who 'instituted himself censor of things in general, and began the great task of reprobating everything and everybody [. . .] Accordinging to him nobody was true, and not only nobody, but nothing; a man could not take off his hat to a lady without telling a lie; – the lady would lie again in smiling. The ruffles of the gentleman's shirt would be fraught with deceit, and the lady's flounces full of falsehood. Was ever anything more severe than that attack of his on chip bonnets, or the anathemas with which he endeavoured to dust the powder out of the bishops' wigs?' See also Carlyle on Trollope, page 111.

living and moving, as his conscience keeps telling him. They will not be patient neither understand that they must begin with an Idea of the world in order not to be prevailed over by the world's multitudinousness: or if they cannot get that, at least with isolated ideas: and all other things shall (perhaps) be added unto them.

Letter to Arthur Clough, 1848/9, in John Keats:
The Critical Heritage, ed. G.M. Matthews (1995)

George Gordon, Lord Byron (1788–1824) on Keats

Here are Johnny Keats's piss a-bed poetry [...] There is such a trash of Keats and the like upon my tables, that I am ashamed to look at them [...] No more Keats, I entreat: flay him alive; if some of you don't I must skin him myself: there is no bearing the driveling idiotism of the Mankin.

The *Edinburgh* praises Jack Keats or Ketch, or whatever his names are [...] why, his is the *Onanism* of Poetry – something like the pleasure an Italian fiddler extracted out of being suspended daily by a Street Walker in Drury Lane. This went on for some weeks: at last the Girl went to get a pint of Gin – met another, chatted too long, and Cornelli was *hanged outright before she returned*. Such like is the trash they praise, and such will be the end of the *outstretched* poesy of this miserable Self-polluter of the human mind.

Mr Keats, whose poetry you enquire after, appears to me what I have already said: such writing is a sort of mental masturbation – he is always frigging his *Imagination*. I don't mean he is *indecent*, but viciously soliciting his ideas into a state, which is neither poetry nor any thing else but a Bedlam vision produced by raw pork and opium.[59]

Letters to John Murray, 12 August–9 September 1820, in The Routledge
Literary Sourcebook on the Poems of John Keats, ed. J. Strachan (2003)

Thomas De Quincey (1785–1859) on Keats

As a man, and viewed in relation to social objects, Keats was nothing. It was as mere an affectation when he talked with apparent zeal of

---

[59] Byron was not an admirer of the Lake Poets: he felt that Keats, as a camp-follower of the school ('a tadpole of the Lakes'), exhibited all their faults and worse. But after Keats's death – widely attributed by Shelley and others to the scabrous comments of the literary quarterlies and critics such as Byron – he

liberty, or human rights, or human prospects, as is the hollow enthusiasm which innumerable people profess for music, or most poets for external nature. For these things Keats fancied that he cared; but in reality, from all I can learn, he cared next to nothing. Upon them, or any of their aspects, he had thought too little, and too indeterminately, to feel for them as personal concerns. Whereas Shelley, from his earliest days, was mastered and shaken by the great moving realities of life, as a prophet is by the burden of wrath or of promise which he has been commissioned to reveal. Had there been no such thing as literature, Keats would have dwindled into a cipher. Shelley, in the same event, would hardly have lost one plume from his crest. It is in relation to literature, and to the boundless questions as to the true and the false arising out of literature and poetry, that Keats challenges a fluctuating interest, sometimes an interest of strong disgust, sometimes of deep admiration. There is not, I believe, a case on record throughout European Literature where feelings so repulsive of each other have centred in the same individual.

Review in *Tait's Edinburgh Magazine*, 1845/6, in *De Quincey as Critic*,
ed. J.E. Jordan (1973)

Thomas Carlyle (1795–1881) on Keats

[On Monckton Milne's *Life of Keats*] An attempt to make us eat dead dog by exquisite currying and cooking [. . .] The kind of man that Keats was gets ever more horrible to me. Force of hunger for every pleasure of every kind, and want of all other force – that is a combination! Such a structure of soul, it would once have been very evident, was a chosen 'Vessel of Hell' [. . .]

In J.A. Froude, *Thomas Carlyle: A History of His Life in London, 1834–1881*
(1884)

---

modified his position, writing in 1821: 'My indignation at Mr Keats's deprecia-
tion of Pope has hardly permitted me to do justice to his own genius, which,
malgre all the fantastic fopperies of his style, was undoubtedly of great promise.
His fragment of Hyperion seems actually inspired by the Titans, and is as sublime
as Aeschylus. He is a loss to our literature.'

VICTOR HUGO 1802–1885

Charles Baudelaire (1821–67) on Hugo

Hugo, like a priest, always has his head bowed – bowed so low that he can see nothing except his own navel.

Intimate Journals, 1887, ed. and trans. C. Isherwood (1930)

Thomas Carlyle (1795–1881) on Hugo

A glittering humbug.

In Henry Brewster Stanton, *Random Recollections* (1887)

Jean Cocteau (1889–1963) on Hugo

Victor Hugo was a madman who thought he was Victor Hugo.

Opium: The Diary of a Cure (1932)

HENRY WADSWORTH LONGFELLOW 1807–1882

Edgar Allan Poe (1809–1849) on Longfellow

In no literary circle out of BOSTON – or, indeed, out of the small coterie of abolitionists, transcendentalists and fanatics in general, which is the Longfellow junto – have we heard a seriously dissenting voice on this point. It is universally, in private conversation – out of the knot of rogues and madmen aforesaid – admitted that the poetical claims of Mr. LONGFELLOW have been vastly overrated, and that the individual himself would be esteemed little without the accessaries of wealth and position. It is usually said, that he has a sufficient scholarship, a fine taste, a keen appreciation of the beautiful, a happy memory, a happier tact at imitation or transmutation, felicity of phrase and some fancy. A few insist on his imagination – thus proving the extent of their own – and showing themselves to be utterly unread in the old English and modern German literature, to one or other of which, the author of 'Outre Mer' is unquestionably indebted for whatever imagination or traces of invention his works may display. No phrenologist, indeed, would require to be told that Mr. LONGFELLOW was not the man of genius his friends would have us believe him – his head giving no indication of ideality. Nor, when we speak of phrenologists, do we mean to insist on implicit faith in the marvels and inconsistencies of the FOWLERS *et id genus omne.* Common observation, independently of either GAIL or SPURZHEIM, would suffice to teach all mankind that very many of the salient points of phrenological science are undisputable truths – whatever falsity may be detected in the principles kindly furnished to the science by hot-headed and asinine votaries. Now, one of these salient points, is the fact that what men term 'poetical genius', and what the phrenologists generally term the organ of ideality, are always found co-existent in the same individual. We should as soon expect to see our old friend, SATAN, presiding at a temperance meeting, as to see a veritable poem – of his own – composed by a man whose head was flattened at the temples, like that of Professor LONGFELLOW. Holding these views, we confess that we were not a little surprised to hear Mr. POE, in a late lecture, on the Poetry of AMERICA, claim for the Professor a preeminence over all poets of this country on the score of the 'loftiest poetical quality – imagination.' There is no doubt in our minds, that an opinion so crude as this, must arise from a want of leisure or inclination to compare the works of the writer in question with the sources from which they were stolen. A defensive letter written by an unfortunate wight who called himself 'OUTIS', seems to have stirred up the critic to make the proper examination, and we will make an even wager of a pound avoirdupois of nothing against LONGFELLOW originality, that the rash opinion would not be given again. The simple truth is, that, whatever may be the talents of Professor LONGFELLOW, he is the GREAT MOGUL of the Imitators. There is, perhaps, no other country than our own, under the sun, in which it would have been possible for him to have attained his present eminence; and no other, certainly, in which, after having attained it by accident or chicanery, he would not have been hurled from it in a very brief period after its attainment.[60]

'Longfellow's Poems', *The Aristidean*, April 1845, in *Essays and Reviews by Edgar Allan Poe*, ed. G.R. Thompson (1984)

---

[60]   This was an anonymous review, very probably written by Poe, and took issue both with 'Mr. POE' and with 'OUTIS', another pseudonym of Poe's. Poe was, in a highly convoluted manner, fomenting a controversy that came to be known as the 'Longfellow Wars', and, remarkably, taking all sides in it himself, virulently attacking and staunchly defending Longfellow in different guises. Some commentators penetrated this ventriloquism, and one journal, the *Town*, published a parody of a Poe review, in which the same book was described as 'a mass of insufferable trash' and 'one of the most delightful books'. Longfellow himself stayed out of the Longfellow Wars.

THOMAS BABINGTON MACAULAY 1800–1859

Thomas Carlyle (1795–1881) on Macaulay

Macaulay is well for a while, but one wouldn't live under Niagara.

In R.M. Milnes, *Notebooks* (1838)

Sydney Smith (1771–1845) on Macaulay

Yes, I agree, he is certainly more agreeable since his return from India. His enemies might perhaps have said before (though I never did so) that he talked rather too much; but now he has occasional flashes of silence, that make his conversation perfectly delightful.

Remark in Lady Saba Holland, *A Memoir of the Reverend Sydney Smith* (1855)

EDWARD BULWER-LYTTON 1803–1873

Nathaniel Hawthorne (1804–1864) on Bulwer-Lytton

Bulwer nauseates me; he is the very pimple of the age's humbug. There is no hope of the public, so long as he retains an admirer, a reader, or a publisher.[61]

Mosses from an Old Manse (1851)

---

[61]   This opinion is delivered under the cloak of one 'P', a friend of Hawthorne's who has lost his reason – he thinks he has encountered Napoleon Bonaparte in Pall Mall, and fancies Dickens died shortly after completing *The Pickwick Papers*, among other delusions. The cover enables Hawthorne to deliver himself of some satirical opinions on figures such as Burns, Byron, Bulwer-Lytton, Scott and Shelley.

4 VENOM FOR THE VICTORIANS

The Victorian era, from the point of view of invective, was a period of full-blown, extended and often public disagreement. There were the famous quarrels between Dickens and Thackeray; Tolstoy and Turgenev; Twain and Harte; James and Wells; and Wells and Shaw. Sometimes these were over matters of literary style; more often there were personal reasons. Basic forces such as ambition and sex often lay at their root (Dickens and Thackeray quarrelled over Dickens's relationship with the actress Ellen Ternan; Tolstoy and Turgenev over Turgenev's illegitimate daughter).

In fact the Victorian era was a period of painful struggles over sex in literature. The most famous of these was the 'Fleshly School' controversy, in which conservative critics such as Buchanan and Morley pitted themselves against poets of licence such as Swinburne, Morris and Rossetti. Buchanan wrote:

> We cannot forbear expressing our wonder, by the way, at the kind of women whom it seems the unhappy lot of these gentlemen to encounter. We have lived as long in the world as they have, but never yet came across persons of the other sex who conduct themselves in the manner described. Females who bite, scratch, scream, bubble, munch, sweat, writhe, twist, wriggle, foam, and in a general way slaver over their lovers, must surely possess some extraordinary qualities to counteract their otherwise most offensive mode of conducting themselves.

Buchanan was comprehensively worsted in the onslaught that followed; his naïve remarks ruined his reputation for ever. Such was the impact of the controversy that Ezra Pound still felt his readers would recognize the name 'Buchanan' when he wrote his 'Hugh Selwyn Mauberley' in 1920:

> Fœtid Buchanan lifted up his voice
> When that faun's head of hers
> Became a pastime for
> Painters and adulterers.

But Swinburne too could be a prude, and attacked Tennyson in language not so very dissimilar to Buchanan's, describing the theme of 'Merlin and Vivien' as: 'the erotic fluctuations and vacillations of a dotard under the moral and physical manipulation of a prostitute. The conversation of Vivien is exactly described in the poet's own phrase – it is "as the poached filth that floods the middle street".'

From the perspective of the literary era we now inhabit – the one which produced *Ulysses* and *Tropic of Cancer* – it is quite a spectator sport to watch the Victorians falling over one another. This was a time with no Freud, no Havelock Ellis, and consequently none of the tools to do the job. In some moments it just wanted sex to go away. Or as Buchanan wrote: 'At times, in reading such books as this, one cannot help wishing that things had remained for ever in the asexual state described in Mr. Darwin's great chapter on Palingenesis.'

If there is a single figure who symbolizes Victorian literature it is probably Dickens. What his colleagues made of him was not always something good. Henry James, younger and more 'modern', was one of his most vocal critics, and he surely put his finger on the strange familial repulsiveness of Dickens's style when he said (of *Our Mutual Friend*) that his characters were 'a mere bundle of eccentricities, animated by no principle of nature whatever'. James had a bad word for everyone: Trollope was 'gross and importunate'; Baudelaire was 'ludicrously puerile'; Hardy was 'ingeniously verbose' – this from James!; Wilde was 'clumsy, feeble and vulgar'.

But there was no shortage of curmudgeons: Trollope and Carlyle were busy doing down their fellow writers, and among those they did down most energetically were each other: Carlyle sneered at Trollope as 'a dirtyish little pug' and Trollope described Carlyle as 'a man who was always in danger of going mad in literature and who has now done so.'

The Victorian era is also marked by another phenomenon: the rise of the great American writers and the first stirrings of the Great American Novel. And where there are great writers there other great writers prepared to be revolted by them.

RALPH WALDO EMERSON 1803–1882

Herman Melville (1819–1891) on Emerson

I could readily see in Emerson, notwithstanding his merit, a gaping flaw. It was, the insinuation, that had he lived in those days when the world was made, he might have offered some valuable suggestions. These men are all cracked right across the brow.

> Letter to Evert Duyckinck, 3 March 1849, in *Herman Melville:*
> *Representative Selections*, ed. W. Thorp (1938)

Algernon Charles Swinburne (1837–1909) on Emerson

A foul mouth is so ill matched with a white beard that I would gladly believe the newspaper scribes alone responsible for the bestial utterances which they declare to have dropped from a teacher whom such disciples as these exhibit, to our disgust and compassion, as performing on their obscene platform the last tricks of tongue now possible to a gap-toothed and hoary-headed ape, carried first into notice on the shoulder of Carlyle, and who now, in his dotage, spits and chatters from a dirtier perch of his own finding and fouling: coryphaeus or choragus of his Bulgarian tribe of autocoprophagous baboons, who make the filth they feed on.[62]

> *New York Daily Tribune*, 25 February 1874, in *Modern Language Notes*,
> March 1933

BENJAMIN DISRAELI 1804–1881

Anthony Trollope (1815–1882) on Disraeli

There is one other name, without which the list of the best known English novelists of my own time would certainly be incomplete, and that is the name of the present Prime Minister of England. Mr. Disraeli has written so many novels, and has been so popular as a novelist that, whether for good or for ill, I feel myself compelled to

---

[62] Swinburne was reacting to an article in *Frank Leslie's Illustrated Newspaper* for 3 January 1874, in which Emerson was reported to have described him as a 'perfect leper' and a 'mere sodomite' ('mere' in the archaic sense of 'pure' or 'thoroughgoing'.)

speak of him. To me they have all had the same flavour of paint and unreality. In whatever he has written he has affected something which has been intended to strike his readers as uncommon and therefore grand. Because he has been bright and a man of genius, he has carried his object as regards the young. He has struck them with astonishment and aroused in their imagination ideas of a world more glorious, more rich, more witty, more enterprising, than their own. But the glory has been the glory of pasteboard, and the wealth has been a wealth of tinsel. The wit has been the wit of hairdressers, and the enterprise has been the enterprise of mountebanks. An audacious conjurer has generally been his hero, – some youth who, by wonderful cleverness, can obtain success by every intrigue that comes to his hand. Through it all there is a feeling of stage properties, a smell of hair-oil, an aspect of buhl, a remembrance of tailors, and that pricking of the conscience which must be the general accompaniment of paste diamonds. I can understand that Mr. Disraeli should by his novels have instigated many a young man and many a young woman on their way in life, but I cannot understand that he should have instigated any one to good. Vivian Grey has had probably as many followers as Jack Sheppard,[63] and has led his followers in the same direction.

An Autobiography (1883)

NATHANIEL HAWTHORNE 1804–1864

Oliver Wendell Holmes (1809–1894) on Hawthorne
Hawthorne was named among other authors, probably by Fields, whose house had just published his 'Marble Faun,' and who had recently come home on the same steamer with him. Doctor Holmes asked if I had met Hawthorne yet, and when I confessed that I had hardly yet even hoped for such a thing, he smiled his winning smile, and said: 'Ah, well! I don't know that you will ever feel you have really met him. He is like a dim room with a little taper of personality burning on the corner of the mantel.'

In William Dean Howells, *Literary Friends and Acquaintances* (1900)

---

[63] A notorious burglar and thief (1702–24) who was hanged at Tyburn.

GEORGE SAND 1804–1876

Charles Baudelaire (1821–1867) on Sand

On George Sand. – That woman is the Prudhomme of immorality.

She has always been a moralist.

Only there was a time when her conduct was anti-moral.

Besides, she was never an artist. She has the famous 'flowing style', dear to the bourgeoisie.

She is stupid, heavy and garrulous. Her ideas on morals have the same depth of judgment and delicacy of feeling as those of janitresses and kept women.

What she says about her mother.

What she says about poetry.

Her love of the working-class.

The fact that there are men who could become enamoured of this slut is indeed a proof of the abasement of the men of this generation.

Compare the preface to *Mademoiselle La Quintinie,* where she claims that true Christians do not believe in Hell.

La Sand speaks for *the God of the respectable,* the God of janitresses and knavish lackeys.

She has good reasons to wish to abolish Hell.

The Devil and George Sand. – It must not be supposed that the Devil tempts only men of genius. He doubtless despises imbeciles, but he does not disdain their support. Quite on the contrary, he founds his greatest hopes upon such people.

George Sand, for example. She is, above all else, a *ponderous* animal; but also she is *possessed*. It was the Devil who persuaded her to rely on her 'good heart' and her 'good sense', so that she might persuade all the other ponderous animals to rely upon *their* good heart and good sense.

I cannot think of this stupid creature without a sort of shudder of repulsion. If I met her, I would be unable to refrain from throwing a stoup of holy-water at her head.

My Heart Laid Bare, 1864-66, trans. N. Cameron (1975)

Thomas Carlyle (1795–1881) on Sand

In the general putrescence of your 'religions,' as you call them, a strange new religion, named of Universal Love, with Sacraments mainly of – *Divorce*, with Balzac, Sue and Company for Evangelists, and Madame Sand for Virgin, will come, – and results fast following therefrom which will astonish you very much!

Latter Day Pamphlets (1850)

ELIZABETH BARRATT BROWNING 1806–1861

G.K. Chesterton (1874–1936) on Elizabeth Barratt Browning

It is not unnoticeable that as Miss Austen spent most of her life in a village, Miss Barrett spent most of her life on a sofa. The godlike power of guessing seems (for some reason I do not understand) to grow under such conditions. Unfortunately Mrs. Browning was like all the other Victorians in going a little lame, as I have roughly called it, having one leg shorter than the other. But her case was, in one sense, extreme. She exaggerated both ways. She was too strong and too weak, or (as a false sex philosophy would express it) too masculine and too feminine. I mean that she hit the centre of weakness with almost the same emphatic precision with which she hit the centre of strength. She could write finally of the factory wheels 'grinding life down from its mark,' a strong and strictly true observation. Unfortunately she could also write of Euripides 'with his droppings of warm tears.' She could write in *A Drama of Exile*, a really fine exposition, touching the later relation of Adam and the animals: unfortunately the tears were again turned on at the wrong moment at the main; and the stage direction commands a silence, only broken by the dropping of angel's tears. How much noise is made by angel's tears? Is it a sound of emptied buckets, or of garden hose, or of mountain cataracts? That is the sort of question which Elizabeth Barrett's extreme love of the extreme was always tempting people to ask. [. . .] As to the critic who thinks her poetry owed anything to the great poet who was her husband, he can go and live in the same hotel with the man who can believe that George Eliot owed anything to the extravagant imagination of Mr. George Henry Lewes. So far from Browning inspiring or interfering, he did not in one sense interfere enough. Her real inferiority to him in literature is that he was consciously while she was unconsciously absurd.

The Victorian Age in Literature (1913)

Edward Fitzgerald (1809–83) on Elizabeth Barratt Browning

Mrs. Browning's death is rather a relief to me, I must say: no more Aurora Leighs, thank God. A woman of real genius, I know; but what is the upshot of it all? She and her sex had better mind the kitchen and her children; and perhaps the poor: except in such things as little novels, they only devote themselves to what men do much better, leaving that which men do worse or not at all.[64]

Letter to W.H. Thompson, 15 July 1861, in *Letters and Literary Remains* (1889)

EDWARD FITZGERALD 1809–1883

Robert Browning (1812–1889) on Fitzgerald

I chanced upon a new book yesterday:
I opened it, and where my finger lay
'Twixt page and uncut page, these words I read
– Some six or seven at most – and I learned thereby
That you, Fitzgerald, whom by ear and eye
She never knew, 'thanked God my wife was dead.'

Ay, dead! and you were yourself alive, good Fitz,
How to return you thanks would task my wits:
Kicking you seems the common lot of curs –
While more appropriate greeting lends you grace:
Surely to spit there glorifies your face –
Spitting – from lips once sanctified by Hers.[65]

Athenaeum, 13 July 1889

---

[64] See Browning's furious response, below.

[65] The desire to spit in FitzGerald's face – the dead FitzGerald's face, since FitzGerald had died six years before, in 1883 – was occasioned by reading the letter from FitzGerald in his posthumous *Letters and Literary Remains*, in which FitzGerald had expressed relief that Mrs Browning had died. See above.

EDGAR ALLAN POE 1809–1849

T.S. Eliot (1888–1965) on Poe

That Poe had a powerful intellect is undeniable, but it seems to me the intellect of a highly gifted young person before puberty. The forms which his lively curiosity takes are those in which a pre-adolescent mentality delights: wonders of nature and of mechanics and of the supernatural, cryptograms and cyphers, puzzles and mazes, mechanical chess-players and wild flights of speculation. The variety and ardour of his curiosity delight and dazzle: yet in the end the eccentricity and lack of coherence of his interests tire. There is just that lacking which gives dignity to the mature man: a consistent view of life. An attitude can be mature and consistent, and yet be highly sceptical: but Poe was no sceptic. He appears to yield himself completely to the idea of the moment: the effect is that all of his ideas seem to be *entertained* rather than believed. What is lacking is not brain power, but that maturity of intellect which comes only with the maturing of the man as a whole, the development and coordination of his various emotions. I am not concerned with any possible psychological or pathological explanation: it is enough for my purpose to record that the work of Poe is such as I should expect of a man of very exceptional mind and sensibility, whose emotional development has been in some respect arrested at an early age. His most vivid imaginative realizations are the realization of a dream: significantly, the ladies in his poems and tales are always ladies lost, or ladies vanishing before they can be embraced. Even in *The Haunted Palace*, where the subject appears to be his own weakness of alcoholism, the disaster has no moral significance; it is treated impersonally as an isolated phenomenon; it has not behind it the terrific force of such lines as those of François Villon when he speaks of his own fallen state.

'From Poe to Valéry', 1948, in *To Criticize the Critic and Other Writings* (1965)

Henry James (1843–1916) on Poe

With all due respect to the very original genius of the author of the 'Tales of Mystery', it seems to us that to take him with more than a certain degree of seriousness is to lack seriousness one's self. An enthusiasm for Poe is the mark of a decidedly primitive stage of reflection.

'Charles Baudelaire', *The Nation*, 27 April 1876, in *The Portable Henry James*,
ed. J. Auchard (2004)

James Russell Lowell (1819–1891) on Poe

There comes Poe, with his raven, like Barnaby Rudge,
Three fifths of him genius and two fifths sheer fudge,
Who talks like a book of iambs and pentameters,
In a way to make people of common sense damn metres,
Who has written some things quite the best of their kind,
But the heart somehow seems all squeezed out by the
mind [. . .].[66]

'A Fable for Critics', 1848, in *Nineteenth-century American Poetry*, ed. W.C.
Spengemann and J.F. Roberts (1996)

ALFRED TENNYSON, 1809–1892

Anon. on Tennyson

When Tennyson entered the Oxford Theatre to receive his honorary
degree of D.C.L., his locks hanging in admired disorder on his
shoulders, dishevelled and unkempt, a voice from the gallery was heard
crying out to him, 'Did your mother call you early, dear?'

In Julian Charles Young, *A Memoir of Charles Mayne Young*, 1871, in
The Oxford Book of Literary Anecdotes, ed. J. Sutherland (1975)

Robert Browning (1812–1889) on Tennyson

I send with this Tennyson's new vol., and, alas, the old with it – that is,
what he calls old. You will see, and groan! The alterations are insane.
Whatever is touched is spoiled. There is some woeful infirmity in the

---

[66] Poe had previously praised Lowell, and so when 'A Fable for Critics' came
out, it seemed like rank ingratitude. Poe reviewed it for more than one journal,
saying of it that 'no failure was ever more complete or more pitiable'. He went
on (in reference to Lowell's Northern abolitionist politics) to excommunicate
Lowell entirely: 'no Southerner who does not wish to be insulted, and at the
same time revolted by a bigotry the most obstinately blind and deaf, should ever
touch a volume by this author.'

man – he was months buried in correcting the press of the last volume, and in that time began spoiling the new poems (in proof) as hard as he could [. . .] I have been with Moxon this morning, who tells me that he is miserably thin-skinned, sensitive to criticism (foolish criticism), wishes to see no notices that contain the least possible depreciatory expressions – poor fellow! But how good when good he is – that noble *Locksley Hall*, for instance – and *St Simeon Stylites* – which I think perfect.

Letter to Alfred Domett, 13 July 1842,

in *The Poets and Their Critics*, ed. H.S. Davies (1962)

G.K. Chesterton (1874–1936) on Tennyson

He really did hold a great many of the same views as Queen Victoria, though he was gifted with a more fortunate literary style. If Dickens is Cobbett's democracy stirring in its grave, Tennyson is the exquisitely ornamental extinguisher on the flame of the first revolutionary poets. England has settled down; England has become Victorian. The compromise was interesting, it was national and for a long time it was successful: there is still a great deal to be said for it. But it was as freakish and unphilosophic, as arbitrary and untranslatable, as a beggar's patched coat or a child's secret language. Now it is here that Browning had a certain odd advantage over Tennyson; which has, perhaps, somewhat exaggerated his intellectual superiority to him. [. . .] Browning is the Englishman taking himself wilfully, following his nose like a bull-dog, going by his own likes and dislikes. We cannot help feeling that Tennyson is the Englishman taking himself seriously – an awful sight. One's memory flutters unhappily over a certain letter about the Papal Guards written by Sir Willoughby Patterne.[67] It is here chiefly that Tennyson suffers by that very Virgilian loveliness and dignity of diction which he put to the service of such a small and anomalous national scheme. Virgil had the best news to tell as well as the best words to tell it in. His world might be sad; but it was the largest world one could live in before the coming of Christianity. If he

---

[67]   Sir Willoughby is the hero of *The Egoist* (1879) by George Meredith: the Swiss Guards 'affected [i.e. excited] his sense of humour', of which Meredith makes it clear that there was in fact none.

told the Romans to spare the vanquished and to war down the mighty, at least he was more or less well informed about who *were* mighty and who *were* vanquished. But when Tennyson wrote verses like –

> 'Of freedom in her regal seat,
> Of England; not the schoolboy heat,
> The blind hysterics of the Celt'

he quite literally did not know one word of what he was talking about; he did not know what Celts are, or what hysterics are, or what freedom was, or what regal was or even of what England was – in the living Europe of that time.

His religious range was very much wider and wiser than his political; but here also he suffered from treating as true universality a thing that was only a sort of lukewarm local patriotism. Here also he suffered by the very splendour and perfection of his poetical powers. He was quite the opposite of the man who cannot express himself; the inarticulate singer who dies with all his music in him. He had a great deal to say; but he had much more power of expression than was wanted for anything he had to express. He could not think up to the height of his own towering style.

The Victorian Age in Literature (1913)

Bertrand Russell (1872–1970) on Tennyson

Tennyson was an appalling exhibitionist. He thought of himself as a combination of Homer and Sir Henry Irving. He used to go swaggering along country lanes reciting aloud and swinging a cloak. He had an almost theatrically pink complexion and two red spots on his cheeks. I think he used makeup.

In Alistair Cooke, *Six Men* (1977)

Algernon Charles Swinburne (1837–1909) on Tennyson

The Vivien of Mr. Tennyson's idyl seems to me, to speak frankly, about the most base and repulsive person ever set forth in serious literature. Her impurity is actually eclipsed by her incredible and incomparable vulgarity – (*'O ay,' said Vivien, 'that were likely too'*). She is such a sordid creature as plucks men passing by the sleeve. I am of course aware that this figure appears the very type and model of a beautiful and fearful temptress of the flesh, the very embodied and ennobled ideal of danger and desire, in the chaster eyes of the virtuous journalist[68] who grows sick with horror and disgust at the license of other French and English writers; but I have yet to find the French or English contemporary poem containing a passage that can be matched against the loathsome dialogue in which Merlin and Vivien discuss the nightly transgressions against chastity, within doors and without, of the various knights of Arthur's court. I do not remember that any modern poet whose fame has been assailed on the score of sensual immorality – say for instance the author of 'Mademoiselle de Maupin' or the author of the 'Fleurs du Mal'[69] – has ever devoted an elaborate poem to describing the erotic fluctuations and vacillations of a dotard under the moral and physical manipulation of a prostitute. The conversation of Vivien is exactly described in the poet's own phrase – it is 'as the poached filth that floods the middle street.'

Under the Microscope (1872)

HARRIET BEECHER STOWE 1811–1896

William Dean Howells (1837–1920) on Stowe

As for the author of 'Uncle Tom's Cabin' her syntax was such a snare to her that it sometimes needed the combined skill of all the proof-readers and the assistant editor to extricate her. Of course, nothing was ever written into her work, but in changes of diction, in correction of solecisms, in transposition of phrases, the text was largely rewritten on the margin of her proofs.

In William Dean Howells, *Literary Friends and Acquaintances* (1900)

---

[68]   Robert Buchanan, who had attacked Rossetti and Swinburne. See page 126.

[69]   Théophile Gautier and Charles Baudelaire respectively.

WILLIAM MAKEPEACE THACKERAY 1811–1863

Arnold Bennett (1867–1931) on Thackeray

Again and again in *Vanity Fair* you see Thackeray approaching a
difficulty whose solution will demand honesty and bravery, and you ask
yourself: 'How is he going to get through this?' Well, he doesn't get
through it. He curves away from it, or he stops dead. He is a coward.

In *Arnold Bennett: The Evening Standard Years*, ed. A. Mylett (1974)

John Ruskin (1819–1900) on Thackeray

Scott made his romance so ridiculous, that, since his day, one can't help
fancying helmets were always pasteboard, and horses were always hobby.
Dickens made everybody laugh, or cry, so that they could not go about
their business till they had got their faces in wrinkles; and Thackeray
settled like a meatfly on whatever one had got for dinner, and made
one sick of it.

Fors Clavigera (1871–84)

Anthony Trollope (1815–1882) on Thackeray

Late in Thackeray's life, – he never was an old man, but towards the end
of his career, – he failed in his power of charming, because he allowed
his mind to become idle. In the plots which he conceived, and in the
language which he used; I do not know that there is any perceptible
change; but in The Virginians and in Philip the reader is introduced to
no character with which he makes a close and undying acquaintance.
And this, I have no doubt, is so because Thackeray himself had no such
intimacy. His mind had come to be weary of that fictitious life which
is always demanding the labour of new creation, and he troubled
himself with his two Virginians and his Philip only when he was seated
at his desk.[70]

An Autobiography (1883)

---

[70] Trollope was a friend and generally an admirer of Thackeray, calling his style
the 'purest' and 'most harmonious' of novelists.

CHARLES DICKENS 1812–1870

Arnold Bennett (1867–1931) on Dickens

Of Dickens, dear friend, I know nothing. About a year ago, from idle curiosity, I picked up *The Old Curiosity Shop*, & of all the rotten vulgar un-literary writing . . .! Worse than George Eliot's. If a novelist can't *write* where *is* the beggar?[71]

Letter to George Sturt, 6 February 1898,
in *Charles Dickens: The Critical Heritage*, ed. P. Collins (1995)

George Eliot (1819–1880) on Dickens

We have one great novelist who is gifted with the utmost power of rendering the external traits of our town population; and if he could give us their psychological character – their conceptions of life, and their emotions – with the same truth as their idiom and manners, his books would be the greatest contribution Art has ever made to the awakening of social sympathies. But while he can copy Mrs Plornish's colloquial style with the delicate accuracy of a sun-picture, while there is the same startling inspiration in his description of the gestures and phrases of 'Boots', as in the speeches of Shakespeare's mobs or numbskulls, he scarcely ever passes from the humorous and external to the emotional and tragic, without becoming as transcendent in his unreality as he was a moment before in his artistic truthfulness. But for the precious salt of his humour, which compels him to reproduce external traits that serve, in some degree, as a corrective to his frequently false psychology, his preternaturally virtuous poor children and artisans, his melodramatic boatmen and courtezans, would be as noxious as Eugène Sue's idealized proletaries in encouraging the miserable fallacy that high morality and refined sentiment can grow out of harsh social relations, ignorance and want; or that the working-classes are in a condition to enter at once into a millennial state of *altruism*, wherein everyone is caring for everyone else, and no one for himself.[72]

---

[71]   Bennett was a consistent dismisser of Dickens, considering himself part of a new wave of post-Dickensian modernists. Elsewhere he criticized Dickens's 'grossness', 'common mind and inferior style' and claimed: 'Ninety percent of Dickens bores me.'

[72]   Eliot had in July 1856 not yet published a novel. Her relations with Dickens were later friendly, though when she met him she was not impressed: 'His

The Westminster Review, July 1856, in *Charles Dickens:*
The Critical Heritage, ed. P. Collins (1995)

Henry James (1843–1916) on Dickens

Our Mutual Friend is, to our perception, the poorest of Mr Dickens's works. And it is poor with the poverty not of momentary embarrassment, but of permanent exhaustion. It is wanting in inspiration. For the last ten years it has seemed to us that Mr Dickens has been unmistakably forcing himself. *Bleak House* was forced; *Little Dorrit* was labored; the present work is dug out as with a spade and pickaxe. [. . .] To say that the conduct of the story, with all its complications, betrays a long-practised hand, is to pay no compliment worthy the author. If this were, indeed, a compliment, we should be inclined to carry it further, and congratulate him on his success in what we should call the manufacture of fiction; for in so doing we should express a feeling that has attended us throughout the book. Seldom, we reflected, had we read a book so intensely *written*, so little seen, known, or felt.

In all Mr Dickens's works the fantastic has been his great resource; and while his fancy was lively and vigorous it accomplished great things. But the fantastic, when the fancy is dead, is a very poor business. The movement of Mr Dickens's fancy in Mrs Wilfer and Mr Boffin and Lady Tippins, and the Lammles and Miss Wren, and even in Eugene Wrayburn, is, to our mind, a movement lifeless, forced, mechanical. It is the letter of his old humor without the spirit. It is hardly too much to say that every character here put before us is a mere bundle of eccentricities, animated by no principle of nature whatever. In former days there reigned in Mr Dickens's extravagances a comparative consistency; they were exaggerated statements of types that really existed. We had, perhaps, never known a Newman Noggs, nor a Pecksniff, nor a Micawber; but we had known persons of whom these figures were but the strictly logical consummation. But among the grotesque creatures who occupy the pages before us, there is not one whom we can refer to as an existing type. In all Mr Dickens's stories, indeed, the reader has been called upon, and has willingly

---

appearance is certainly disappointing,' she wrote, 'no benevolence in the face and I think little in the head – the anterior lobe not by any means remarkable.'

consented, to accept a certain number of figures or creatures of pure fancy, for this was the author's poetry. He was, moreover, always repaid for his concession by a peculiar beauty or power in these exceptional characters. But he is now expected to make the same concession with a very inadequate reward. What do we get in return for accepting Miss Jenny Wren as a possible person? This young lady is the type of a certain class of characters of which Mr Dickens has made a speciality, and with which he has been accustomed to draw alternate smiles and tears, according as he pressed one spring or another. But this is very cheap merriment and very cheap pathos. Miss Jenny Wren is a poor little dwarf, afflicted, as she constantly reiterates, with a 'bad back' and 'queer legs,' who makes dolls' dresses, and is for ever pricking at those with whom she converses, in the air, with her needle, and assuring them that she knows their 'tricks and their manners.' Like all Mr Dickens's pathetic characters, she is a little monster; she is deformed, unhealthy, unnatural; she belongs to the troop of hunchbacks, imbeciles, and precocious children who have carried on the sentimental business in all Mr Dickens's novels; the little Nells, the Smikes, the Paul Dombeys. [. . .]

[L]et us boldly declare it, there is no humanity here. Humanity is nearer home than the Boffins, and the Lammles, and the Wilfers, and the Veneerings. It is in what men have in common with each other, and not in what they have in distinction. The people just named have nothing in common with each other, except the fact that they have nothing in common with mankind at large. What a world were this world if the world of *Our Mutual Friend* were an honest reflection of it! But a community of eccentrics is impossible. Rules alone are consistent with each other; exceptions are inconsistent. Society is maintained by natural sense and natural feeling. We cannot conceive a society in which these principles are not in some manner represented. Where in these pages are the depositaries of that intelligence without which the movement of life would cease? Who represents nature? Accepting half of Mr Dickens's persons as intentionally grotesque, where are those exemplars of sound humanity who should afford us the proper measure of their companions' variations? [. . .] If we might hazard a definition of his literary character, we should, accordingly, call him the greatest of superficial novelists. We are aware that this definition confines him to an inferior rank in the department of letters which he adorns; but we accept this consequence of our proposition. It were, in our opinion, an offence against humanity to place Mr Dickens among the greatest novelists. For, to repeat what we have already intimated, he has created nothing but figure.

> *The Nation*, 21 December 1865, in *Charles Dickens:*
> *The Critical Heritage*, ed. P. Collins (1995)

George Meredith (1828–1909) on Dickens

Not much of Dickens will live, because it has so little correspondence to life. He was the incarnation of cockneydom, a caricaturist who aped the moralist; he should have kept to short stories. If his novels are read at all in the future, people will wonder what we saw in them, save some possible element of fun meaningless to them. The world will never let Mr. Pickwick, who to me is full of the lumber of imbecility, share honors with Don Quixote.[73]

> In Edward Clodd, *Memories* (1916)

Anthony Trollope (1815–1882) on Dickens

Of Dickens's style it is impossible to speak in praise. It is jerky, ungrammatical, and created by himself in defiance of rules – almost as completely as that created by Carlyle. To readers who have taught themselves to regard language, it must therefore be unpleasant. But the critic is driven to feel the weakness of his criticism, when he acknowledges to himself – as he is compelled in all honesty to do – that with the language, such as it is, the writer has satisfied the great mass of the readers of his country. Both these great writers [Dickens and Carlyle] have satisfied the readers of their own pages; but both have done infinite harm by creating a school of imitators. No young novelist should ever dare to imitate the style of Dickens. If such a one wants a model for his language, let him take Thackeray.

> *An Autobiography* (1883)

---

[73] These opinions were part of a conversation Meredith had with George Gissing when Gissing and Clodd called on Meredith.

ROBERT BROWNING 1812–1889

Thomas Carlyle (1795–1881) on Browning

My wife has read through 'Sordello' without being able to make out whether 'Sordello' was a man, or a city, or a book.

In William Sharp, *The Life of Robert Browning* (1890)

G.K. Chesterton (1874–1936) on Browning

Almost every poem of Browning, especially the shortest and most successful ones, was moulded or graven in some special style, generally grotesque, but invariably deliberate. In most cases whenever he wrote a new song he wrote a new kind of song. The new lyric is not only of a different metre, but of a different shape. No one, not even Browning, ever wrote a poem in the same style as that horrible one beginning 'John, Master of the Temple of God,' with its weird choruses and creepy prose directions. No one, not even Browning, ever wrote a poem in the same style as *Pisgah-sights*. No one, not even Browning, ever wrote a poem in the same style as *Time's Revenges*, no one, not even Browning, ever wrote a poem in the same style as *Meeting at Night* and *Parting at Morning*. No one, not even Browning, ever wrote a poem in the same style as *The Flight of the Duchess*, or in the same style as *The Grammarian's Funeral*, or in the same style as *A Star*, or in the same style as that astounding lyric which begins abruptly 'Some people hang pictures up.'[74] These metres and manners were not accidental; they really do suit the sort of spiritual experiment Browning was making in each case. Browning, then, was not chaotic; he was deliberately grotesque. But there certainly was, over and above this grotesqueness, a perversity and irrationality about the man which led him to play the fool in the middle of his own poems; to leave off carving gargoyles and simply begin throwing stones. His curious complicated puns are an example of this: Hood had used the pun to make a sentence or a sentiment especially pointed and clear. In Browning the word with two meanings seems to mean rather less, if

---

[74] The first line is 'Some people hang portraits up' and the poem is entitled 'A Likeness'. In calling it 'astounding' Chesterton is perhaps remarking on its somewhat anarchic metrical scheme, or on the proliferation of Browningesque rhymes, mating, for example, 'crony owes' with 'Marc Antonios' or 'leaps ache' with 'keepsake'.

anything, than the word with one. It also applies to his trick of setting himself to cope with impossible rhymes. It may be fun, though it is not poetry, to try rhyming to ranunculus; but even the fun presupposes that you *do* rhyme to it; and I will affirm, and hold under persecution, that 'Tommy-make-room-for-your-uncle-us' does not rhyme to it.

The Victorian Age in Literature (1913)

Edward FitzGerald (1809–1883) on Browning

In Browning I could but see little but Cockney Sublime, Cockney Energy, etc; and as you once very wittily said to me that Miss Brontë was a 'great Mistress of the Disagreeable', so, if B. has power, I must consider it of that sort [. . .] Cowell tells me that even at Oxford and Cambridge Browning is considered the deepest! But 'this will also pass away'.

Letter to W.F. Pollock, 20 November 1869,
in *More Letters of Edward FitzGerald* (1901)

Gerard Manley Hopkins (1844–1889) on Browning

But Browning has, I think, many frigidities. Any untruth to nature, to human nature, is frigid. Now he has got a great deal of what came in with Kingsley and the Broad Church school, a way of talking (and making his people talk) with the air and spirit of a man bouncing up from the table with his mouth full of bread and cheese and saying that he meant to stand no blasted nonsense.

Letter to R.W. Dixon, 1881, in *The Correspondence of Gerard Manley Hopkins and Richard Watson Dixon*, ed. C.C. Abbott (1935)

Alfred Tennyson (1809–1892) on Browning

Lord Tennyson manfully tackled [*Sordello*], but is reported to have admitted in bitterness of spirit: 'There were only two lines in it that I understood, and they were both lies: "Who will may hear Sordello's story told" and "Who would has heard Sordello's story told."'[75]

In William Sharp, *The Life of Robert Browning* (1890)

---

[75] *Sordello* was the particular bugbear of Browning's detractors, though productions such as *The Ring and the Book* are not much less obscure. Browning himself is reported to have said of *Sordello*: 'When it was written, God and Robert Browning knew what it meant; now only God knows.'

ANTHONY TROLLOPE 1815–1882

Thomas Carlyle (1795–1881) on Trollope

Ruskin's *Sesame and Lillies* must be a pretty little thing. Trollope, in reviewing it with considerable insolence stupidity and vulgarity, produces little specimens far beyond any Trollope sphere of speculation. A dirtyish little pug, that Trollope; irredeemably imbedded in commonplace, and grown fat upon it, and prosperous to an unwholesome degree. Don't *you* return his love; nasty gritty creature, with no eye for 'the Beautiful the' etc. – and awfully 'interesting to himself' he be.[76]

Letter to Jane Welsh Carlyle, 27 July 1865, in *Thomas Carlyle: Letters to His Wife*, ed. T Bliss (1953)

George Eliot (1819–1880) on Trollope

I suppose you have seen in the papers that our friend Mr Trollope has resigned his place in the Post Office. I cannot help being rather sorry, though one is in danger of being rash in such judgements. But it seems to me a thing greatly to be dreaded for a man that he should be in any way led to excessive writing.

Letter to John Blackwood, 18 October 1867, in *Trollope: Interviews and Recollections*, ed. R.C. Terry (1987)

H. Rider Haggard (1856–1925) on Trollope

Anthony Trollope has been out here [South Africa]. The first I saw of that distinguished author was one morning when I met him in a towering rage (at a roadside inn) because he could not get any breakfast. He stopped in the country about twelve days, and now is going home to write a book about it – in which, no doubt, he will express his opinions with a certainty that an old resident would hesitate to adopt. I talked with him a good deal, he has the most peculiar ideas and is as obstinate as a pig. I call such a proceeding downright dishonesty: making use of a great name to misrepresent a country.

Trollope: Interviews and Recollections, ed. R.C. Terry (1987)

---

[76] See Trollope on Carlyle, page 87. Ten years earlier in 1855 Trollope had published *The Warden*, which contained a ludicrous caricature of Carlyle. See note to page 87.

Henry James (1843–1916) on Trollope

Trollope's fecundity was prodigious: there was no limit to the work that he was ready to do. It is not unjust to say that he sacrificed quality for quantity. Abundance, certainly, is in itself a great merit; almost all the greatest writers have been abundant. But Trollope's fertility was gross, importunate; he himself contended, we believe, that he had given to the world a greater number of printed pages of fiction than any of his literary contemporaries. Not only did his novels follow each other without visible intermission, overlapping and treading on each other's heels, but most of these works are of extraordinary length. *Orley Farm, Can You Forgive Her?, He Knew He Was Right,* are exceedingly voluminous tales. *The Way We Live Now* is one of the longest of modern novels. Trollope produced, moreover, in the intervals of larger labour a great number of short stories, many of them charming, as well as various books of travel, and two or three biographies. He was the great *improvvisatore* of these latter years. Two distinguished story-tellers of the other sex – one in France and one in England – have shown an extraordinary facility of composition; but Trollope's pace was brisker even than that of the wonderful Madame Sand and the delightful Mrs Oliphant. He had taught himself to keep this pace, and had reduced his admirable faculty to a system. Every day of his life he wrote a certain number of pages of his current tale, a number sacramental and invariable, independent of mood and place.

Century, July 1883, in *Anthony Trollope: The Critical Heritage,* ed. D. Smalley
(1995)

[Of Trollope's novel *Can You Forgive Her?*] The question is, Can we forgive Miss Vavasor? Of course we can, and forget her, too, for that matter. What does Mr. Trollope mean by this question? It is a good instance of the superficial character of his work that he has been asking it once a month for so long a time without being struck by its flagrant impertinence. What are we to forgive? Alice Vavasor's ultimate acceptance of John Grey makes her temporary ill-treatment of him, viewed as a moral question, a subject for mere drawing-room gossip. There are few of Mr Trollope's readers who will not resent being summoned to pass judgment on such a sin as the one here presented, to establish by precedent the criminality of the conscientious flutterings of an excellent young lady. Charming women, thanks to the talent of their biographers, have been forgiven much greater improprieties. Since forgiveness was to be brought into the question, why did not Mr. Trollope show us an error that we might really forgive – an error that would move us to indignation? It is too much to be called upon to take cognizance in novels of sins against convention, of improprieties; we have enough of these in life. We can have charity and pity only for real sin and real misery. We trust to novels to maintain us in the practice of great indignations and great generosities. Miss Vavasor's dilemma is doubtless considerable enough in itself, but by the time it is completely unfolded by Mr. Trollope it has become so trivial, it is associated with so much that is of a merely accidental interest, it is so defloral of the bloom of a serious experience, that when we are asked to enter into it judicially, we feel almost tempted to say that it really is Miss Vavasor's own exclusive business.

Nation magazine, September 1865, in *Anthony Trollope:*
The Critical Heritage, ed. D. Smalley (1995)

CHARLOTTE BRONTË 1816–1855

George Eliot (1819–1880) on Charlotte Brontë
I have read 'Jane Eyre', and shall be glad to know what you admire in it. All self-sacrifice is good, but one would like it to be in a somewhat nobler cause than that of a diabolical law which chains a man soul and body to a putrefying carcase. However, the book *is* interesting; only I wish the characters would talk a little less like the heroes and heroines of police reports.

Letter to Charles Bray, June 1848, in *Life and Letters:*
The Works of George Eliot (2004)

Anne Thackeray[77] (1837–1919) on Charlotte Brontë
She enters in mittens, in silence, in seriousness; our hearts are beating with wild excitement. This then is the authoress, the unknown power whose books have set all London talking, reading, speculating; some

---

[77]   The daughter of W.M. Thackeray, and author of several novels including *The Story of Elizabeth* and *Miss Angel*.

people even say our father wrote the books – the wonderful books. To
say that we little girls had been given *Jane Eyre* to read scarcely represents
the facts of the case; to say that we had taken it without leave, read bits
here and bits there, been carried away by an undreamed-of and hitherto
unimagined whirlwind into things, times, places, all utterly absorbing
and at the same time absolutely unintelligible to us, would more
accurately describe our states of mind on that summer's evening as we
look at Jane Eyre – the great Jane Eyre – the tiny little lady. The moment
is so breathless that dinner comes as a relief to the solemnity of the
occasion, and we all smile as my father stoops to offer his arm; for, genius
though she may be, Miss Brontë can barely reach his elbow. [. . .]

It was a gloomy and a silent evening. Every one waited for the
brilliant conversation which never began at all. Miss Brontë retired to
the sofa in the study, and murmured a low word now and then to our
kind governess, Miss Truelock. The room looked very dark, the lamp
began to smoke a little, the conversation grew dimmer and more dim,
the ladies sat round still expectant, my father was too much perturbed
by the gloom and the silence to be able to cope with it at all. Mrs.
Brookfield, who was in the doorway by the study, near the corner in
which Miss Brontë was sitting, leant forward with a little
commonplace, since brilliance was not to be the order of the evening.
'Do you like London, Miss Brontë', she said; another silence, a pause,
then Miss Brontë answers, 'Yes and No', very gravely; Mrs. Brookfield
has herself reported the conversation. My sister and I were much too
young to be bored in those days; alarmed, oppressed we might be, but
not yet bored. A party was a party, a lioness was a lioness; and – shall I
confess it? – at that time an extra dish of biscuits was enough to mark
the evening. We felt all the importance of the occasion; tea spread in
the dining-room, ladies in the drawing-room; we roamed about
inconveniently, no doubt, and excitedly, and in one of my excursions
crossing the hall, after Miss Brontë had left, I was surprised to see my
father opening the front door with his hat on. He put his fingers to his
lips, walked out into the darkness, and shut the door quietly behind
him. When I went back to the drawing-room again, the ladies asked
me where he was. I vaguely answered that I thought he was coming
back. I was puzzled at the time, nor was it all made clear to me till long
afterwards, when one day Mrs. Procter asked me if I knew what had
happened once when my father had invited a party to meet Jane Eyre

at his house. It was one of the dullest evenings she had ever spent in her life, she said. And then with a good deal of humour she described the situation – the ladies who had all come expecting so much delightful conversation, and the gloom and the constraint, and how finally, overwhelmed by the situation, my father had quietly left the room, left the house, and gone off to his club.

Chapters from some Memoirs (1894)

D.H. Lawrence (1885–1930) on Charlotte Brontë

And I'm sure poor Charlotte Bronte, or the authoress of *The Sheik*,[78] did *not* have any deliberate intention to stimulate sex feelings in the reader. Yet I find *Jane Eyre* verging towards pornography and Boccaccio seems to me always fresh and wholesome. [. . .] Wagner and Charlotte Bronte were both in the state where the strongest instincts have collapsed, and sex has become something slightly obscene, to be wallowed in, but despised. Mr Rochester's sex passion is not 'respectable' till Mr Rochester is burned, blinded, disfigured, and reduced to helpless dependence. Then, thoroughly humbled and humiliated, it may be merely admitted.

'Pornography and Obscenity', 1929, in *Late Essays and Articles*,
ed. J. T. Boulton (2004)

GEORGE ELIOT 1819–1880

Arnold Bennett (1867–1931) on George Eliot

I dipped into *Adam Bede,* and my impression that George Eliot will never be among the classical writers was made a certainty. Her style, though not without shrewdness, is too rank to have any enduring vitality. People call it 'masculine'. Quite wrong! It is downright, aggressive, sometimes rude, but genuinely masculine, never. On the contrary it is transparently feminine – feminine in its lack of restraint, its wordiness, and the utter absence of feeling for form which characterises it. The average woman italicises freely. George Eliot, of course, had trained herself too well to do that, at least formally; yet her

---

[78] The sensational book on which the Valentino film was based, by Edith Maude Hull.

constant, undue insistence springs from the same essential weakness, and amounts practically to the same expedient.

> Journal for 13 May 1896, in *The Journals of Arnold Bennett*,
> ed. N. Flower (1932–3)

E.M. Forster (1879–1970) on George Eliot

George Eliot talks about God, but never alters her focus; God and the tables and chairs are all in the same plane, and in consequence we have not for a moment the feeling that the whole universe needs pity and love – they are only needed in Hetty's cell.[79]

> *Aspects of the Novel* (1927)

Henry James (1843–1916) on George Eliot

Why is it that in George Eliot the sun sinks forever to the west, and the shadows are long, and the afternoon wanes, and the trees vaguely rustle, and the color of the day is much inclined to yellow?

> 'The Lesson of Balzac', 1905, in *Henry James: Literary Criticism*,
> ed. L. Edel and M. Wilson (1984)

George Moore (1852–1933) on George Eliot

And if I did not believe that Providence bestows names upon us in harmony with the books we are ordained to write, the name of George Eliot would convert me. The writer's real name was Marian Evans, a chaw-bacon, thick-loined name, but withal pleasing, redeemed by its character, like the shire horse. But the Providence that shapes the writer to its ends required a hollow, barren name, without sign of human presence upon it, one reminiscent of the strange sea-shells that are found only on the mantelpieces of Pentonville front parlours – striped backed, white-lipped shells in which it is impossible to believe that a living creature ever dwelt. I will put it to the reader's honour. Hand on your heart, reader, could the name George Eliot have written Miss Austen's novels?

> *Avowals* (1919)

---

[79] Hetty is from *Adam Bede*. She is condemned to death for the murder of her child.

Anthony Trollope (1815–1882) on George Eliot

Her imagination is no doubt strong, but it acts in analysing rather than in creating. Everything that comes before her is pulled to pieces so that the inside of it shall be seen, and be seen if possible by her readers as clearly as by herself. This searching analysis is carried so far that, in studying her latter writings, one feels oneself to be in company with some philosopher rather than with a novelist. I doubt whether any young person can read with pleasure either *Felix Holt*, *Middlemarch*, or *Daniel Deronda*. I know that they are very difficult to many that are not young.

Her personifications of character have been singularly terse and graphic, and from them has come her great hold on the public, – though by no means the greatest effect which she has produced. The lessons which she teaches remain, though it is not for the sake of the lessons that her pages are read. Seth Bede, Adam Bede, Maggie and Tom Tulliver, old Silas Marner, and, much above all, Tito, in *Romola*, are characters which, when once known, can never be forgotten. I cannot say quite so much for any of those in her later works, because in them the philosopher so greatly overtops the portrait-painter, that, in the dissection of the mind, the outward signs seem to have been forgotten. In her, as yet, there is no symptom whatever of that weariness of mind which, when felt by the reader, induces him to declare that the author has written himself out. It is not from decadence that we do not have another Mrs. Poyser, but because the author soars to things which seem to her to be higher than Mrs. Poyser.

It is, I think, the defect of George Eliot that she struggles too hard to do work that shall be excellent. She lacks ease. Latterly the signs of this have been conspicuous in her style, which has always been and is singularly correct, but which has become occasionally obscure from her too great desire to be pungent. It is impossible not to feel the struggle, and that feeling begets a flavour of affectation. In *Daniel Deronda*, of which at this moment only a portion has been published, there are sentences which I have found myself compelled to read three times before I have been able to take home to myself all that the writer has intended. Perhaps I may be permitted here to say, that this gifted woman was among my dearest and most intimate friends.

An Autobiography (1883)

HERMAN MELVILLE 1819–1891

D.H. Lawrence (1885–1930) on Melville

Nobody can be more clownish, more clumsy and sententiously in bad taste, than Herman Melville, even in a great book like *Moby Dick*. He preaches and holds forth because he's not sure of himself. And he holds forth, often, so amateurishly.

The artist was so *much* greater than the man. The man is rather a tiresome New Englander of the ethical-mystical-transcendentalist sort: Emerson, Longfellow, Hawthorne, etc. So unrelieved, the solemn ass even in humour. So hopelessly *au grand sérieux*, you feel like saying: Good God, what does it matter? If life is a tragedy, or a farce, or a disaster, or anything else, what do I care! Let life be what it likes. Give me a drink, that's what I want just now.

For my part, life is so many things I don't care what it is. It's not my affair to sum it up. Just now it's a cup of tea. This morning it was wormwood and gall. Hand me the sugar.

One wearies of the *grand sérieux*. There's something false about it. And that's Melville. Oh dear, when the solemn ass brays! brays! brays![80]

Studies in Classic American Literature (1923)

Gore Vidal (1925–) on Melville

I do detest *Moby Dick* and I never finished *Pierre, or The Ambiguities*. But then I don't like Melville's writing. It is windy and pretentious, it is bogus Shakespeare.

Conversations with Gore Vidal, ed. R. Peabody and L. Ebersole (2005)

WALT WHITMAN 1819–1892

D.H. Lawrence (1885–1930) on Whitman

I AM HE THAT ACHES WITH AMOROUS LOVE

Walter, leave off. You are not HE. You are just a limited Walter. And

---

[80] As with his remarks on page 121 on Whitman, Lawrence is later more generous: 'But he was a deep, great artist, even if he was rather a sententious man. He was a real American in that he always felt his audience in front of him. But

your ache doesn't include all Amorous Love, by any means. If you ache you only ache with a small bit of amorous love, and there's so much more stays outside the cover of your ache, that you might be a bit milder about it.

I AM HE THAT ACHES WITH AMOROUS LOVE

CHUFF! CHUFF! CHUFF!

CHU-CHU-CHU-CHU-CHUFF!

Reminds one of a steam engine. A locomotive. They're the only things that seem to me to ache with amorous love. All that steam inside them. Forty million foot-pound pressure. The ache of AMOROUS LOVE. Steam-pressure. CHUFF!

An ordinary man aches with love for Belinda, or his Native Land, or the Ocean, or the Stars, or the Oversoul: if he feels that an ache is in the fashion.

It takes a steam-engine to ache with AMOROUS LOVE. [...]

And Walt's great poems are really huge fat tomb-plants, great rank graveyard growths.

All that false exuberance. All those lists of things boiled in one pudding-cloth! No, no!

I don't want all those things inside me, thank you.

'I reject nothing,' says Walt.

If that is so, one might be a pipe open at both ends, so everything runs through.

Post-mortem effects.

'I embrace ALL,' says Whitman. 'I weave all things into myself.'

Do you really! There can't be much left of *you* when you've done. When you've cooked the awful pudding of One Identity.

'And whoever walks a furlong without sympathy walks to his own funeral dressed in his own shroud.'

Take off your hat then, my funeral procession of one is passing.

This awful Whitman. This post-mortem poet. This poet with the private soul leaking out of him all the time. All his privacy leaking out in a sort of dribble, oozing into the universe.

Walt becomes in his own person the whole world, the whole

---

when he ceases to be American, when he forgets all audience, and gives us his sheer apprehension of the world, then he is wonderful, his book commands a stillness in the soul, an awe.'

universe, the whole eternity of time, as far as his rather sketchy knowledge of history will carry him, that is. Because to *be* a thing he had to know it. In order to assume the identity of a thing, he had to know that thing. He was not able to assume one identity with Charlie Chaplin, for example, because Walt didn't know Charlie. What a pity! He'd have done poems, paeans and what not, Chants, songs of Cinematernity.

'O Charlie my Charlie, another film is done—'

As soon as Walt *knew* a thing, he assumed a One Identity with it. If he knew that an Eskimo sat in a kyak, immediately there was Walt being little and yellow and greasy, sitting in a kyak.

Now will you tell me exactly what a kyak is?

Who is he that demands petty definition? Let him behold me *sitting in a kyak.*

I behold no such thing. I behold a rather fat old man full of a rather senile, self-conscious sensuosity.

DEMOCRACY. EN MASSE. ONE IDENTITY.

The universe in short, adds up to ONE.

ONE.

I.

Which is Walt.[81]

Studies in Classic American Literature (1923)

Algernon Charles Swinburne (1837–1909) on Whitman

But under the dirty clumsy paws of a harper whose plectrum is a muck-rake, any tune will become a chaos of discords, though the motive of the tune may be the first principle of nature – the passion of man for woman or the passion of woman for man. And the unhealthily demonstrative and obtrusive animalism of the Whitmaniad is as unnatural, as incompatible with the wholesome instincts of human passion, as even the filthy and inhuman asceticism of SS Macarius and Simeon Stylites. [. . .] Mr. Whitman's Eve is a drunken apple-woman, indecently sprawling on the

---

[81]   This extraordinary, almost Whitmanesque response to Whitman runs on for several more pages, largely in this tone but conceding, finally: 'Whitman, the great poet, has meant so much to me. Whitman, the one man breaking a way ahead. Whitman, the one pioneer. And only Whitman. No English pioneers, no French. No European pioneer-poets. In Europe the would-be pioneers are mere innovators. The same in America. Ahead of Whitman, nothing.'

slush and garbage of the gutter amid the rotten refuse of her
overturned fruit-stall; but Mr. Whitman's Venus is a Hottentot wench
under the influence of cantharides and adulterated rum.

Fortnightly Review, 1887, in *The Complete Works of Algernon Charles
Swinburne,* ed. E. Gosse and T.J. Wise (1926)

CHARLES BAUDELAIRE 1821–1867

Henry James (1843–1916) on Baudelaire

'Les Fleurs du Mal' was a very happy title for Baudelaire's verses, but it
is not altogether a just one. Scattered flowers incontestably do bloom in
the quaking swamps of evil, and the poet who does not mind
encountering bad odours in his pursuit of sweet ones is quite at liberty
to go in search of them. But Baudelaire has, as a general thing, not
plucked the flowers – he has plucked the evil-smelling weeds (we take
it that he did not use the word flowers in a purely ironical sense) and he
has often taken up mere cupfuls of mud and bog-water. He had said to
himself that it was a great shame that the realm of evil and unclean
things should be fenced off from the domain of poetry; that it was full
of subjects, of chances and effects; that it had its light and shade, its logic
and its mystery; and that there was the making of some capital verses in
it. So he leaped the barrier and was soon immersed in it up to his neck.
Baudelaire's imagination was of a melancholy and sinister kind, and, to a
considerable extent, this plunging into darkness and dirt was doubtless
very spontaneous and disinterested. But he strikes us on the whole as
passionless, and this, in view of the unquestionable pluck and acuteness
of his fancy, is a great pity. He knew evil not by experience, not as
something within himself, but by contemplation and curiosity, as
something outside of himself, by which his own intellectual agility was
not in the least discomposed, rather, indeed (as we say his fancy was of a
dusky cast) agreeably flattered and stimulated. In the former case,
Baudelaire, with his other gifts, might have been a great poet. But, as it
is, evil for him begins outside and not inside, and consists primarily of a
great deal of lurid landscape and unclean furniture. This is an almost
ludicrously puerile view of the matter. Evil is represented as an affair of
blood and carrion and physical sickness – there must be stinking

corpses and starving prostitutes and empty laudanum bottles in order that the poet shall be effectively inspired.

A good way to embrace Baudelaire at a glance is to say that he was, in his treatment of evil, exactly what Hawthorne was not – Hawthorne, who felt the thing at its source, deep in the human consciousness. Baudelaire's infinitely slighter volume of genius apart, he was a sort of Hawthorne reversed. It is the absence of this metaphysical quality in his treatment of his favourite subjects (Poe was his metaphysician, and his devotion sustained him through a translation of 'Eureka!'[82]) that exposes him to that class of accusations of which M. Edmond Schérer's accusation of feeding upon *pourriture* is an example; and, in fact, in his pages we never know with what we are dealing. We encounter an inextricable confusion of sad emotions and vile things, and we are at a loss to know whether the subject pretends to appeal to our conscience or – we were going to say – to our olfactories. 'Le Mal?' we exclaim; 'you do yourself too much honour. This is not Evil; it is not the wrong; it is simply the nasty!' Our impatience is of the same order as that which we should feel if a poet, pretending to pick 'the flowers of good', should come and present us, as specimens, a rhapsody on plumcake and *eau du Cologne*.

'Charles Baudelaire', *The Nation*, 27 April 1876,
in *The Portable Henry James*, ed. J. Auchard (2004)

FYODOR DOSTOEVSKY 1821–1881

Vladimir Nabokov (1899–1977) on Dostoevsky

Dostoevski's lack of taste, his monotonous dealings with persons suffering with pre-Freudian complexes, the way he has of wallowing in the tragic misadventures of human dignity – all this is difficult to admire. I do not like this trick his characters have of 'sinning their way to Jesus' or, as a Russian author Ivan Bunin put it more bluntly, 'spilling Jesus all over the place.'

Lectures on Russian Literature, ed. F.T. Bowers (1981)

---

[82]   'Eureka!' was Poe's tract on cosmology.

Nikolay Strakhov (1828–1896) on Dostoevsky

All the while I was writing the biography I had to fight off a revulsion that kept rising within me, and I have tried to stifle this evil feeling. Help me to find some solution. [. . .] He was vicious, envious, depraved and spent his entire life in a state of emotional upheaval and exasperation [. . .] Viskovatov told me that he bragged one day of having — with a little girl whom his governess had brought him, in the public baths [. . .] Note that along with his bestial sensuality he was utterly lacking in taste, and had no sense of beauty or feminine charm.

Letter to Leo Tolstoy, 28 November 1883,
in Henri Troyat, *Tolstoy* (1980)

GUSTAVE FLAUBERT 1821–80

George Moore (1852–1933) on Flaubert

Flaubert bores me. What nonsense has been talked about him! Impersonal! He is the most personal writer. But his odious pessimism! How weary I am of it, it never ceases, it is lugged in *à tout propos* and the little lyrical phrase with which he winds up every paragraph, how boring it is!

Confessions of a Young Man (1888)

Rudyard Kipling (1865–1936) on Flaubert

Remind me that I bear a grudge against Mrs Ross. She has insulted by sending the English version of Madame Bovary embellished by bad Woodbury or autotype pictures. To mark my deep contempt I have thrown it at the lame black cat who is my constant companion and from her language I gather that she approves of Flaubert as little as I do. Happy thought! Perhaps Flaubert had indigestion and that suggested killing his crazy heroine with arsenic. You've read the thing haven't you? Didn't you resent it?

Twasn't so bad in its French but when I unearthed it in all the bald brutality of the British tongue I kicked . . . as the black cat knoweth.

Letter to Edmonia Hill, 22 April 1888,
in *The Letters of Rudyard Kipling*, ed. T. Pinney (1990)

GEORGE MEREDITH 1828–1909

E.M. Forster (1879–1970) on Meredith

Meredith is not the great name he was twenty or thirty years ago, when much of the universe and all Cambridge trembled. I remember how depressed I used to be by a line in one of his poems: 'We breathe but to be sword or block.' I did not want to be either and I knew that I was not a sword. It seems, though, that there was no real cause for depression, for Meredith is himself now rather in the trough of a wave, and though fashion will turn and raise him a bit he will never be the spiritual power he was about the year 1900. His philosophy has not worn well. His heavy attacks on sentimentality – they bore the present generation, which pursues the same quarry but with neater instruments, and is apt to suspect anyone carrying a blunderbuss of being a sentimentalist himself. And his visions of Nature – they do not endure like Hardy's, there is too much Surrey about them, they are fluffy and lush.

He could no more write the opening chapter of *The Return of the Native* than Box Hill could visit Salisbury Plain. What is really tragic and enduring in the scenery of England was hidden from him, and so is what is really tragic in life. When he gets serious and noble-minded there is a strident overtone, a bullying that becomes distressing. I feel indeed that he was like Tennyson in one respect: through not taking himself quietly enough he strained his inside. And his novels: most of the social values are faked. The tailors are not tailors, the cricket matches are not cricket, the railway trains do not even seem to be trains, the county families give the air of having been only just that moment unpacked, scarcely in position before the action starts, the straw still clinging to their beards. It is surely very odd, the social scene in which his characters are set; it is partly due to his fantasy, which is legitimate, but partly a chilly fake, and wrong.

Aspects of the Novel (1927)

Ezra Pound (1885–1972) on Meredith

Meredith is to me chiefly a stink. I should never write on him, as I detest him too much ever to trust myself as critic of him.

Letter to John Quinn, 3 April 1918, in *The Selected Letters of Ezra Pound to John Quinn, 1915–1924*, ed. T. Materer (1991)

Oscar Wilde (1854–1900) on Meredith

As a writer he has mastered everything except language: as a novelist
he can do everything, except tell a story: as an artist he is everything,
except articulate. Somebody in Shakespeare –Touchstone, I think –
talks about a man who is always breaking his shins over his own wit,
and it seems to me that this might serve as the basis for a criticism of
Meredith's method. But whatever he is, he is not a realist. Or rather I
would say that he is a child of realism who is not on speaking terms
with his father. By deliberate choice he has made himself a romanticist.
He has refused to bow the knee to Baal, and after all, even if the man's
fine spirit did not revolt against the noisy assertions of realism, his style
would be quite sufficient of itself to keep life at a respectful distance.
By its means he has planted round his garden a hedge full of thorns,
and red with wonderful roses.[83]

'The Decay of Lying', in *Intentions* (1891)

DANTE GABRIEL ROSSETTI 1828–1882

Robert Buchanan[84] (1841–1901) on Rossetti

Mr. Rossetti has been known for many years as a painter of
exceptional powers, who, for reasons best known to himself, has
shrunk from publicly exhibiting his pictures, and from allowing
anything like a popular estimate to be formed of their qualities. He
belongs, or is said to belong, to the so-called Pre-Raphaelite school, a

---

[83]   It is not quite fair to say this is Wilde speaking as Wilde: the quotation comes
from Wilde's dramatic essay 'The Decay of Lying', in which the main character,
Vivian, is a Wilde stand-in. The main thesis of 'The Decay of Lying' is, in Vivian's words: 'the more we study Art, the less we care for Nature. What Art really
reveals to us is Nature's lack of design, her curious crudities, her extraordinary
monotony, her absolutely unfinished condition.'

[84]   Robert Buchanan (1841–1901) was a poet, novelist, playwright, essayist and
journalist much better known in his own day than in this, who raised a literary storm with his prudish essay, 'The Fleshly School of Poetry'. Rossetti and
Swinburne both published devastating replies to Buchanan, and Buchanan later
regretted his words. Ezra Pound remembered Buchanan in 1920 when he wrote
in 'Hugh Selwyn Mauberley': 'Foetid Buchanan lifted up his voice/When that
faun's head of hers/Became a pastime for/Painters and adulterers.'

school which is generally considered to exhibit much genius for colour, and great indifference to perspective. It would be unfair to judge the painter by the glimpses we have had of his works, or by the photographs which are sold of the principal paintings. Judged by the photographs, he is an artist who conceives unpleasantly, and draws ill. Like Mr. Simeon Solomon, however, with whom he seems to have many points in common, he is distinctively a colourist, and of his capabilities in colour we cannot speak, though we should guess that they are great; for if there is any good quality by which his poems are specially marked, it is a great sensitiveness to hues and tints as conveyed in poetic epithet. These qualities, which impress the casual spectator of the photographs from his pictures, are to be found abundantly among his verses. There is the same thinness and transparence of design, the same combination of the simple and the grotesque, the same morbid deviation from healthy forms of life, the same sense of weary, wasting, yet exquisite sensuality; nothing virile, nothing tender, nothing completely sane; a superfluity of extreme sensibility, of delight in beautiful forms, hues, and tints, and a deep-seated indifference to all agitating forces and agencies, all tumultuous griefs and sorrows, all the thunderous stress of life, and all the straining storm of speculation. Mr. Morris is often pure, fresh, and wholesome as his own great model; Mr. Swinburne startles us more than once by some fine flash of insight; but the mind of Mr. Rossetti is like a glassy mere, broken only by the dive of some water-bird or the hum of winged insects, and brooded over by an atmosphere of insufferable closeness, with a light blue sky above it, sultry depths mirrored within it, and a surface so thickly sown with water-lilies that it retains its glassy smoothness even in the strongest wind. Judged relatively to his poetic associates, Mr. Rossetti must be pronounced inferior to either. He cannot tell a pleasant story like Mr. Morris, nor forge alliterative thunderbolts like Mr. Swinburne. It must be conceded, nevertheless, that he is neither so glibly imitative as the one, nor so transcendently superficial as the other. [. . .]

We at once recognise as his own property such passages as this: –

> I looked up
> And saw where a brown-shouldered harlot leaned
> Half through a tavern window thick with vine.

Some man had come behind her in the room
And caught her by her arms, and she had turned
With that coarse empty laugh on him, as now
He *munched her neck with kisses, while the vine*
Crawled in her back.

Or this: –

As I stooped, her own lips rising there
Bubbled with brimming kisses at my mouth.

Or this: –

Have seen your lifted silken skirt
Advertise dainties through the dirt!

Or this: –

What more prize than love to impel thee,
Grip and *lip* my limbs as I tell thee!

Passages like these are the common stock of the walking gentlemen of the fleshly school. We cannot forbear expressing our wonder, by the way, at the kind of women whom it seems the unhappy lot of these gentlemen to encounter. We have lived as long in the world as they have, but never yet came across persons of the other sex who conduct themselves in the manner described. Females who bite, scratch, scream, bubble, munch, sweat, writhe, twist, wriggle, foam, and in a general way slaver over their lovers, must surely possess some extraordinary qualities to counteract their otherwise most offensive mode of conducting themselves. It appears, however, on examination, that their poet-lovers conduct themselves in a similar manner. They, too, bite, scratch, scream, bubble, munch, sweat, writhe, twist, wriggle, foam, and slaver, in a style frightful to hear of. Let us hope that it is only their fun, and that they don't mean half they say. At times, in reading such books as this, one cannot help wishing that things had remained for ever in the asexual state described in Mr. Darwin's great chapter on

Palingenesis. We get very weary of this protracted hankering after a person of the other sex; it seems meat, drink, thought, sinew, religion for the fleshly school.

Contemporary Review, October 1871, in *Notorious Literary Attacks*,
ed. A. Mordell (1926)

COUNT LEO TOLSTOY 1828–1910

Anton Chekhov (1860–1904) on Tolstoy

It is all old stuff. Saying of art that it has grown decrepit, drifted into a blind alley, that it isn't what it ought to be, and so forth and so on, is the same as saying that the desire to eat and drink has grown obsolete, seen its day and isn't what it ought to be. Of course hunger is an old story, and in our desire to eat we have entered a blind alley, but we still have to do it and we will keep on eating, whatever the philosophers and angry old men may go to the trouble of saying.[85]

Letter to Alexei Suvorin, 4 January 1898, in *The Selected Letters of Anton Chekhov*, ed. L. Hellman (1955)

George Orwell (1903–1950) on Tolstoy

A sort of doubt has always hung around the character of Tolstoy, as round the character of Gandhi. He was not a vulgar hypocrite, as some people declared him to be, and he would probably have imposed even greater sacrifices on himself than he did, if he had not been interfered with at every step by the people surrounding him, especially his wife. But on the other hand it is dangerous to take such men as Tolstoy at their disciples' valuation. There is always the possibility – the probability, indeed – that they have done no more than exchange one form of egoism for another. Tolstoy renounced wealth, fame and privilege; he abjured violence in all its forms and was ready to suffer for doing so; but it is not easy to believe that he abjured the principle of coercion, or at least the *desire* to coerce

---

[85]   Chekhov was of course a great admirer of Tolstoy, knew him personally and said: 'I have never loved anyone as much as I love him.' The bone of contention was a Tolstoy pamphlet on art.

others. There are families in which the father will say to his child, 'You'll get a thick ear if you do that again', while the mother, her eyes brimming over with tears, will take the child in her arms and murmur lovingly, 'Now, darling, *is* it kind to Mummy to do that?' And who would maintain that the second method is less tyrannous than the first? The distinction that really matters is not between violence and non-violence, but between having and not having the appetite for power.

'Lear, Tolstoy and the Fool', in *Polemic*, March 1947,

in *The Collected Essays, Journalism and Letters of George Orwell* (1968)

Ivan Turgenev (1818–1883) on Tolstoy

Today, at last, I received the letter Tolstoy sent in September via Davidov the bookseller (admirable punctuality of our Russian businessmen!), in which he states that he had insulted me intentionally and apologizes, etc. And almost at the same moment, owing to certain gossip I think I told you about, I challenged him to a duel. [. . .] What can we do? We must act as though we lived on different planets or in different centuries.[86]

Letter to Afanasy Fet, 7 January 1862,

in Henri Troyat, *Tolstoy* (1980)

---

[86] Turgenev and Tolstoy had fallen out after a trivial quarrel about Turgenev's daughter in 1861 (Tolstoy had made references to the fact that she was illegitimate). According to the poet Afanasy Fet, who witnessed the quarrel, Turgenev threatened to slap Tolstoy, then rushed from the scene. Tolstoy sent him a note demanding an apology, which Turgenev duly wrote, but it was delivered to the wrong address. Tolstoy, still seething, then challenged Turgenev to a duel. Baffled by this turn of events, and not knowing about the misdelivery of the letter, Turgenev wrote again: 'I say in all sincerity that I would gladly stand under your fire in order to wipe out my truly insane words' (even though Tolstoy had been by far the more insulting). Tolstoy replied: 'You are afraid of me, but I scorn you and do not want to have anything to do with you.' Three months later he changed his mind and wrote to Turgenev apologizing, but this letter never reached Turgenev, who was abroad. Turgenev then heard 'certain gossip' that Tolstoy was showing Turgenev's craven letter to all his friends. He then challenged Tolstoy to a duel – shortly before receiving Tolstoy's letter of apology. It was in the aftermath of this pointless feud, caused entirely by the lack of email, that Turgenev wrote the letter above.

EMILY DICKINSON 1830–1886

Woody Allen (1935–) on Dickinson

How wrong Emily Dickinson was! Hope is not 'the thing with feathers'. The thing with feathers has turned out to be my nephew. I must take him to a specialist in Zurich.

Without Feathers (1975)

WILLIAM MORRIS 1834–96

Rudyard Kipling (1865–1936) on Morris

I see by this week's P[all].M[all]. Gazette that the worthy William Morris has been giving his opinion on the Hundred best books. Lord! Lord! what a lying world it is. He has gravely stuck down the Mahabarat and I will wager everything I have that he hasn't the ghost of a conception what he means when he advises the study of that monstrous midden. [. . .] But I suppose we must accept the dictum of William the poet and it would be flat blasphemy to hint that one decent primer on Sanitary Engineering and sewage disposal is worth more than all the tomes of sacred smut ever produced.

Letter to W.C. Crofts, 18–27 February 1886,
in *The Letters of Rudyard Kipling*, ed. T. Pinney (1990)

MARK TWAIN 1835–1910

William Faulkner (1897–1962) on Twain

[A] hack writer who would not have been considered fourth rate in Europe, who tricked out a few of the old proven 'sure fire' literary skeletons with sufficient local color to intrigue the superficial and the lazy.[87]

'Books & Things: American Drama: Inhibitions',
in *The Mississippian*, March 1922

---

[87]   Much later, in 1958, Faulkner recognized Twain's greatness: he was 'among the masters from whom we learned our craft' and, perhaps a little improbably, 'all of our grandfather'.

George Orwell (1903–1950) on Twain

He had in him an iconoclastic, even revolutionary vein which he obviously wanted to follow up and yet somehow never did follow up. He might have been a destroyer of humbugs and a prophet of democracy more valuable than Whitman, because healthier and more humorous. Instead he became that dubious thing a 'public figure', flattered by passport officials and entertained by royalty, and his career reflects the deterioration in American life that set in after the Civil War.

Mark Twain has sometimes been compared with his contemporary, Anatole France. This comparison is not so pointless as it may sound. Both men were the spiritual children of Voltaire, both had an ironical, sceptical view of life, and a native pessimism overlaid by gaiety; both knew that the existing social order is a swindle and its cherished beliefs mostly delusions. Both were bigoted atheists and convinced (in Mark Twain's case this was Darwin's doing) of the unbearable cruelty of the universe. But there the resemblance ends. Not only is the Frenchman enormously more learned, more civilized, more alive aesthetically, but he is also more courageous. He does attack the things he disbelieves in; he does not, like Mark Twain, always take refuge behind the amiable mask of the 'public figure' and the licensed jester. He is ready to risk the anger of the Church and to take the unpopular side in a controversy – in the Dreyfus case, for example. Mark Twain, except perhaps in one short essay 'What is Man?', never attacks established beliefs in a way that is likely to get him into trouble. Nor could he ever wean himself from the notion, which is perhaps especially an American notion, that success and virtue are the same thing.

In *Life on the Mississippi* there is a queer little illustration of the central weakness of Mark Twain's character. In the earlier part of this mainly autobiographical book the dates have been altered. Mark Twain describes his adventures as a Mississippi pilot as though he had been a boy of about seventeen at the time, whereas in fact he was a young man of nearly thirty. There is a reason for this. The same part of the book describes his exploits in the Civil War, which were distinctly inglorious. Moreover, Mark Twain started by fighting, if he can be said to have fought, on the Southern side, and then changed his allegiance before the war was over. This kind of behaviour is more excusable in a boy than in a man, whence the adjustment of the dates. It is also clear enough, however, that he changed sides because he saw that the North was going to win; and this tendency to side with the stronger whenever possible, to believe that might must be right, is apparent throughout his career. In *Roughing It* there is an interesting account of a bandit named Slade, who, among countless other outrages, had committed twenty-eight murders. It is perfectly clear that Mark Twain admires this disgusting scoundrel. Slade was successful; therefore he was admirable. This outlook, no less common today, is summed up in the significant American expression 'to *make good*'.

> 'Mark Twain – The Licensed Jester', in *Tribune*, 26 November 1943, in *The Collected Essays, Journalism and Letters of George Orwell* (1968)

BRET HARTE 1836–1902

Mark Twain (1835–1910) on Harte

Harte is a liar, a thief, a swindler, a snob, a sot, a sponge, a coward, a Jeremy Diddler, he is brim full of treachery, & he conceals his Jewish birth as carefully as if he considered it a disgrace. How do I know? By the best of all evidence, personal observation. [. . .] If he had only been made a home official, I think I could stand it; but to send this nasty creature to puke upon the American name in a foreign land is too much.[88]

> Letter to William Dean Howells, 27 June 1878, in *Mark Twain-Howells Letters*, ed. H.N. Smith, W.M. Gibson and F. Anderson (1960)

ALGERNON CHARLES SWINBURNE 1837–1909

Edmund Gosse (1849–1928) on Swinburne

Outside poetry, and, in lesser measure, his family life, Swinburne's interests were curiously limited. He had no 'small talk', and during the discussion of the common topics of the days his attention at once

---

[88] Twain and Harte, the two most celebrated American writers of their day, had fallen out over the production of a play. Bret Harte left the USA to become a commercial agent in Krefeld, Germany, in 1878, and never returned.

flagged and fell off, the glazed eye betraying that the mind was far away. For science he had no taste whatever, and his lack of a musical ear was a byword among his acquaintances. I once witnessed a practical joke played upon him, which made me indignant at the time, but which now seems innocent enough, and not without interest. A lady, having taken the rest of the company into her confidence, told Swinburne that she would render on the piano a very ancient Florentine ritornello which had just been discovered. She then played 'Three Blind Mice', and Swinburne was enchanted. He found that it reflected to perfection the cruel beauty of the Medicis – which perhaps it does.

Portraits and Sketches (1912)

Gerard Manley Hopkins (1844–1889) on Swinburne

Swinburne has a new volume out, which is reviewed in its own style: 'the rush and the rampage, the pause and the pull-up of these lustrous and lumpophorous lines.' It is all now a 'self-drawing web', a perpetual functioning of genius without truth, feeling, or any adequate matter to be at function on. There is some heavydom, in long waterlogged lines (he has no real understanding of rhythm, and though he sometimes hits brilliantly at other times he misses badly) about the *Armada*, that pitfall of the patriotic muse, and *rot* about babies, a blethery bathos into which Hugo and he from opposite coasts have long driven Channel-tunnels.

Letter to Robert Bridges, 29 April 1889, in *Gerard Manley Hopkins: The Major Works*, ed. C. Phillips (2002)

John Morley[89] (1838–1923) on Swinburne

It is of no use, therefore, to scold Mr. Swinburne for grovelling down among the nameless shameless abominations which inspire him with such frenzied delight. They excite his imagination to its most vigorous efforts, they seem to him the themes most proper for poetic treatment, and they suggest ideas which in his opinion, it is highly to be wished that English men and women should brood upon and make their own.

---

[89] John Morley was a Liberal politician who wrote numerous biographies and works of literary criticism; here he prefigures Robert Buchanan (see page 126) in the attack on the 'Fleshly School of Poetry' of Swinburne, Rossetti and Morris.

He finds that these fleshly things are his strong part, so he sticks to
them. Is it wonderful that he should? And at all events he deserves
credit for the audacious courage with which he has revealed to the
world a mind all aflame with the feverish carnality of a schoolboy over
the dirtiest passages in Lemprière. It is not every poet who would ask
us all to go hear him tuning his lyre in a stye. [. . .]

We should be sorry to be guilty of anything so offensive to Mr.
Swinburne as we are quite sure an appeal to the morality of all the
wisest and best men would be. The passionate votary of the goddess
whom he hails as 'Daughter of Death and Priapus' has got too high for
this. But it may be presumed that common sense is not too insulting a
standard by which to measure the worth and place of his new volume.
Starting from this sufficiently modest point, we may ask him whether
there is really nothing in women worth singing about except
'quivering flanks' and 'splendid supple thighs,' 'hot sweet throats' and
'hotter hands than fire,' and their blood as 'hot wan wine of love'? Is
purity to be expunged from the catalogue of desirable qualities? Does
a poet show respect to his own genius by gloating, as Mr. Swinburne
does, page after page and poem after poem, upon a single subject, and
that subject kept steadily in a single light? Are we to believe that
having exhausted hot lustfulness, and wearied the reader with a
luscious and nauseating iteration of the same fervid scenes and fervid
ideas, he has got to the end of his tether?

Saturday Review, 4 August 1866, in *The Eclectic Magazine*,
ed. J.H. Agnew and W.H. Bidwell (1866)

THOMAS HARDY 1840–1928

T.S. Eliot (1888–1965) on Hardy

He seems to me to have written as nearly for the sake of 'self-
expression' as a man well can; and the self which he had to express does
not strike me as a particularly wholesome or edifying communication.
He was indifferent even to the prescripts of good writing: he wrote
sometimes overpoweringly well, but always very carelessly; at times his
style touches sublimity without ever having passed through the stage of
being good. In consequence of his self-absorption, he makes a great

deal of landscape; for romantic landscape is a passive creature which lends itself to an author's mood. It is fitted too for the purposes of an author who is interested not at all in men's minds, but only in their emotions; and perhaps only in men as vehicles for emotions. It is only, indeed, in their emotional paroxysms that most of his characters come alive. This extreme emotionalism seems to me a symptom of decadence; it is a cardinal point of faith in a romantic age, to believe that there is something admirable for its own sake in violent emotion, whatever the emotion or whatever its object. But it is by no means self-evident that human beings are most real when most violently excited; violent passions do not in themselves differentiate men from each other, but rather tend to reduce them to the same state; and the passion has significance only in relation to the character and behaviour of the man at other moments of his life and in other contexts. Furthermore, strong passion is only interesting or significant in strong men; those who abandon themselves without resistance to excitements which tend to deprive them of reason, become merely instruments of feeling and lose their humanity; and unless there is moral resistance and conflict there is no meaning. But as the majority is capable neither of strong emotion nor of strong resistance, it always inclines, unless instructed to the contrary, to admire passion for its own sake; and, if somewhat deficient in vitality, people imagine passion to be the surest evidence of vitality. This in itself may go towards accounting for Hardy's popularity.

'Personality and Demonic Possession', 1934, in *We Write for Our Own Time:*
Selected Essays from Seventy-Five Years of the Virginia Quarterly Review,
ed. A. Burnham (2000)

Henry James (1843–1916) on Hardy

Mr Hardy puts his characters through a variety of comical movements; he fills their mouths with quaint turns of speech; he baptizes them with odd names ('Joseph Poorgrass' for a bashful, easily-snubbed Dissenter is excellent); he pulls the wires, in short, and produces a vast deal of sound and commotion; and his novel, at a cursory glance, has a rather promising air of life and warmth. But by critics who prefer a grain of substance to a pound of shadow it will, we think, be pronounced a decidedly delusive performance; it has a fatal lack of magic. We have found it hard to read, but its shortcomings are easier to summarize than to encounter in order. Mr Hardy's novel is very long, but his subject is very short and simple, and the work has been distended to its rather formidable dimensions by the infusion of a large amount of conversational and descriptive padding and the use of an ingeniously verbose and redundant style. It is inordinately diffuse, and, as a piece of narrative, singularly inartistic. The author has little sense of proportion, and almost none of composition.

[. . .] But we cannot say that we either understand or like Bathsheba. She is a young lady of the inconsequential, wilful, mettlesome type which has lately become so much the fashion for heroines, and of which Mr. Charles Reade is in a manner the inventor – the type which aims at giving one a very intimate sense of the young lady's *womanishness*. But Mr. Hardy's embodiment of it seems to us to lack reality; he puts her through the Charles Reade paces, but she remains alternatively vague and coarse, and seems always artificial. This is Mr Hardy's trouble; he rarely gets beyond ambitious artifice – the mechanical simulation of heat and depth and wisdom that are absent. Farmer Boldwood is a shadow, and Sergeant Troy an elaborate stage-figure. Everything human in the book strikes us as factitious and insubstantial; the only things we believe in are the sheep and the dogs. But, as we say, Mr Hardy has gone astray very cleverly, and his superficial novel is a really curious imitation of something better.

Review of *Far from the Madding Crowd* in *The Nation*, 24 December 1874, in *Thomas Hardy: The Critical Heritage*, ed. R.G. Cox (1995)

But oh yes, dear Louis, she [Tess] is vile. The pretence of 'sexuality' is only equalled by the absence of it, and the abomination of the language by the author's reputation for style.

Letter to R.L. Stevenson, 17 February 1893, in *Thomas Hardy: The Critical Heritage*, ed. R.G. Cox (1995)

Katherine Mansfield (1888–1923) on Hardy

Last night (this letter is like kalter aufschnitt,[90] please forgive it) I read *The Well-Beloved* by Thomas Hardy. It really is *appallingly bad, simply rotten* – withered, bony and pretentious. This is very distressing. I

---

[90]   Cold meat or cold cuts.

thought it was going to be such a find and hugged it home from the library as though I were a girl of fifteen. Of course, I wouldn't say this about it to another human being but you, c'est entendu. The style is so PREPOSTEROUS, too. I've noticed that before in Hardy occasionally – a pretentious, snobbish, schoolmaster vein (Lawrence echoes it), an 'all about Berkeley Square-ishness,' too. And then to think, as he does, that it is the study of a temperament! I hope to God he's ashamed of it now at any rate. You won't like me writing like this about him. But don't you know the feeling? If a man is 'wonderful' you want to fling up your arms and cry 'Oh, do *go on* being wonderful. Don't be less wonderful.' (Which is unreasonable, of course.)

Letter to John Middleton Murry, 5 June 1918,
in *The Letters of Katherine Mansfield*, ed. J.M. Murry (1928)

EMILE ZOLA 1840–1902

Anatole France (1844–1924) on Zola

His work is evil, and he is one of those unhappy beings of whom one can say that it would be better had he never been born. I will not, certainly, deny his detestable fame. No one before him has raised so lofty a pile of ordure. That is his monument, and its greatness cannot be disputed.

On Life and Letters (1911)

Edmond de Goncourt (1822–1896) on Zola

Then came the sweetly hypocritical compliments, the questions which are traps, the declarations which, if you follow him, he will suddenly interrupt with an 'Oh, my dear fellow, I wouldn't go as far as you!' followed by a virtual recantation of his previous arguments. In fact that art of talking without saying anything of which the Man of Médan is the master.

Pages from the Goncourt Journal, trans. R. Baldick (1962)

Oscar Wilde (1854–1900) on Zola

M. Zola, true to the lofty principle that he lays down in one of his pronunciamientos on literature, 'L'homme de génie n'a jamais d'esprit,' is determined to show that, if he has not got genius, he can at least be dull. And how well he succeeds! He is not without power. Indeed at times, as in Germinal, there is something almost epic in his work. But his work is entirely wrong from beginning to end, and wrong not on the ground of morals, but on the ground of art. From any ethical standpoint it is just what it should be. The author is perfectly truthful, and describes things exactly as they happen. What more can any moralist desire? We have no sympathy at all with the moral indignation of our time against M. Zola. It is simply the indignation of Tartuffe on being exposed. But from the standpoint of art, what can be said in favour of the author of L'Assommoir, Nana, and Pot-Bouille? Nothing. Mr. Ruskin once described the characters in George Eliot's novels as being like the sweepings of a Pentonville omnibus, but M. Zola's characters are much worse. They have their dreary vices, and their drearier virtues. The record of their lives is absolutely without interest. Who cares what happens to them? In literature we require distinction, charm, beauty, and imaginative power. We don't want to be harrowed and disgusted with an account of the doings of the lower orders.[91]

'The Decay of Lying', in *Intentions* (1891)

HENRY JAMES 1843–1916

Arnold Bennett (1867–1931) on James

It took me years to ascertain that Henry James's work was giving me little pleasure [. . .] In each case I asked myself: 'What the dickens is this novel about, and where does it think it's going to?' Question unanswerable! I gave up. To-day I have no recollection whatever of any characters or any events in either novel.[92]

In *Arnold Bennett: The Evening Standard Years*, ed. A. Mylett (1974)

---

[91]   It would be a mistake to take this as entirely Wilde's opinion: the quote comes from a dramatic essay, 'The Decay of Lying', in which Wilde, through the character Vivian, upholds the supremacy of Art over Nature.

[92]   Bennett had chosen *The Ambassadors* and *The Golden Bowl* as likely to represent the pinnacle of James's art.

Hugh Walpole (1884–1941) on James

I remember once walking with him in the fields beyond Rye, and two very small and grubby children opened the gate for us. James smiled beneficently, felt in his deep pocket for coppers, found some and then began an elaborate explanation of what the children were to buy. They were to go to a certain sweet shop because there the sweets were better than any other; they were to see that they were not deceived and offered an inferior brand, for those particular sweets had a peculiar taste of nuts and honey, with, he fancied, an especial flavour that was almost the molasses of his own country. If the children took care to visit the right shop and insisted that they should have only that particular sweet called, he fancied, 'Honey-nut' – or was it something with 'delight' in it? 'Rye's Delight' or 'Honey Delights' or – But at that moment the children, who had been listening open-mouthed, their eyes fixed on the pennies, of a sudden took fright and turned, running and roaring with terror across the fields.

He stood bewildered, the pennies in his hand. What had he done? What had he said? He had meant nothing but kindness. Why had they run from him crying and screaming? He was greatly distressed, going over every possible corner of it in his mind. He alluded to it for days afterwards.

The Apple Trees (1932)

H.G. Wells (1866–1946) on James

It was an extremely weak drama.[93] James was a strange unnatural human being, a sensitive man lost in an immensely abundant brain, which had had neither a scientific nor a philosophical training, but which was by education and natural aptitude alike, formal, formally aesthetic, conscientiously fastidious and delicate. Wrapped about in elaborations of gesture and speech, James regarded his fellow creatures with a face of distress and a remote effort at intercourse, like some victim of enchantment placed in the centre of an immense bladder. [. . .]

Guy Domville was one of those rare ripe exquisite Catholic Englishmen of ancient family conceivable only by an American mind,

---

[93]   Wells was the theatre critic for the *Pall Mall*, and on 5 January 1895 witnessed the opening night of James's doomed theatre experiment, *Guy Domville*. For James's terrible premonition of the play's probable reception, see page 147.

who gave up the woman he loved to an altogether coarser cousin, because his religious vocation was stronger than his passion. I forget the details of the action. There was a drinking scene in which Guy and the cousin, for some obscure purpose of discovery, pretended to drink and, instead, poured their wine furtively into a convenient bowl of flowers upon the table between them. Guy was played by George Alexander, at first in a mood of refined solemnity, and then, as the intimations of gathering disapproval from the pit and gallery increased, with stiffening desperation. Alexander at the close had an incredibly awkward exit. He had to stand at a door in the middle of the stage, say slowly, 'Be keynd to Her ... *Be* keynd to Her,' and depart. By nature Alexander had a long face, but at that moment with audible defeat before him, he seemed the longest and dismalest face, all face, that I had ever seen. The slowly closing door reduced him to a strip, to a line, of perpendicular gloom. The uproar burst like a thunder-storm as the door closed and the stalls responded with feeble applause. Then the tumult was mysteriously allayed. There were some minutes of uneasy apprehension. 'Author,' cried voices, 'Au-thor!' The stalls, not understanding, redoubled their clapping.

Disaster was too much for Alexander that night. A spasm of hate for the writer of those fatal lines must surely have seized him. With incredible cruelty he led the doomed James, still not understanding clearly how things were with him, to the middle of the stage, and there the pit and gallery had him. James bowed; he knew it was the proper thing to bow. Perhaps he had selected a few words to say, but if so they went unsaid. I have never heard any sound more devastating than the crescendo of booing that ensued. The gentle applause of the stalls was altogether overwhelmed. For a moment or so James faced the storm, his round face white, his mouth opening and shutting, and then Alexander, I hope in a contrite mood, snatched him back into the wings.[94]

Experiment in Autobiography (1934)

---

[94] Ford Madox Ford gave another explanation for James's terrible treatment on this occasion. Those who had booed James, Ford claimed, were members of a dramatic society, venting their spleen not on James but on Alexander, the actor-manager who had that evening introduced a charge for programmes. It is possible that Wells knew this but deliberately withheld it here for personal reasons.

His people nose out suspicions, hint by hint, link by link. Have you ever known living human beings do that? The thing his novel is *about* is always there. It is like a church lit but with no congregation to distract you, with every light and line focussed on the high altar. And on the altar, very reverently placed, intensely there, is a dead kitten, an eggshell, a bit of string. [. . .] His vast paragraphs sweat and struggle; they could not sweat and elbow and struggle more if God Himself was the processional meaning to which they sought to come. And all for tales of nothingness. It is leviathan retrieving pebbles. It is a magnificent but painful hippopotamus resolved at any cost, even at the cost of its dignity, upon picking up a pea which has got into the corner of its den.[95]

Boon (1915)

Oscar Wilde (1854–1900) on James

Mr. Henry James writes fiction as if it were a painful duty, and wastes upon mean motives and imperceptible 'points of view' his neat literary style, his felicitous phrases, his swift and caustic satire.[96]

'The Decay of Lying', in *Intentions* (1891)

Virginia Woolf (1882–1941) on James

I have finished the Wings of the Dove, & make this comment. His manipulations become so elaborate towards the end that instead of feeling the artist you merely feel the man who is posing the subject. And then I think he loses the power to feel the crisis. He becomes merely excessively ingenious. This, you seem to hear him saying, is the way to do it. Now just when you expect a crisis, the true artist evades it. Never do the thing, & it will be all the more impressive. Finally, after all this juggling & arranging of silk pocket handkerchiefs, one ceases to have any feeling for the figures behind. Milly thus manipulated, disappears. He overreaches himself. And then one can never read it again. The mental grasp & stretch are magnificent. Not a flabby or

---

[95] This attack marked the end of the friendship between Wells and James, those two very different writers. The *casus belli* was James's cool assessment of the merits of Wells's books in his *Notes on Novelists*, published the year before – see page 158.

[96] This is not quite Wilde speaking: it comes from a dramatic essay, 'The Decay of Lying', in which the Wilde-figure, Vivian, denounces Nature and upholds Art.

slack sentence, but much emasculated by this timidity or consciousness or whatever it is. Very highly American, I conjecture, in the determination to be highly bred, & the slight obtuseness as to what high breeding is.[97]

Diary for 12 September 1921, in *The Diary of Virginia Woolf*,
ed. A.O. Bell (1977–84)

GERARD MANLEY HOPKINS 1844–1889

Yvor Winters[98] (1900–1968) on Hopkins

For more than thirty years I have bred and exhibited Airedales in a small way, and I have owned some very fine ones. At the present time I own a young dog who seems to me exceptionally beautiful, especially when he is in motion. No less than Hopkins' falcon,[99] he is one of God's little creatures; he is probably a much better specimen of his kind and better adapted to his peculiar ends, and if one is sufficiently scholarly and sufficiently perceptive, one will be aware of this probability; in addition, I am fairly certain that his moral character is more admirable than that of the bird. Yet it would never occur to me to write a poem describing his beauty and then stating that the beauty of Christ was similar but merely greater. To do so would seem to me ludicrous, and to many it would seem blasphemous. Yet there is no essential difference between my dog and Hopkins' bird; the bird has the advantage merely of the Romantic and sentimental feeling attached to birds as symbols of the free and unrestrained spirit, a feeling derived very largely from Shelley's *Skylark* and from a handful of similar – and similarly bad – poems of the past century and a half. Hopkins' poem employs a mechanical and a very easy formula. His image resembles the image of the anvil in *No worst, there is none*, in

---

[97]   Woolf nevertheless admired James greatly and elsewhere praised what even his fans did not always notice: 'his vitality – his vernacular – his pounce and grip and swing'. She kept a photograph of James on her writing table.

[98]   Yvor Winters was a notoriously combative American poet and critic with some idiosyncratic ideas about the literary canon. His collections of poetry are numerous and include *Diadems and Fagots* (1921) and *The Proof* (1930).

[99]   i.e. 'The Windhover'.

which we get the physical embodiment of the meaning, without the meaning, or with too small a part of it. To defend this sort of thing with pretentious remarks about the 'sacramental view of nature' is merely foolish, no matter how numerous, pious, and ancient the precedents which one may be in a position to cite. [. . .]

In my terms, it is the business of the poet, not to communicate his own inscape, but to arrive at a true judgment of his subject, whatever it may be; we all have individuality, but few of us have intelligence. [. . .]

If, however, we have a poet who is concerned with the expression of his own inscape (self-expression) and with the inscapes of natural objects and with little else, we may expect him to produce poems which are badly organised, and loosely emotional, and which endeavor to express emotions obscure in their origins and to express these emotions in terms of natural details of landscape to which the emotions are irrelevant. And poems of this kind are what Hopkins most often wrote. [. . .]

I believe that Hopkins is a poet who will find his most devout admirers among the young; at the age of eighteen I myself was among his most devout admirers, but my opinion has changed with the passage of time. The young as a matter of necessity do not know the best English poetry in sufficiently rich detail to be critical and are more likely to be impressed by novelty than by achievement; they are likely to be somewhat emotional and hence uncritical of emotion in others; they are likely to be given to self-pity at odd moments, and hence sympathetic with chronic self-pity in others. I am not one of those who find failure more impressive than success, though I realise that I am in a minority.

On Modern Poets (1959)

ROBERT LOUIS STEVENSON 1850–1894

George Moore (1852–1933) on Stevenson

I will state frankly that Mr. R.L. Stevenson never wrote a line that failed to delight me; but he never wrote a book. You arrive at a strangely just estimate of a writer's worth by the mere question: 'What is he the author of?' for every writer whose work is destined to live is the author of one book that outshines the other, and, in popular imagination, epitomises his talent and position. What is Shakespeare the author of? What is Milton the author of? What is Fielding the author of? What is Byron the author of? What is Carlyle the author of? What is Thackeray the author of? What is Zola the author of? What is Mr. Swinburne the author of? Mr. Stevenson is the author of shall I say, 'Treasure Island,' or what?

Confessions of a Young Man (1888)

Oscar Wilde (1854–1900) on Stevenson

Stevenson's letters are most disappointing also – I see that romantic surroundings are the worst surroundings possible for a romantic writer. In Gower Street Stevenson would have written a new *Trois Mousquetaires*. In Samoa he wrote letters to the *Times* about Germans. I see also the traces of a terrible strain to lead a natural life. To chop wood with any advantage to oneself or profit to others, one should not be able to describe the process. In point of fact the natural life is the unconscious life. Stevenson merely extended the sphere of the artificial by taking to digging. The whole dreary book has given me a lesson. If I spend my future life reading Baudelaire in a *café* I shall be leading a more natural life than if I take to hedger's work or plant cacao in mud-swamps.

Letter to Robert Ross, 6 April 1897, in *The Complete Letters of Oscar Wilde*, ed. M. Holland and R. Hart-Davis (2000)

GEORGE MOORE[100] 1852–1933

G.K. Chesterton (1874–1936) on Moore

Mr. Moore's egoism is not merely a moral weakness, it is a very constant and influential aesthetic weakness as well. We should really be

---

[100] George Moore, the prolific, now little-read, Irish novelist and dramatist. Ford Madox Ford said of Moore: 'I have never met a critic with any pretensions to knowledge of letters who would not acknowledge when challenged that Moore was infinitely the most skilful man of letters of his day. The most skilful in the whole world . . . Yet in an infinite number of reviews and *comptes rendus* of the literature of the world that I have read – and written – George Moore is almost invariably forgotten. That is due perhaps to the fact that he belonged to no school in England; perhaps to his want of personal geniality, perhaps to something more subtle.' See also Moore on George Eliot, page 117, Flaubert, page 124, and Robert Louis Stevenson, page 144.

much more interested in Mr. Moore if he were not quite so interested in himself. We feel as if we were being shown through a gallery of really fine pictures, into each of which, by some useless and discordant convention, the artist had represented the same figure in the same attitude. 'The Grand Canal with a distant view of Mr. Moore,' 'Effect of Mr. Moore through a Scotch Mist,' 'Mr. Moore by Firelight,' 'Ruins of Mr. Moore by Moonlight,' and so on, seems to be the endless series. He would no doubt reply that in such a book as this he intended to reveal himself. But the answer is that in such a book as this he does not succeed. [. . .] In reading [Moore's *Confessions of a Young Man*] we do not feel the presence of a clean-cut personality like that of Thackeray and Matthew Arnold. We only read a number of quite clever and largely conflicting opinions which might be uttered by any clever person, but which we are called upon to admire specifically, because they are uttered by Mr. Moore. He is the only thread that connects Catholicism and Protestantism, realism and mysticism – he or rather his name. He is profoundly absorbed even in views he no longer holds, and he expects us to be. And he intrudes the capital 'I' even where it need not be intruded – even where it weakens the force of a plain statement. Where another man would say, 'It is a fine day,' Mr. Moore says, 'Seen through my temperament, the day appeared fine.' Where another man would say 'Milton has obviously a fine style,' Mr. Moore would say, 'As a stylist Milton had always impressed me.' The Nemesis of this self-centred spirit is that of being totally ineffectual. Mr. Moore has started many interesting crusades, but he has abandoned them before his disciples could begin. Even when he is on the side of the truth he is as fickle as the children of falsehood. Even when he has found reality he cannot find rest.

Heretics (1905)

OSCAR WILDE 1854–1900

Noël Coward (1899–1973) on Wilde
Am reading more of Oscar Wilde. What a tiresome, affected sod.

> Diary for 14 July 1946, in *The Noel Coward Diaries*,
> ed. S. Morley and G. Payn (1982)

Henry James (1843–1916) on Wilde

On the night of the 5th, too nervous to do anything else, I had the ingenious thought of going to some other theatre and seeing some other play as a means of being coerced into quietness from 8 till 10.45. I went accordingly to the Haymarket, to a new piece by the said O.W. that had just been produced – *An Ideal Husband*. I sat through it and saw it played with every appearance (so far as the crowded house was an appearance) of complete success, and *that* gave me the most fearful apprehension. The thing seemed to me so helpless, so crude, so bad, so clumsy, feeble and vulgar, that as I walked away across St James's Square to learn my own fate, the prosperity of what I had seen seemed to me to constitute a dreadful presumption of the shipwreck of *G.D.*, and I stopped in the middle of the Square, paralyzed by the terror of this probability – afraid to go on and learn more. 'How *can* my piece do anything with a public for whom *that* is a success?' It couldn't . . .[101]

Letter to William James, 2 February 1895,
in *Letters of Henry James*, ed. P. Lubbock (1920)

George Moore (1852–1933) on Wilde

You would put him in the first class as a writer and I should put him in the third or fourth. It is not a long time since I read a book of his called *Intentions*, and it seems to me very thin and casual, without depth, therefore, unoriginal; no man is original in the surface of his mind; to be original we must go deep, right down to the roots, and Oscar Wilde's talent seems to me essentially rootless; something growing in a glass in a little water. I was struck by his lack of style; by style, I mean rhythm. It is all quite clear and correct but his sentences do not sway. There is no current and I return to glass for an image, it is all very glassy. He had a certain dramatic gift, he moves his characters deftly and his dialogue is not without grace. It is often to the point. He had a pretty ingenious drawing-room wit, and these qualities enabled him to write plays that are not intolerable to a man of letters, and

---

[101]   This was the fateful night of the first performance of *Guy Domville* (see page 140), James's disastrous play that came off after a few weeks. It was replaced in the same theatre by another play of Wilde's which went on to do very well – *The Importance of Being Earnest*. James had met Wilde on one occasion in 1882 and thought him little more than a poseur. (See also Wilde on James, page 142.)

superficial enough to attract audiences. If I understand your letter rightly you seem to think that Wilde's abnormal impulses mark him out as an interesting subject for literary study. It might be so if Wilde were a great writer. He is that in your opinion,[102] but in my opinion, as I have already said, he is in the third or fourth class and, therefore, not worth troubling about, and I do not think that anybody would have troubled about him if the Marquis of Queensbury had not written him a post card; had it not been for that unlucky post card Wilde and his literature would be sleeping comfortably in the dust at the bottom of an almost forgotten drawer in company with Frank Miles' drawings.[103]

Letter to Frank Harris in *Pearson's Magazine*, March 1918,
in *Oscar Wilde: The Critical Heritage*, ed. K. Beckson (1997)

James McNeill Whistler (1834–1903) on Wilde

What has Oscar in common with Art? except that he dines at our tables and picks from our platters the plums for the pudding he peddles in the provinces. Oscar – the amiable, irresponsible, esurient Oscar – with no more sense of a picture than of the fit of a coat, has the courage of the opinions – of others! [104]

The World, 17 November 1886, in *The Gentle Art of Making Enemies* (1890)

GEORGE BERNARD SHAW 1856–1950

G.K. Chesterton (1874–1936) on Shaw

But the sensation connected with Mr. Shaw in recent years has been his sudden development of the religion of the Superman. He who had to all

---

[102] Harris had said that he thought *The Ballad of Reading Gaol* would last longer than anything written in England between 1875 and 1900.

[103] Frank Harris was the editor of *Pearson's* magazine, and had also completed a biography of Wilde: Harris invited Moore, who he knew had an antipathy to Wilde, to write this assessment. One story about Wilde and Moore is that Wilde was once asked if he knew Moore. His reply was, 'Know him? I know him so well that I haven't spoken to him for ten years.'

[104] Wilde had joined the committee of the National Art Exhibition, and Whistler (whose friendship with Oscar had cooled) objected. Wilde replied a week later in the same organ that 'With our James, "vulgarity begins at home", and should be allowed to stay there.'

appearance mocked at the faiths in the forgotten past discovered a new god in the unimaginable future. He who had laid all the blame on ideals set up the most impossible of all ideals, the ideal of a new creature. But the truth, nevertheless, is that anyone who knows Mr. Shaw's mind adequately, and admires it properly, must have guessed all this long ago.

For the truth is that Mr. Shaw has never seen things as they really are. If he had he would have fallen on his knees before them. He has always had a secret ideal that has withered all the things of this world. He has all the time been silently comparing humanity with something that was not human, with a monster from Mars, with the Wise Man of the Stoics, with the Economic Man of the Fabians, with Julius Caesar, with Siegfried, with the Superman. Now, to have this inner and merciless standard may be a very good thing, or a very bad one, it may be excellent or unfortunate, but it is not seeing things as they are. It is not seeing things as they are to think first of a Briareus with a hundred hands, and then call every man a cripple for only having two. It is not seeing things as they are to start with a vision of Argus with his hundred eyes, and then jeer at every man with two eyes as if he had only one. And it is not seeing things as they are to imagine a demigod of infinite mental clarity, who may or may not appear in the latter days of the earth, and then to see all men as idiots. And this is what Mr. Shaw has always in some degree done. When we really see men as they are, we do not criticize, but worship; and very rightly. For a monster with mysterious eyes and miraculous thumbs, with strange dreams in his skull, and a queer tenderness for this place or that baby, is truly a wonderful and unnerving matter. It is only the quite arbitrary and priggish habit of comparison with something else which makes it possible to be at our ease in front of him. A sentiment of superiority keeps us cool and practical; the mere facts would make our knees knock under as with religious fear. It is the fact that every instant of conscious life is an unimaginable prodigy. It is the fact that every face in the street has the incredible unexpectedness of a fairy-tale. The thing which prevents a man from realizing this is not any clear-sightedness or experience, it is simply a habit of pedantic and fastidious comparisons between one thing and another. Mr. Shaw, on the practical side perhaps the most humane man alive, is in this sense inhumane. He has even been infected to some extent with the primary intellectual weakness of his new master,

Nietzsche, the strange notion that the greater and stronger a man was the more he would despise other things. The greater and stronger a man is the more he would be inclined to prostrate himself before a periwinkle. That Mr. Shaw keeps a lifted head and a contemptuous face before the colossal panorama of empires and civilizations, this does not in itself convince one that he sees things as they are. I should be most effectively convinced that he did if I found him staring with religious astonishment at his own feet. 'What are those two beautiful and industrious beings,' I can imagine him murmuring to himself, 'whom I see everywhere, serving me I know not why? What fairy godmother bade them come trotting out of elfland when I was born? What god of the borderland, what barbaric god of legs, must I propitiate with fire and wine, lest they run away with me?'[105]

Heretics (1905)

Katherine Mansfield (1888–1923) on Shaw

G.B.S. on Butler[106] is very fine indeed. He has such a grip of his subject. I admire his tenacity as a reviewer and the way in which his mind follows Butler with a steady light – does not waver over him, find him, lose him, travel over him. At the same time it's queer he should be (G. B. S.) so uninspired. There is not the faintest hint of inspiration in that man. This chills me. You know the feeling that a great writer gives you: 'My spirit has been fed and refreshed: it has partaken of something new.' One could not possibly feel that about Shaw. It's the clang of the gate that remains with you when all's over. What it amounts to is that Shaw is anything you like, but he's not an artist. Don't you get when you read his plays a sense of extraordinary *flatness*? They may be extremely amusing at moments, but you are always laughing *at* and never *with*. Just the same in his prose: You may agree as much as you like, but he is writing *at* not *with*. There's no getting over it: he's a kind of concierge in the house of literature – sits in a glass case, sees everything, knows

---

[105] Chesterton and Shaw were, despite this attack, great friends and co-disputers. One story goes that Chesterton once remarked to Shaw (who was thin), 'To look at you, anyone would think there was a famine in England.' Shaw retorted to Chesterton (who was fat), 'To look at you, anyone would think you caused it.'

[106] i.e. Samuel Butler: Shaw had just written a review of a book on Butler in *The Manchester Guardian*.

everything, examines the letters, *cleans the stairs*, but has no part, no part in the life that is going on. But as I wrote that, I thought: Yes, but who *is* living there, living there as we mean life? Dostoevsky, Tchehov and Tolstoy and Hardy.[107] I can't think of *anybody else*.

> Letter to John Middleton Murry, 13 December 1919,
> in *The Letters of Katherine Mansfield*, ed. J.M. Murry (1928)

John Osborne (1929–1994) on Shaw

Having recently seen *Saint Joan* in London and *Caesar and Cleopatra* in Sydney, it is clearer to me than ever that Shaw is the most fraudulent, inept writer of Victorian melodramas ever to gull a timid critic or fool a dull public.

He writes like a Pakistani who has learned English when he was 12-years-old in order to become a chartered accountant.

> Letter in *The Guardian*, 23 June 1977

Roger Scruton (1944–) on Shaw

Concerning no subject would he be deterred by the minor accident of complete ignorance from penning a definitive opinion.

> *The Philosopher on Dover Beach* (1990)

H.G. Wells (1866–1946) on Shaw

One of those perpetual children who live in a dream world of make-believe [. . .]. It is almost as if there was no pain in the world. It is under the inspiration of such delightful dreams that Mr. Shaw now flings himself upon his typewriter and rattles out his broadsides. And nothing will stop him. All through the war we shall have this Shavian accompaniment going on, like an idiot child screaming in a hospital, distorting, discrediting, confusing. He is at present . . . an almost unendurable nuisance.[108]

> *The Daily Chronicle*, 31 December 1914, in Stanley Weintraub,
> *Journey to Heartbreak* (1971)

---

[107] Here Mansfield ranks Hardy with these other giants: elsewhere (see page 137) she is less charitable.

[108] Shaw opposed the First World War in *Common Sense about the War* (1914); and Wells, who felt it necessary to continue the war, opposed Shaw.

JOSEPH CONRAD 1857–1924

D.H. Lawrence (1885–1930) on Conrad

Melville doesn't sentimentalize the ocean and the sea's unfortunates. Snivel in a wet hanky like Lord Jim.[109]

Studies in Classic American Literature (1923)

George Moore (1852–1933) on Conrad

Mr. Conrad has paid us a pretty compliment by learning to write the English language correctly, and the journalists are so pleased that they have assigned to him a place in our literature, forgetful that a man gets a place in English literature by bringing into the language something that was not there before, or shall I say that was not obvious before.

Conversations in Ebury Street (1924)

Virginia Woolf (1882–1941) on Conrad

After the middle period Conrad never again was able to bring his figures into perfect relation with their background. He never believed in his later, and more highly sophisticated characters as he had believed in his early seamen. When he had to indicate their relation to that other unseen world of novelists, the world of values and convictions, he was far less sure what those values were. Then, over and over again, a single phrase, 'He steered with care', coming at the end of a storm, carried in it a whole morality. But in this more crowded and complicated world such terse phrases became less and less appropriate. Complex men and women of many interests and relations would not submit to so summary a judgement; or, if they did, much that was important in them escaped the verdict. And yet it was very necessary to Conrad's genius, with its luxuriant and romantic power, to have some law by which its creations could be tried. Essentially – such remained his creed – this world of civilised and self-conscious people is based upon 'a few very simple ideas'; but where, in the world of thoughts and personal relations, are we to find them? There are no masts in drawing-rooms; the typhoon does not test the worth of politicians and business men. Seeking and not finding such supports,

---

[109] And yet see Lawrence on Melville, page 118.

the world of Conrad's later period has about it an involuntary obscurity, an inconclusiveness, almost a disillusionment which baffles and fatigues.[110]

The Common Reader (1925)

ARTHUR CONAN DOYLE 1859–1930

Ezra Pound (1885–1972) on Doyle

Sir A. Conan Doyle has never stooped to literature. Wells, Benett [sic], and the rest of them have wobbled about in penumbras, but here is the man who has 'done it', who has contributed a word to the language, a 'character' to the fiction of the Caucasian world, for there is no European language in which the 'Great Detective' can be hid under any disguise. Herlock Sholmes, spell it as you like, is KNOWN. Caines and Corellis lie by the wayside. Sherlock has held us all spellbound. Let us see what is requisite. Let us see what we are asked to believe.

In the first place, there is a residue in the minds of everyone who sees this name on the magazine cover. We all know something about Mr. Holmes. We have no difficulty in calling to mind this figure. He is perfectly fearless, possessed of inordinate strength, is absolutely impervious to the action of all known drugs and narcotics, and possessed, if not of eternal youth, at least of an eternal prime, of an invulnerable energy. He is also an eunuch (though I have no doubt Sir Arthur would fit him out with a past full of romance if ever the public desire it).

[. . .] Sherlock is unique, but mankind remains amazingly unaltered and unalterable. He likes a relief from reality, he likes fairy stories, he likes stories of giants, he likes genii from bottles. Sherlock with his superhuman strength, his marvelous acumen, his deductive reasoning (which is certainly not shared with the reader), has all the charms of the giant. He is also a moral Titan: right is never too right. The logical end of these likes is, or was, God. The first clever Semite who went out for monotheism made a corner in giantness. We got a giant 'really'

---

[110] Woolf was elsewhere a considerable admirer of Conrad, and wrote to Pernel Strachey in 1923 that he was 'a much better writer than all of us put together'.

bigger than all other possible giants. Whenever art gets beyond itself, and laps up too great a public, it at once degenerates into religion. Sherlock is on the way to religion, a modern worship of efficiency, acumen, inhumanity. Only a man on familiar terms with his public as Sir Arthur, as habituated to writing for that public, would dare 'lay it on so thick.' His Sherlock's peroration (supposedly, August 2, 1914) is a mixture of moving – prognostication of the 'cold and bitter' wind which will blow over England and wither many in its blast, and a hurry to cash a £500 cheque before the arrested spy (then actually in their Ford motor-car, and about to be taken to Scotland Yard) has time to stop payment. Watson is urged to 'start her up'.

Sir Arthur is as illogical as any other sort of fanatic. He is loud in praise of Sherlock's faculty of reason, but his own flesh or mind, or whatever it is, falls a little short of divinity.

'Studies in Contemporary Mentality', in *The New Age*, 13 September 1917

A.E. HOUSMAN 1859–1936

John Berryman (1914–1972) on Housman

Housman is one of my heroes and always has been. He was a detestable and miserable man. Arrogant, unspeakably lonely, cruel, and so on, but an absolutely marvellous minor poet, I think, and a great scholar.

The Paris Review, Winter 1972

Edith Sitwell (1887–1964) on Housman

But to return to 'The Shropshire Lad'; a spurious pathos, springing, however, from a perfectly genuine feeling, is gained from time to time by the juxtaposition of such themes as cricket and death:

> See the son of grief at cricket
> Trying to be glad.
>
> Try I will: no harm in trying.
> Wonder 'tis how little mirth
> Keeps the bones of man from lying
> On the bed of earth.

It is claimed by admirers of cricket and of war that Waterloo was won on the playing fields of Eton. If this may be held to be true, cricket did, on that occasion, bring a great many men to their death. But I do not think that Professor Housman has explained to us clearly enough how it is that cricket has saved men from dying. If he means us to understand that cricket, and cricket alone, has prevented men from committing suicide, then their continuation on this earth seems hardly worth while.

Aspects of Modern Poetry (1934)

RUDYARD KIPLING 1865–1936

Max Beerbohm (1872–1956) on Kipling

'You spoke to me of Kipling,' Beerbohm said.[111] 'When first I met him, in Baltimore, he received me so nicely. He was charming. And later . . . so sympathetic, so kind. And then – you know – his books kept coming out, and occasionally I was asked to review them. I couldn't, you know, abide them. He was a genius, a very great genius, and I felt that he was debasing his genius by what he wrote. And I couldn't refrain from saying so. It went on and on. Friends of his and mine kept telling me that he was so pained and shocked by what I wrote, but I couldn't stop. You know, I couldn't stop. As his publication increased, so did my derogation. He didn't stop; I *couldn't* stop. I meant to. I wanted to. But I couldn't.'

After a pause, Beerbohm continued:

'After that meeting in Baltimore, I saw him twice. Once in a hansom. I was in another hansom, and we passed each other in the Strand. He saw me and he knew that I had seen him. But as the hansoms passed, we each of us averted our eyes. Then, some years later, I saw him again, in White's Club. There was a table between us, and, looking across it, over the heads of the diners, I caught his eye. He was looking at me. I wished to get up. I very much wanted to go over to him and to say, 'Mr. Kipling, I admire you. I admire your very great

---

[111] Beerbohm is being interviewed by S.N. Behrman for his book *Conversations with Max*.

genius. If I have written harshly of you, it is because I do not believe
you are living up to the possibilities of your genius.' I so much wished
to do this. But I didn't. Why didn't I do it? Why didn't I unbend? Why
did I go on persecuting him? And now he is dead and it is too late.'

In Myrick Land, *The Fine Art of Literary Mayhem* (1963)

T.S. Eliot (1888–1965) on Kipling

Mr. Kipling is a laureate without laurels. He is a neglected celebrity.
The arrival of a new book of his verse is not likely to stir the slightest
ripple on the surface of our conversational intelligentsia. He has not
been crowned by the elder generation; malevolent fate has not even
allowed him to be one of the four or five or six greatest living poets. A
serious contemporary has remarked of the present volume that 'in
nearly all our poetical coteries the poetry of Kipling has long been
anathema, with field sports, Imperialism, and public schools.' This is
wide of the mark. Mr Kipling is not anathema; he is merely not
discussed. Most of our discerning critics have no more an opinion on
Mr. Kipling than they have on the poetry of Mr. John Oxenham.[112]

Review of *The Years Between* in *The Athenaeum*, 9 May 1919,
in *Rudyard Kipling, The Critical Heritage*, ed. R.L. Green (1997)

W.B. YEATS 1865–1939

George Orwell (1903–1950) on Yeats

Translated into political terms, Yeats's tendency is Fascist. Throughout
most of his life, and long before Fascism was ever heard of, he had had
the outlook of those who reach Fascism by the aristocratic route. He is
a great hater of democracy, of the modern world, science, machinery,
the concept of progress – above all, of the idea of human equality.
Much of the imagery of his work is feudal, and it is clear that he was
not altogether free from ordinary snobbishness. Later these tendencies
took clearer shape and led him to 'the exultant acceptance of

---

[112] This quotation is actually a defence of Kipling, and should not strictly
speaking be included here – but it does show the general negative opinion of
Kipling in the after-war years. The defence is perhaps surprising, coming from
Eliot, a modernist poet, in 1919.

authoritarianism as the only solution. Even violence and tyranny are
not necessarily evil because the people, knowing not evil and good,
would become perfectly acquiescent to tyranny . . . Everything must
come from the top. Nothing can come from the masses.' Not much
interested in politics, and no doubt disgusted by his brief incursions
into public life, Yeats nevertheless makes political pronouncements. He
is too big a man to share the illusions of Liberalism, and as early as
1920 he foretells in a justly famous passage ('The Second Coming') the
kind of world that we have actually moved into. But he appears to
welcome the coming age, which is to be 'hierarchical, masculine, harsh,
surgical', and is influenced both by Ezra Pound and by various Italian
Fascist writers. He describes the new civilisation which he hopes and
believes will arrive: 'an aristocratic civilisation in its most completed
form, every detail of life hierarchical, every great man's door crowded
at dawn by petitioners, great wealth everywhere in a few men's hands,
all dependent upon a few, up to the Emperor himself, who is a God
dependent on a greater God, and everywhere, in Court, in the family,
an inequality made law.' The innocence of this statement is as
interesting as its snobbishness. To begin with, in a single phrase, 'great
wealth in a few men's hands', Yeats lays bare the central reality of
Fascism, which the whole of its propaganda is designed to cover up.
The merely political Fascist claims always to be fighting for justice:
Yeats, the poet, sees at a glance that Fascism means injustice, and
acclaims it for that very reason. But at the same time he fails to see that
the new authoritarian civilisation, if it arrives, will not be aristocratic,
or what he means by aristocratic. It will not be ruled by noblemen
with Van Dyck faces, but by anonymous millionaires, shiny-bottomed
bureaucrats and murdering gangsters. Others who have made the same
mistake have afterwards changed their views and one ought not to
assume that Yeats, if he had lived longer, would necessarily have
followed his friend Pound, even in sympathy. But the tendency of the
passage I have quoted above is obvious, and its complete throwing
overboard of whatever good the past two thousand years have achieved
is a disquieting symptom.

'W.B. Yeats', in *Horizon*, January 1943, in *The Collected Essays,
Journalism and Letters of George Orwell* (1968)

H.G. WELLS 1866–1946

Henry James (1843–1916) on Wells

Such things as *The New Machiavelli, Marriage, The Passionate Friends*, are
so very much more attestations of the presence of material than of an
interest in the use of it that we ask ourselves again and again why so
fondly neglected a state of leakage comes not to be fatal to *any* provision
of quantity, or even to stores more specially selected for the ordeal than
Mr Wells's always strike us as being. Is not the pang of witnessed waste
in fact great just in proportion as we are touched by our author's fine off-
handedness as to the value of the stores, about which he can for the time
make us believe what he will? so that, to take an example susceptible of
brief statement, we wince at a certain quite peculiarly gratuitous sacrifice
to the casual in *Marriage* very much as at seeing some fine and
indispensable little part of a mechanism slip through profane fingers
and lose itself.[113]

Notes on Novelists (1914)

George Orwell (1903–1950) on Wells

H.G. Wells, though later on he was to write a history of the world, looks
at the past with the same sort of surprised disgust as a civilized man
contemplating a tribe of cannibals.

'The Rediscovery of Europe', in *The Listener*, 19 March 1942,
in *The Collected Essays, Journalism and Letters of George Orwell* (1968)

Rebecca West (1892–1983) on Wells

I have tried to leave H. G. innumerable times, but never without his
following me and asking me to come back. I have as a matter of fact left
him at the moment but I am dreading another attempt to get me to come
back. It is also, as I have a steady monogamous nature, and would have been
the most wifely wife on earth, extremely difficult not to take the job again.
My only hope therefore of getting and keeping clear is to go to America!

Letter to S.K. Ratcliffe, 21 March 1923, in Anthony West,
H.G. Wells: Aspects of a Life (1984)

---

[113] This tone of disdain led to Wells's savage response in *Boon* in which he made
his famous characterization of James as 'a hippopotamus picking up a pea' (see page
142). The metaphor of picking up a small dropped object – a pea – seems to derive
directly from the 'little mechanism' metaphor of the above passage.

ARNOLD BENNETT 1867–1931

Wyndham Lewis (1882–1957) on Bennett

He was the Hitler of the book-racket. The book-trade said that he could make a book overnight. If he praised it on Thursday evening, by the week-end it was selling like hot cakes.

Blasting and Bombardiering (1937)

P.G. Wodehouse (1881–1975) on Bennett

Disraeli once said that the author who talks about his books is as bad as the mother who talks about her children, but Walpole and Bennett had either not come across this dictum or had mutually agreed to ignore it. 'It would be affectation to say that the Clayhanger trilogy is not good,' said Bennett, among a great number of other things. 'Either I'm a good writer or I have been deceiving myself as well as trying to deceive the public. I place it upon record frankly – the Clayhanger trilogy is *good*.' Hugh Walpole was starting to say something about the Herries series, of which his previous conversation had shown that he approved, but Bennett rolled over him like a placid steam-roller. 'The scene, for instance, where Darius Clayhanger dies that lingering death could scarcely be bettered . . . And why?' said Bennett. 'Because I took infinite pains over it. All the time my father was dying, I was at the bedside making copious notes. You can't just slap these things down. You have to take trouble.'

Bring on the Girls (1954)

Virginia Woolf (1882–1941) on Bennett

I dined with Arnold Bennett the other night. Do you know him? He is a kind old walrus, who suddenly shuts his eyes like a dead fish and waits three minutes before he can finish his sentence. He makes enormous sums of money; but has horrible dinners; slabs of fish; huge potatoes; everything half cold; and then he took me to look at his bed. I should say that I had led to this by talking about comfort. All his furniture is very solid, but not comfortable; and uglier than you can even begin to imagine. So was his bed. He says that great artists need all the comfort they can get. But is he a great artist? I detest all novels, so I can't say.

Letter to Lady Cecil, 28 December 1927, in *The Letters of Virginia Woolf*, ed. N. Nicolson and J. Trautmann (1975–1980)

JOHN GALSWORTHY 1867–1933

George Orwell (1903–1950) on Galsworthy

Well, the thing that strikes one about Galsworthy is that though he's trying to be iconoclastic, he has been utterly unable to move his mind outside the wealthy bourgeois society he is attacking. With only slight modifications he takes all its values for granted. All he conceives to be wrong is that human beings are a little too inhumane, a little too fond of money, and aesthetically not quite sensitive enough. When he sets out to depict what he conceives as the desirable type of human being, it turns out to be simply a cultivated, humanitarian version of the upper-middle-class *rentier*, the sort of person who in those days used to haunt picture galleries in Italy and subscribe heavily to the Society for the Prevention of Cruelty to Animals. And this fact – the fact that Galsworthy hasn't any really deep aversion to the social types he thinks he is attacking – gives you the clue to his weakness. It is, that he has no contact with anything outside contemporary English society. He may think he doesn't like it, but he is part of it. Its money and security, the ring of battleships that separated it from Europe, have been too much for him. At the bottom of this heart he despises foreigners, just as much as any illiterate businessman in Manchester.

'The Rediscovery of Europe', in *The Listener*, 19 March 1942,
in *The Collected Essays, Journalism and Letters of George Orwell* (1968)

Anthony Powell (1905–2000) on Galsworthy

One hot summer afternoon [in the offices of Duckworth], I was reading a manuscript, when the door opened quietly. A tall man, dressed in the deepest black, stood there in silence, clothes and bearing suggesting a clergyman. He smiled – to use an epithet he might well have employed in his own writing – 'quizzically'. I withdrew my feet from the desk, but he seemed to expect more than that; indeed instant acknowledgment of something in himself. A further survey convinced me that here was John Galsworthy. He gave off the redolence of boundless vanity, a condition not at all uncommon among authors, in this case more noticeable than usual.

I was about to alert Lewis, bent double at his desk over a sheaf of estimates, which, according to habit, he was examining at a range of about two inches off the paper, but Galsworthy, making the conventional gesture of finger to lips, indicated silence. He was just within sight of Lewis round the corner of the desk, the implication being that by sheer personality Galsworthy would send out rays which would compel Lewis to look up.

We both awaited a respectful burst of recognition. For some reason the magnetism did not work. Galsworthy stood there smiling with benevolent condescension; the smile becoming increasingly fixed, as Lewis continued to ponder the estimates. Finally Galsworthy gave it up as a bad job. He announced his presence abruptly by word of mouth. He was evidently disappointed in Lewis's lack of antennae, where famous writers were concerned. Lewis raised his head to see who had spoken, then, taking in at a glance one of the firm's most lucrative properties, jumped up full of apologies, and hurried the Great Man into the Senior Partner's room.

Messengers of Day (1978)

MARCEL PROUST 1871–1922

Evelyn Waugh (1903–1966) on Proust
I am reading Proust for the first time. Very poor stuff. I think he was mentally defective. I remember how small I used to feel when people talked about him & didn't dare admit I couldn't get through him. Well, I can get through him now, of course – because I can read anything that isn't about politics. Well the chap was plain barmy. He never tells you the age of the hero and on one page he is being taken to the WC in the Champs Elysées by his nurse & the next page he is going to a brothel. Such a lot of nonsense.

Letter to John Betjeman, ?February 1948, in *The Letters of Evelyn Waugh*, ed. M. Amory (1980)

BERTRAND RUSSELL 1872–1970

T.S. Eliot (1888–1965) on Russell

> When Mr. Apollinax visited the United States
> His laughter tinkled among the teacups.
> I thought of Fragilion, that shy figure among the birch-trees,
> And of Priapus in the shrubbery
> Gaping at the lady in the swing.
> In the palace of Mrs. Phlaccus, at Professor Channing-
> Cheetah's
> He laughed like an irresponsible foetus.
> His laughter was submarine and profound
> Like the old man of the sea's
> Hidden under coral islands
> Where worried bodies of drowned men drift down in the
> green silence,
> Dropping from fingers of surf.[114]

Prufrock and Other Observations (1917)

A.E. Housman (1859–1936) on Russell

If I were the Prince of Peace I would choose a less provocative ambassador.

In Ronald William Clark, *The Life and Times of Bertrand Russell* (1976)

---

[114] From 'Mr. Apollinax', aka Russell. Russell was Eliot's tutor at Harvard: the relations between the two men were those of wary respect. Russell himself recognized the caricature (the poem goes on to give lines of overheard talk about Mr. Apollinax – 'His pointed ears … He must be unbalanced'), and did not seem to mind it: he wrote to Barry Fox in 1927: 'Do you know T.S. Eliot's little poem about me, called "Mr. Apollinax"? He seems to have noticed the madness.'

5 MALICE FOR THE MODERNS

Experimentation attracts particular types of invective. Desire to innovate sometimes looks like desire to shock; difficulty sometimes looks like obscurantism; dissension like perversity. Modernist writers, for whom experimentation became a central part of the business of writing, are particularly vulnerable to these charges. Often the charges were levelled by other modernist writers.

Three of the greatest literary faultfinders of the twentieth century were three of its greatest artists: D.H. Lawrence, Virginia Woolf and Ernest Hemingway. Lawrence often seemed irritated to the point of fury by his fellow-writers, tending to dash off essays or letters that read like livid prose-poems. Woolf had a particular gift for the backhanded compliment, combining praise and damnation in the same sentence – she said that E.M. Forster was 'Very good, I think, though impeded, shrivelled, and immature.' Hemingway saved his best bile until last, though it was a life not free of good bile: *A Moveable Feast* appeared posthumously, and in it he described Gertrude Stein as a pitiable old lesbian, Ford Madox Ford as an ambulatory hogshead, and Wyndham Lewis as having 'the eyes of an unsuccessful rapist'.

James Joyce of course is the figure who sits at the centre of literary modernism, the influence of influences, without whom twentieth-century literature as we know it would have been impossible (even as straight-laced a writer as George Orwell echoed the 'Circe' episode of *Ulysses* in *A Clergyman's Daughter*). It is interesting to see his contemporaries' reactions to him. Woolf did not like him at all ('an insignificant man [. . .] dull, self-centred, & perfectly self assured'); Lawrence despised him ('James Joyce bores me stiff – too terribly would-be and done-on-purpose, utterly without spontaneity or real life') and everyone from Shaw to Forster to Pound expressed reservations that we nowadays do not hear very much about. When we read early-twentieth-century opinions of *Ulysses* or *Finnegans Wake* we realize that Joyce has now to an extent been fossilized in place in the canon. We are no longer able to sneer at Joyce, it seems: we have lost the knack.

In the latter half of the century the palm for Most Feuding Nation must surely go to the USA, with the excellent fights it provided between Mailer and Vidal, Updike and Vidal, Wolfe and Updike, Wolfe and Irving and various other permutations of that enormously competitive generation, all jostling to don the cursed mantle of the Great American Novel. Mailer's trustees would not release for publication here the worst things he had to say about Vidal; so you can imagine how bad they were.

ROBERT FROST 1874–1963

James Dickey (1923–1997) on Frost

If it were thought that anything I wrote was influenced by Robert Frost, I would take that particular work of mine, shred it, and flush it down the toilet, hoping not to clog the pipes. [. . .] a more sententious, holding-forth old bore, who expected every hero-worshiping, adenoidal little twerp of a student-poet to hang on his every word I never saw.

Writers at Work: The Paris Review Interviews, ed. G. Plimpton (1981)

AMY LOWELL 1874–1925

D.H. Lawrence (1885–1930) on Lowell

Why don't you always be yourself. Why go to France or anywhere else for your inspiration. If it doesn't come out of your own heart, real Amy Lowell, it is no good, however many colours it may have. I wish one saw more of your genuine strong, sound self in this book, full of common-sense and kindness and the restrained, almost bitter, Puritan passion. Why do you deny the bitterness in your nature, when you write poetry? Why do you take a pose? It causes you always to shirk your issues, and find a banal resolution at the end. So your romances are spoiled. When you are full of your own strong gusto of things, real old English strong gusto it is, like those tulips, then I like you very much. But you shouldn't compare the sun to the yolk of an egg, except playfully. And you shouldn't spoil your story-poems with a sort of vulgar, artificial 'flourish of ink'. If you had followed the real tragedy of your man, or woman, it had been something.

I suppose you think me damned impertinent. But I hate to see you posturing, when there is thereby a real person betrayed in you.

Please don't be angry with what I say. Perhaps it really is impertinence.

At any rate, thank you very much for your book of poems, which I like because they all they have a lot of you in them – but how much nicer, finer, bigger you are, intrinsically, than your poetry is.[115]

Letter to Amy Lowell, 18 November 1914, in *The Letters of D. H. Lawrence*, ed. J.T. Boulton and G.J. Zytaruk (2000)

W. SOMERSET MAUGHAM 1874–1965

Edmund Wilson (1895–1972) on Maugham

It has happened to me from time to time to run into some person of taste who tells me that I ought to take Somerset Maugham seriously, yet I have never been able to convince myself that he was anything but second-rate. His swelling reputation in America, which culminated the other day in his solemn presentation to the Library of Congress of the manuscript of *Of Human Bondage*, seems to me a conspicuous sign of the general decline of our standards. Thirty or thirty-five years ago the English novelists that were read in America were as least men like Wells and Bennett, who, though not quite of top rank, were at least by vocation real writers. Mr. Maugham, I cannot help feeling, is not, in the sense of 'having the métier,' really a writer at all.

'Somerset Maugham and an Antidote', *New Yorker*, 8 June 1946, in *W. Somerset Maugham: The Critical Heritage*, ed. A. Curtis and J. Whitehead (1987)

Virginia Woolf (1882–1941) on Maugham

Then there was Somerset Maugham, a grim figure; rat eyed; dead man cheeked, unshaven; a criminal I should have said had I met him in a bus.

Letter to Vanessa Bell, 2 November 1938, in *The Letters of Virginia Woolf*, ed. N. Nicolson and J. Trautmann (1975–80)

---

[115] 'Bigger'? Perhaps the least judicious choice of words in this already injudicious critique. Lowell was built on a large scale: the poet Witter Bynner described her as a 'hippo-poetess', a description also taken up by Ezra Pound.

GERTRUDE STEIN 1874–1946

Ernest Hemingway (1899–1961) on Stein

The maidservant opened the door before I rang and told me to come in and to wait. Miss Stein would be down at any moment. It was before noon but the maidservant poured me a glass of *eau-de-vie*, put it in my hand and winked happily. The colorless alcohol felt good on my tongue and it was still in my mouth when I heard someone speaking to Miss Stein as I had never heard one person speak to another; never, anywhere, ever.

Then Miss Stein's voice came pleading and begging, saying 'Don't, pussy. Don't. Don't, please don't. I'll do anything, pussy, but please don't do it. Please don't. Please don't, pussy.' I swallowed the drink and put the glass down on the table and started for the door. The maidservant shook her finger at me and whispered, 'Don't go. She'll be right down.'

'I have to go,' I said, and tried not to hear any more as I left, but it was still going on and the only way I could not hear it was to be gone. It was bad to hear and the answers were worse.

In the courtyard I said to the maidservant, 'Please say I came to the courtyard and met you. That I could not wait because a friend is sick. Say bon voyage for me. I will write.'

'C'est entendu, Monsieur. What a shame you cannot wait.'

'Yes,' I said. 'What a shame.'[116]

A Moveable Feast (1964)

Wyndham Lewis (1882–1957) on Stein

Gertrude Stein's prose-song is a cold, black suet-pudding. We can represent it as a cold suet-roll of fabulously reptilian length. Cut it at any point, it is the same thing; the same heavy, sticky, opaque mass all

---

[116] The 'someone' is unnamed but Hemingway undoubtedly intended to suggest Alice B. Toklas, Stein's companion. Stein, Hemingway and Sherwood Anderson formed a tight literary alliance in the Paris of the 1920s, and both Stein and Anderson were influences on the Hemingway style. Hemingway later felt the need to distance himself from his old mentors by making disparaging remarks about Stein and by publishing *The Torrents of Spring*, a parody of Anderson; Stein took her revenge in *The Autobiography of Alice B. Toklas* (see page 202).

through, and all along. It is weighted, projected, with a sibylline urge. It is mournful and monstrous, composed of dead and inanimate material. It is all fat, without nerve. Or the evident vitality that informs it is vegetable rather than animal. Its life is a low-grade, if tenacious one, of the sausage, by-the-yard, variety.

Time and Western Man (1927)

Edith Sitwell (1887–1964) on Stein

A lecture was given at the American Women's Club here the other day, on the subject of G. Stein, and I am *told*, though I cannot vouch for the truth of the rumour, that G. wore a white Grecian robe, with her various chests surrounded by a gold – cestus, I think is the word – anyhow, you will know what I mean. It must have been an impressive spectacle, and I can't think how she managed about her lingerie, for she usually wears dark grey knitted plus fours underneath everything.[117]

Letter to Charlotte Franken Haldane, 5 December 1933, in
Geoffrey Elborn, *Edith Sitwell: A Biography* (1981)

E.M. FORSTER 1879–1970

D.H. Lawrence (1885–1930) on Forster

We have had E. M. Forster here for three days. There is more in him than ever comes out. But he is not dead yet. I hope to see him pregnant with his own soul. We were on the edge of a fierce quarrel all the time. He went to bed muttering that he was not sure we – my wife and I – weren't just playing round his knees: he seized a candle and went to bed, neither would he say good night. Which is rather nice. He sucks his dummy – you know, those child's comforters – long after his age. But there is something very real in him, if he will not cause it to die. He is *much* more than his dummy-sucking, clever little habits allow him to be. [. . .]

Forster is not poor, but he is bound hand and foot bodily. Why?

---

[117] Sitwell and Stein were good friends, but Edith was feeling hurt for reasons that may (according to biographer Geoffrey Elborn) have been connected with the publication of a scandalous book, *The Young and Evil*, by friends of Stein, Charles Henri Ford and Parker Tyler.

Because he does not believe that any beauty or any divine utterance is any good any more. Why? Because the world is suffering from bonds, and birds of foul desire which gnaw its liver. Forster knows, as every thinking man now knows, that all his thinking and his passion for humanity amounts to no more than trying to soothe with poetry a man raging with pain which can be cured. Cure the pain, don't give the poetry. Will all the poetry in the world satisfy the manhood of Forster, when Forster knows that his implicit manhood is to be satisfied by nothing but immediate physical action. He tries to dodge himself – the sight is pitiful.

But why can't he act? Why can't he take a woman and fight clear to his own basic, primal being? Because he knows that self-realisation is not his ultimate desire. His ultimate desire is for the continued action which has been called the social passion – the love for humanity – the desire to work for humanity. That is every man's ultimate desire and need. Now you see the vicious circle. Shall I go to my Prometheus and tell him beautiful tales of the free, whilst the vulture gnaws his liver?

> Letter to Bertrand Russell, 12 February 1915, in *The Letters of D.H. Lawrence*, ed. J.T. Boulton and G.J. Zytaruk (2000)

Katherine Mansfield (1888–1923) on Forster

Putting my weakest books to the wall last night I came across a copy of *Howard's End* and had a look into it. Not good enough. E.M. Forster never gets any further than warming the teapot. He's a rare fine hand at that. Feel this teapot. Is it not beautifully warm? Yes, but there ain't going to be no tea.

And I can never be perfectly certain whether Helen was got with child by Leonard Bast or by his fatal forgotten umbrella. All things considered, I think it must have been the umbrella.

> Journal for May 1917, in *The Journal of Katherine Mansfield*, ed. J.M. Murry (1927)

Lytton Strachey (1880–1932) on Forster

He's a mediocre man – and knows it, or suspects it, which is worse; he will come to no good, and in the meantime he's treated rudely by waiters and is not really admired even by middle-class dowagers.

> Letter to James Strachey, 3 February 1914, in Michael Holroyd, *Lytton Strachey: A Critical Biography* (1968)

Virginia Woolf (1882–1941) on Forster

Beneath bicycles and dusters, Sawston and Italy, Philip, Harriet, and Miss Abbott, there always lies for him – it is this which makes him so tolerant a satirist – a burning core. It is the soul; it is reality; it is truth; it is poetry; it is love; it decks itself in many shapes, dresses itself in many disguises. But get at it he must; keep from it he cannot. Over brakes and byres, over drawing-room carpets and mahogany sideboards, he flies in pursuit. Naturally the spectacle is sometimes comic, often fatiguing; but there are moments – and his first novel provides several instances – when he lays his hands on the prize.

Yet, if we ask ourselves upon which occasions this happens and how, it will seem that those passages which are least didactic, least conscious of the pursuit of beauty, succeed best in achieving it. When he allows himself a holiday [. . .]

But the second novel, *The Longest Journey*, leaves us baffled and puzzled. The opposition is still the same: truth and untruth; Cambridge and Sawston; sincerity and sophistication. But everything is accentuated. He builds his Sawston of thicker bricks and destroys it with yet stronger blasts. The contrast between poetry and realism is much more precipitous. And now we see much more clearly to what a task his gifts commit him. We see that what might have been a passing mood is in truth a conviction. He believes that a novel must take sides in the human conflict. He sees beauty – none more keenly; but beauty imprisoned in a fortress of brick and mortar whence he must extricate her. Hence he is always constrained to build the cage – society in all its intricacy and triviality – before he can free the prisoner. The omnibus, the villa, the suburban residence, are an essential part of his design. They are required to imprison and impede the flying flame which is so remorselessly caged behind them. At the same time, as we read *The Longest Journey* we are aware of a mocking spirit of fantasy which flouts his seriousness. No one seizes more deftly the shades and shadows of the social comedy; no one more amusingly hits off the comedy of luncheon and tea party and a game of tennis at the rectory. His old maids, his clergy, are the most lifelike we have had since Jane Austen laid down the pen. But he has into the bargain what Jane Austen had not – the impulses of a poet. The neat surface is always being thrown into disarray by an outburst of lyric poetry. [. . .] Here, then, is a difficult family of gifts to persuade to live in harmony together: satire and sympathy; fantasy and fact; poetry and a prim moral sense. No wonder that we are often aware of contrary currents that run counter to each other and prevent the book from bearing down on us and overwhelming us with the authority of a masterpiece. Yet if there is one gift more essential to a novelist than another it is the power of combination – the single vision. The success of the masterpieces seems to lie not so much in their freedom from faults – indeed we tolerate the grossest errors in them all – but in the immense persuasiveness of a mind which has completely mastered its perspective.

'The Novels of E.M. Forster', *Atlantic Monthly*, November 1927, in *E.M. Forster: The Critical Heritage*, ed. P. Gardner (1997)

The book [*A Passage to India*] shows signs of fatigue and disillusionment; but it has chapters of clear and triumphant beauty, and above all it makes us wonder, What will he write next?[118]

'The Novels of E.M. Forster', *Atlantic Monthly*, November 1927, in *E.M. Forster: The Critical Heritage*, ed. P. Gardner (1997)

The middle age of buggers is not to be contemplated without horror.[119]

Diary for 12 March 1922, in *The Diary of Virginia Woolf*, ed. A.O. Bell (1977–82)

P.G. WODEHOUSE 1881–1975

Sean O'Casey (1880–1964) on Wodehouse

It is amusing to read the various wails about the villainy of Wodehouse. The harm done to England's cause and to England's dignity is not the poor man's babble in Berlin, but the acceptance of him by a childish part of the people and the academic government of Oxford, dead from

---

[118] Forster did not publish any novels after *A Passage to India* in 1924, though he lived until 1970. The drying-up was a source of bafflement to his contemporaries.

[119] Woolf liked Forster personally very much, though she later (in 1930) felt the books were, with a characteristic Woolfian oxymoron, 'very good, I think, though impeded, shrivelled and immature.'

the chin up, as a person of any importance whatsoever in English humorous literature, or any literature at all. It is an ironic twist of retribution on those who banished Joyce and honoured Wodehouse.

If England has any dignity left in the way of literature, she will forget for ever the pitiful antics of English Literature's performing flea. If Berlin thinks the poor fish great so much the better for us.[120]

> Letter to the *Daily Telegraph*, 8 July 1941, in Frances Donaldson,
> *P.G. Wodehouse* (1982)

JAMES JOYCE 1882–1941

Arnold Bennett (1867–1931) on Joyce

Here are a few words from one page: limpopo, sar, icis, seints, zezere, hamble, blackburry, dwyergray, meanam, meyne, draves, pharphar, uyar. It ought to be published with a Joyce dictionary.

Someone (I read somewhere) said to Joyce: 'I don't understand it.' Joyce replied: 'But you will.' Joyce is an optimist. Human language cannot be successfully handled with such violence as he has here used to English. And *Anna Livia Plurabelle* will never be anything but the wild caprice of a wonderful creative artist who has lost his way.[121]

> 19 September 1929, *London Evening Standard*, in *James Joyce:*
> *The Critical Heritage*, ed. R.H. Deming (1970)

---

[120] In 1941 P.G. Wodehouse made five broadcast talks to America from Berlin, detailing humorously his experiences as a prisoner-of-war, and attracted considerable enmity in Britain for doing so. His defenders included Malcolm Muggeridge and George Orwell, but they were much in the minority. O'Casey's famous attack is notable for being a literary rather than a political criticism. Wodehouse embraced O'Casey's epithet, titling a collection of his letters *Performing Flea*, and wrote: 'With Sean O'Casey's statement that I am "English literature's performing flea", I scarcely know how to deal. Thinking it over, I believe he meant to be complimentary, for all the performing fleas I have met have impressed me with their sterling artistry and that indefinable something which makes the good trouper.'

[121] Bennett was reading part of Joyce's 'Work in Progress' which was published in instalments and eventually became *Finnegans Wake*. Among Joyce's many detractors in the 1920s Bennett was, elsewhere, an unlikely and generous supporter, and said, 'I never write fiction without thinking of Joyce's discoveries.'

E.M. Forster (1879–1970) on Joyce

[*Ulysses*] is a dogged attempt to cover the universe with mud, an inverted Victorianism, an attempt to make crossness and dirt succeed where sweetness and light failed, a simplification of the human character in the interests of Hell. All simplifications are fascinating, all lead away from the truth (which lies nearer the muddle of *Tristram Shandy*), and *Ulysses* must not detain us on the ground that it contains a morality – otherwise we shall also have to discuss Mrs Humphry Ward. We are concerned with it because, through a mythology, Joyce has been able to create the peculiar stage and characters he required.

The action of those 400,000 words occupies a single day, the scene is Dublin, the theme is a journey – the modern man's journey from morn to midnight, from bed to the squalid tasks of mediocrity, to a funeral, newspaper office, library, pub, lavatory, lying-in hospital, a saunter by the beach, brothel, coffee-stall, and so back to bed. And it coheres because it depends from the journey of a hero through the seas of Greece, like a bat hanging to a cornice.

Ulysses himself is Mr Leopold Bloom – a converted Jew – greedy, lascivious, timid, undignified, desultory, superficial, kindly, and always at his lowest when he pretends to aspire. He tries to explore life through the body. Penelope is Mrs Marion Bloom, an overblown soprano, by no means harsh to her suitors. The third character is young Stephen Dedalus, whom Bloom recognizes as his spiritual son much as Ulysses recognizes Telemachus as his actual son. Stephen tries to explore life through the intellect – we have met him before in *A Portrait of the Artist as a Young Man,* and now he is worked into this epic of grubbiness and disillusion. He and Bloom meet halfway through in Night Town (which corresponds partly to Homer's Palace of Circe, partly to his Descent into Hell), and in its supernatural and filthy alleys they strike up their slight but genuine friendship. This is the crisis of the book, and here – and indeed throughout – smaller mythologies swarm and pullulate, like vermin between the scales of a poisonous snake. Heaven and earth fill with infernal life, personalities melt, sexes interchange, until the whole universe, including poor, pleasure-loving Mr Bloom, is involved in one joyless orgy.

Does it come off? No, not quite. Indignation in literature never quite comes off either in Juvenal or Swift or Joyce; there is something in words that is alien to its simplicity. The Night Town scene does not come off except as a superfetation of fantasies, a monstrous coupling of reminiscences. Such satisfaction as can be attained in this direction is attained, and all through the book we have similar experiments – the aim of which is to degrade all things, and more particularly civilization and art, by turning them inside out and upside down.

Aspects of the Novel (1927)

Edmund Gosse (1849–1928) on Joyce

I should very much regret you paying Mr. J. Joyce the compliment of an article in the *Revue des Deux Mondes*. You could only expose the worthlessness and impudence of his writings, and surely it would be a mistake to give him this prominence. I have difficulty in describing to you, *in writing*, the character of Mr. Joyce's notoriety . . . It is partly political; it is partly a perfectly cynical appeal to sheer indecency. He is of course not entirely without talent, but he is a literary charlatan of the extremest order. His principal book, Ulysses, has not parallel that I know of in French. It is an anarchical production, infamous in taste, in style, in everything.

Mr. Joyce is unable to publish or sell his books in England on account of their obscenity. He therefore issues a 'private' edition in Paris, and charges a huge price for each copy. He is a sort of Marquis de Sade, but does not write so well.

Letter to Louis Gillet, 7 June 1924, in Richard Ellmann, *James Joyce* (1959)

D.H. Lawrence (1885–1930) on Joyce

Somebody sent me *Transition* – American number – that Paris modernissimo periodical, James Joyce and Gertrude Stein, etc. What a stupid *olla podrida*[122] of the Bible and so forth James Joyce is: just stewed-up fragments of quotation in the sauce of a would-be-dirty mind. Such effort! Such exertion! sforzato davvero![123]

Letter to Earl Brewster, 15 August 1928, in *The Letters of D.H. Lawrence*, ed. J.T. Boulton and G.J. Zytaruk (2000)

---

[122] A Spanish stew containing scraps of various ingredients.

[123] 'Really too much'.

But James Joyce bores me stiff – too terribly would-be and done-on-purpose, utterly without spontaneity or real life.

> Letter to Harry Crosby, 6 September 1928, in *The Letters of D.H. Lawrence*,
> ed. J.T. Boulton and G.J. Zytaruk (2000)

Ezra Pound (1885–1972) on Joyce

MS [of *Finnegans Wake*] arrived this AM. All I can do is wish you every possible success.

I will have another go at it, but up to present I make nothing of it whatever. Nothing so far as I make out, nothing short of divine vision or a new cure for the clap can possibly be worth all the circumambient peripherization.

> Letter to James Joyce, 15 November 1926, in *The Letters of Ezra Pound*,
> ed. D.D. Paige (1950)

George Bernard Shaw (1856–1950) on Joyce

I have read several fragments of *Ulysses* in its serial form. It is a revolting record of a disgusting phase of civilisation; but it is a truthful one; and I should like to put a cordon round Dublin; round up every male person in it between the ages of 15 and 30; force them to read it; and ask them whether on reflection they could see anything amusing in all that foul mouthed, foul minded derision and obscenity. To you, possibly, it may appeal as art: you are probably (you see I don't know you) a young barbarian beglamoured by the excitements and enthusiasms that art stirs up in passionate material; but to me it is all hideously real: I have walked those streets and know those shops and have heard and taken part in those conversations. I escaped from them to England at the age of twenty; and forty years later have learnt from the books of Mr. Joyce that Dublin is still what it was, and young men are still drivelling in slackjawed blackguardism just as they were in 1870.

> Letter to Sylvia Beach, 11 June 1921, in Sylvia Beach,
> *Shakespeare and Company* (1959)

Virginia Woolf (1882–1941) on Joyce

Joyce himself is an insignificant man, wearing very thick eyeglasses, a little like Shaw to look at, dull, self-centred, & perfectly self assured.

> Diary for 20 September 1920, in *The Diary of Virginia Woolf*,
> ed. A.O. Bell (1977–84)

I dislike *Ulysses* more & more – that is I think it more & more unimportant; and don't even trouble conscientiously to make out its meanings. Thank God, I need not write about it.

> Diary for 26 August 1922, in *The Diary of Virginia Woolf*,
> ed. A.O. Bell (1977–84)

I finished *Ulysses,* & think it a misfire. Genius it has I think; but of the inferior water. The book is diffuse. It is brackish. It is pretentious. It is underbred, not only in the obvious sense, but in the literary sense. A first rate writer, I mean, respects writing too much to be tricky; startling; doing stunts. I'm reminded all the time of some callow board school boy, say like Henry Lamb, full of wits & powers, but so self-conscious & egotistical that he loses his head, becomes extravagant, mannered, uproarious, ill at ease, makes kindly people feel sorry for him, & stern ones merely annoyed; & one hopes he'll grow out of it; but as Joyce is forty that scarcely seems likely. I have not read it carefully; & only once; & it is very obscure; so no doubt I have scamped the virtue of it more than is fair. I feel that myriads of tiny bullets pepper one & spatter one; but one does not get one deadly wound straight in the face – as from Tolstoy, for instance; but it is entirely absurd to compare him with Tolstoy.

> Diary for 6 September 1922, in *The Diary of Virginia Woolf*,
> ed. A.O. Bell (1977–84)

WYNDHAM LEWIS 1882–1957

Ernest Hemingway (1899–1961) on Lewis

Ezra wanted me to teach him to box and it was while we were sparring late one afternoon in his studio that I first met Wyndham Lewis. Ezra had not been boxing very long and I was embarrassed at having him work in front of anyone he knew, and I tried to make him look as good as possible. But it was not very good because he knew how to fence and I was still working to make his left into his boxing hand and move his left foot forward always and bring his right foot up parallel with it. It was just basic moves. I was never able to teach him to throw a left hook and to teach him to shorten his right was something for the future.

Wyndham Lewis wore a wide black hat, like a character in the quarter, and was dressed like someone out of *La Bohème*. He had a face that reminded me of a frog, not a bullfrog but just any frog, and Paris was too big a puddle for him. At that time we believed that any writer or painter could wear any clothes he owned and there was no official uniform for the artist; but Lewis wore the uniform of a pre-war artist. It was embarrassing to see him and he watched superciliously while I slipped Ezra's left leads or blocked them with an open right glove.

I wanted us to stop but Lewis insisted we go on, and I could see that, knowing nothing about what was going on, he was waiting, hoping to see Ezra hurt. Nothing happened. I never countered but kept Ezra moving after me, sticking out his left hand and throwing a few right hands, and then said we were through and washed down with a pitcher of water and towelled off and put on my sweat-shirt.

We had a drink of something and I listened while Ezra and Lewis talked about people in London and Paris. I watched Lewis carefully without seeming to look at him, as you do when you are boxing, and I do not think I had ever seen a nastier-looking man. Some people show evil as a great racehorse shows breeding. They have the dignity of a hard chancre. Lewis did not show evil; he just looked nasty.

Walking home I tried to think what he reminded me of and there were various things. They were all medical except toe-jam and that was a slang word. I tried to break his face down and describe it but I could only get the eyes. Under the black hat, when I had first seen them, the eyes had been those of an unsuccessful rapist.

'I met the nastiest man I've ever seen today,' I told my wife.

'Tatie, don't tell me about him,' she said. 'Please don't tell me about him. We're just going to have dinner.'

About a week afterwards I met Miss Stein and told her I'd met Wyndham Lewis and asked her if she had ever met him.

'I call him "the Measuring Worm",' she said. 'He comes over from London and he sees a good picture and takes a pencil out of his pocket and you watch him measuring it on the pencil with his thumb. Sighting on it and measuring it and seeing exactly how it is done. Then he goes back to London and does it and it doesn't come right. He's missed what it's all about.'

So I thought of him as the Measuring Worm. It was a kinder and more Christian term than what I had thought about him myself. Later I tried to like him and to be friends with him as I did with nearly all of Ezra's friends when he explained them to me. But this was how he seemed to me on the first day I ever met him in Ezra's studio.[124]

A Moveable Feast (1964)

Edith Sitwell (1887–1964) on Lewis

There are men who seem to have been born without relations but with a collar, and Lewis was one of these. He remained immured in this faithful friend and I think it must have figured on his passport. Certainly one had only to add up the rings on it (made by time) as one adds up the rings on a palm tree or on the horns of an antelope, to arrive at some estimate of his age.[125]

Taken Care Of – An Autobiography (1965)

A.A. MILNE 1882–1956

Dorothy Parker (1893–1967) on Milne

'Tiddledy what?' said Piglet. (He took, as you might say, the very words out of our correspondent's mouth.)

'Pom,' said Pooh. 'I put that in to make it more hummy.'

And it is that word 'hummy', my darlings, that marks the first place in *The House at Pooh Corner* at which Tonstant Weader Fwowed up.

Review in Parker's 'Constant Reader' column in the *New Yorker* of Milne's
The House at Pooh Corner, 20 October 1928, in *The Critical Waltz:*
Essays on the Work of Dorothy Parker, ed. R.S. Pettit (2005)

---

[124] *A Moveable Feast* was published in 1964, four decades after the events it describes, and there are many passages where one suspects that long-delayed score-settling is going on. One reason for Hemingway to wish to settle scores with Lewis was Lewis's satirical treatment of Hemingway in his *Men Without Art* of 1934 – see page 201.

[125] Lewis had satirized the Sitwells in *The Apes of God*. He was inordinately sensitive to remarks about his age, and Edith ridiculed him comprehensively in her autobiography, *Taken Care Of* (1965).

VIRGINIA WOOLF 1882–1941

Arnold Bennett (1867–1931) on Woolf

I have heard a good deal about the wonders of Mrs Woolf's style. She sometimes discovers a truly brilliant simile. She often chooses her adjectives and adverbs with beautiful felicity. But there is more in style than this. The form of her sentences is rather tryingly monotonous, and the distance between her nominatives and her verbs is steadily increasing.

In *Arnold Bennett: The Evening Standard Years*, ed. A. Mylett (1974)

Edith Sitwell (1887–1964) on Woolf

Virginia Woolf, I enjoyed talking to her, but thought nothing of her writing. I considered her 'a beautiful little knitter'.[126]

Letter to Geoffrey Singleton, 11 July 1955, in *Selected Letters*,
ed. J. Lehmann and D. Parker (1970)

HUGH WALPOLE 1884–1941

P.G. Wodehouse (1881–1975) on Walpole

I can't remember if I ever told you about meeting Hugh Walpole when I was at Oxford getting my D.Litt. I was staying with the Vice-Chancellor at Magdalen and he blew in and spent the day. It was just after Hilaire Belloc had said that I was the best living English writer. It was just a gag, of course, but it worried Hugh terribly. He said to me, 'Did you see what Belloc said about you?' I said I had. – 'I wonder why he said that.' 'I wonder,' I said. Long silence. 'I can't imagine why he said that,' said Hugh. I said I couldn't, either. Another long silence.

---

[126]   cf. Letter from Sitwell to Virginia Woolf, 11 July 1930: 'My dear Virginia, I cannot tell you how much I appreciated your writing to me, and how much pleasure your letter gave me. You know that you are one of the only living writers whom I can read with joy and perpetual astonishment and satisfaction, and the fact that you like my poems makes me proud and happy. Not only are you one of the only living writers whom I can read with delight, but you are one of the only people whom I really enjoy talking to. I wish I saw you more often, – but I am afraid to suggest coming to see you, or your coming to see me, because of your work.'

'It seems such an extraordinary thing to say!' – 'Most extraordinary.'
Long silence again. 'Ah, well,' said Hugh, having apparently found the
solution, 'the old man's getting very old.'

Performing Flea[127] (1953)

D.H. LAWRENCE 1885–1930

E.M. Forster (1879–1970) on Lawrence

He does not wholly believe in free speech, for the reason that it never
leads further than Dr. Marie Stopes. [. . .] Unlike Mr Lawrence, I
would tolerate everybody, even Nosey Parker and Peeping Tom. Let
them peep and nose until they are sick [. . .].[128]

Nation and Athenaeum, 11 January 1930, in *D.H. Lawrence:*
The Critical Heritage, ed. R.P. Draper (1997)

John Middleton Murry (1889–1957) on Lawrence

He writes of his characters as though they were animals circling round
each other; and on this sub-human plane no human destinies can be
decided. Alvina and Cicio become for us like grotesque beasts in an
aquarium, shut off from our apprehension by the misted glass of an
esoteric language, a quack terminology. Life, as Mr. Lawrence shows
it to us, is not worth living; it is mysteriously degraded by a corrupt
mysticism. Mr Lawrence would have us back to the slime from which
we rose.[129]

Review of *The Lost Girl* in *The Athenaeum*, 17 December 1920,
in *D.H. Lawrence: The Critical Heritage*, ed. R.P. Draper (1997)

---

[127] The title *Performing Flea* is itself an insult. It was the description of
Wodehouse by Sean O'Casey – 'English literature's performing flea' – which
Wodehouse adopted for the title of this collection of letters. See pages 170–1.

[128] Forster, despite an at times difficult relationship with Lawrence (see
Lawrence on Forster, page 167) nevertheless believed to the end that Lawrence
was 'the greatest imaginative novelist of our generation'. He also testified in
favour of the long-dead Lawrence at the Chatterley trial.

[129] This scathing review was Murry's revenge on Lawrence for, among other
things, calling him 'a dirty little worm' earlier that year – see note, page 191.

Edith Sitwell (1887–1964) on Lawrence

Mr. Lawrence looked like a plaster gnome on a stone toadstool in some suburban garden. At the same time he bore some resemblance to a bad self-portrait by Van Gogh. He had a rather matted, dank appearance. He looked as if he had just returned from spending an uncomfortable night in a very dark cave, hiding, perhaps, in the darkness, from something which, at the same time, he on his side was hunting.

His hair, which had been very red, was now dimmed by illness, as though dust, or ash, had quenched that flame. It hung down, at moments, into his bright and eager eyes, hindering him from seeing anything. He had a sad look of illness; at times he had a kind of eager quickness, as if he were afraid of something being left unfinished. At other moments he would lag behind in the conversation as if he were trying to drag time to a standstill. [. . .]

Poor Mr. Lawrence had a very bad chip on his shoulder. He hated men who were magnificent to look at. He hated men who were 'gentlemen'.

At about the same time when we visited him, or soon after, he wrote *Lady Chatterley's Lover*, to me a very dirty and completely worthless book, of no literary importance, and unworthy of the man who could write 'The Snake' and 'The Mountain Lion' – two beautiful and most moving poems. In *Lady Chatterley's Lover* his loathing for Sir Clifford Chatterley amounted practically to a mania. Sir Clifford was so criminally offensive as to be a Baronet, and he, with most men, fought like a tiger in the First World War, instead of remaining safely at home, fornicating and squealing, shrilly, about the oppressions from which he had suffered.

Sir Clifford was also in trouble for being a famous writer. Fame should be left to persons behaving like the denizens of Monkey Hill at the Zoo.

The book contains certain remarkable faults of taste, as when Mr. Mellors, the adulterous gamekeeper, speaking of his master, who had been desperately injured in the war, said 'He as good as told me I was a disreputable character who walked about with my breeches buttons undone' (nothing could have been more true) 'and I as good as told him he'd nothing to unbutton anyway. It's not for a man in the shape you're in, Sir Clifford, to twit me for having a cod between my legs.'

Nobody seems to have thrashed Mr. Mellors, which was what he deserved, and this unutterably filthy, cruel, and smelly speech has been, apparently, accepted by the more idiotic of the British public as being a fine example of the working-man's frank and splendid mode of expression.

No decent working man, no decent man of any class, would have uttered it. It is an utterance worthy of Monkey Hill.[130]

Taken Care Of – An Autobiography (1965)

Virginia Woolf (1882–1941) on Lawrence

I am also reading D.H.L. with the usual sense of frustration: and that he and I have too much in common – the same pressure to be ourselves: so that I don't escape when I read him: am suspended: what I want is to be made free of another world. This Proust does. To me Lawrence is airless, confined: I don't want this, I go on saying. [. . .] Then too I don't like strumming with two fingers – and the arrogance. After all, English has one million words: why confine yourself to 6? and praise yourself for so doing. But it's the preaching that rasps me. Like a person delivering judgment when only half the facts are there: and clinging to the rails and beating the cushion. Come out and see what's up here – I want to say. I mean it's so barren: so easy: giving advice on a system. The moral is, if you want to help, never systematize – not till you're 70: and have been supple and sympathetic and creative and tried out all your nerves and scopes. He died though at 45. And why does Aldous say he was an 'artist'? Art is being rid of all preaching: things in themselves: the sentence in itself beautiful: multitudinous seas; daffodils that come before the swallow dares: whereas Lawrence would only say what proved something. I haven't read him of course. But in the Letters he can't listen beyond a point; must give advice; get you into the system too. Hence his attraction for those who want to be fitted: which I don't; indeed I think it a blasphemy this fitting of Carswells[131] into a Lawrence system. So much more reverent to leave them alone: nothing else to reverence except the Carswellism of Carswell. Hence his schoolboy tweaking and smacking of anyone offered to him:

---

[130] Edith's vitriol is partly explained by her suspicion that Lawrence had used her family home, Renishaw Hall, as a model for Sir Clifford's home, Wragby, in *Lady Chatterley's Lover*.

[131] Lawrence's friends the writers Catherine and Donald Carswell.

Lytton, Bertie, Squire – all are suburban, unclean. His ruler coming down and measuring them. Why all this criticism of other people? Why not some system that includes the good? What a discovery that would be – a system that did not shut out.

Entry for 2 October 1932, in A Writer's Diary, ed. L. Woolf (1959)

EZRA POUND 1885–1972

Conrad Aiken (1889–1973) on Pound

If one might conceive, in the heliotrope future, any Ph. Demon so inspired as to set about compiling a list of dull books by interesting authors, one could hardly doubt that Ezra Pound's *Pavannes and Divisions* would be his first entry. An incredible performance! [. . .] For in point of style, or manner, or whatever, it is difficult to imagine anything much worse than the prose of Mr. Pound. It is ugliness and awkwardness incarnate. Did he always write so badly?

'A Pointless Pointillist', Dial, October 1918, in Ezra Pound,
ed. E. Homberger (1997)

Hilda Doolittle (H.D.) (1886–1961) on Pound

I found Ezra waiting for me on the pavement outside the house, off Oxford Circus, where I had a room. His appearance was again unexpected, unpredictable. He began, 'I as your nearest male relation . . . ,' and hailed a taxi. He pushed me in. He banged with his stick, pounding (*Pounding*), as I have said. 'You are not going with them [a friend and her husband, who were going to the Continent].' I had seen them the day before at their hotel, off Victoria Station. It was all arranged. [. . .] Awkwardly, at Victoria Station, I explained to a married Frances,[132] with a long tulle travelling veil, that I wasn't coming. I had changed my mind. Awkwardly, the husband handed me back the cheque that I had made out for my ticket. Glowering and savage, Ezra waited till the train pulled out.[133]

End to Torment (1979)

---

[132] Frances Gregg, to whom H.D. was romantically attached.

[133] Hilda Doolittle, poet and novelist, became engaged to Pound around 1907, but the wedding never took place. They remained lifelong friends.

Ben Hecht (1894–1964) on Pound

In fact my complaint against Ezra is that, having attracted me time and again with the promise of delightful cerebral embraces, he is forever bidding me adieu with no more than a languid handshake [. . .] He does not present to me a style – but a series of portrayals. [. . .] To me Pound remains the exquisite showman without a show.

The Little Review, November 1918, in *Possum and Ole Ez in the Public Eye*, ed. Burton Raffel (1985)

Archibald MacLeish (1892–1982) on Pound

Pound has too many rules. The rules of revolution are as revolting as the rules of reaction. [. . .] Pound is crazy. Last letter he asked me to learn Arabic so as to write like myself. Also have something to talk to him about when we meet. I'm getting a bit fed up with the Ezraic assumption that he is a Great Man. Let the rest of us say so for a while. Nothing on earth is worse than a literary gent talking about his own stuff. [. . .] I don't get your angle on Pound. Is obsession with *The Past* equivalent to Bergsonian-Whiteheadian-Alexandrian-Time-Durée obsession?[134]

Letter to Ernest Hemingway, 14 February 1927, in *Letters of Archibald MacLeish, 1907–1982*, ed. R.H. Winnick (1983)

George Orwell (1903–1950) on Pound

Now, of course, Pound did not sell himself solely for money. No writer ever does that. Anyone who wanted money before all else would choose some more paying profession. But I think it probable that Pound did sell himself partly for prestige, flattery and a professorship.[135]

The Tribune, 28 January 1944, in *The Collected Essays, Journalism and Letters of George Orwell* (1968)

---

[134] By 1939 Archibald MacLeish had changed his mind. 'He was, and still is, one of the great clearers and cleansers of the cluttered earth,' he wrote in *Atlantic Monthly*. 'If a new generation does not see him in these terms it is because a new generation does not know the architecture he has overthrown.' MacLeish had by this time won the Pulitzer Prize, with work that Edmund Wilson called a 'vulgarized' version of Eliot and Pound.

[135] Pound, of course, had disgraced himself during the war by making anti-Semitic broadcasts from Rome; after the war he was imprisoned by the Allies and released into a mental hospital. He was, however, never deserted by his friends: Hemingway, E.E. Cummings, Eliot, William Carlos Williams and many others.

Gertrude Stein (1874–1946) on Pound

We[136] met Ezra Pound at Grace Lounsbery's house, he came home to dinner with us and he stayed and he talked about japanese prints among other things. Gertrude Stein liked him but did not find him amusing. She said he was a village explainer, excellent if you were a village, but if you were not, not.[137]

The Autobiography of Alice B. Toklas (1933)

Virginia Woolf (1882–1941) on Pound

Not that I've read more than 10 words by Ezra Pound by [*sic*] my conviction of his humbug is unalterable. [. . .] I was so rash as to say to Eliot the other night that Wyndham Lewis and Ezra Pound were the biggest humbugs unhung, and then had to own that this was mere inspiration on my part, as I have never read a word of either of them.

Letter to Roger Fry, 18 November 1918, in *Possum and Ole Ez
in the Public Eye*, ed. Burton Raffel (1985)

EDITH SITWELL 1887–1964

Kingsley Amis (1922–1995) on Sitwell

I've had another letter from the old bag – seen the latest Specr[138] by the way? She forgives me handsomely,[139] adding: 'When you come to

---

[136]   Stein is writing in the voice of Toklas.

[137]   The phrase 'If not, not' was quoted by R.B. Kitaj in his painting of that name, which, in tapestried form, hangs prominently in the British Library.

[138]   *Spectator* magazine.

[139]   This is a complicated story. On 8 January 1954 Anthony Hartley published a review in the *Spectator* of Edith Sitwell's *Gardeners and Astronomers*, claiming that its excesses were a result of the influence of the neo-Symbolist school. He deprecated lines such as: 'Where the wind like peridots and beryls/Rises in the budding fig branches' ('Out of School') and the final lines of 'A Song of Dust': 'If every grain of my dust should be a Satan,/If every atom of my heart were a Lucifer – /If every drop of my blood were an Abaddon,/ –Yet I should love.' Sitwell replied in a letter in the 22 January issue of the *Spectator* that the lines from 'A Song of Dust' were an adaptation of one of Donne's Sermons: 'Would it not have been wiser for your reviewer, before being quite so impertinent, to have read more widely? I shall, no doubt, be told that little Mr. Tomkins (or whatever his name may be), this week's new great poet, does not incorporate in his work, phrasing from the past, giving them a twist,

and importing new meaning. That is so. But more than one great poet does. And it is useless to deny it.' Amis could not resist satirizing what he thought of as pretentious nonsense, and wrote the letter below, which was printed in the *Spectator* on 29 January 1954:

Sir,
As last week's new great poet, I was very glad to see that letter from a Doctor Sitwell telling Mr. Anthony Hartley that it's okay for great poets to copy bits out of dead writers. The lady is wrong, though, if she thinks I never copy bits out of dead writers like she does. Here is a bit out of one of my poems, which I haven't managed to get published yet:

What noise is that? How now, what hath befallen?
I'll tell the news; here comes the general.
Tomorrow – out of joint – the pity of it –
Ripeness is all.

Do you get the way I've twisted the meanings there? I'd like to see Mr. Anthony Hartley having the cheek to teach, not only Doctor Sitwell and that Donne man, but me and the late William Shakespeare how to write.
Personally I think the sap of a tree is more like Double Diamond than peridots and beryls but if Doctor Sitwell likes to say it's like peridots and beryls then that's quite okay by me. It just shows how we great poets differ.
Yours faithfully,
Little Mr. Tomkins
[Name and address supplied].

However, when Amis shortly afterwards (by coincidence?) received a fan letter from Edith Sitwell congratulating him on *Lucky Jim* with an invitation to luncheon, he had to change tack. He replied, mentioning his embarrassment over the *Spectator* letter and revealing his true identity. Edith Sitwell replied generously (8 March 1954) to his apology, as detailed in Amis's letter to Larkin, above. Amis wrote back to Sitwell on 24 March 1954:

Dear Miss Sitwell,
I was most relieved and thankful to receive your letter of the 8th March. I am extremely grateful to you for your magnanimity.
It is very kind of you to want to arrange a luncheon party for me. I too am greatly looking forward to it. Unfortunately I shall have a great deal on hand during the first period you suggest, immediately after Easter, so I should like, if I may, to defer our meeting until June. The latter part of that month would suit me best, as our examinations here start near the beginning of it and entail the usual laborious clearing-up afterwards. Perhaps I may write to you again nearer the time, when things here are more definite.
With renewed thanks and best wishes,
Yours most sincerely,
Kingsley Amis
PS. I do hope the indisposition you mention is now completely at an end.

the luncheon party I shall give for you, you will find me completely oblivious that this has ever happened . . . *Not one* of the persons who has had the impertinence to attack me has even a gleam of talent for poetry. They simply cant write. And it would never enter the head of a poet of any stature to discuss their verses. Not only I, but all my fellow-poets of any importance (as I know from their letters to me on the subject), are entirely amazed that they should have dared to behave as they have. They cannot harm me, all that has happened is that they have made an abjectly ridiculous spectacle of themselves, and are being laughed at, not only all over England, but also in New York . . . Yours very sincerely . . ' Rather pathetic in a way. You know, all this is going to be confoundedly difficult. Bloody funny, though, isn't it?

Letter to Philip Larkin, 14 March 1954, in *The Letters of Kingsley Amis*,
ed. Z. Leader (2000)

Had a corking fine lunch with my pal the Dame. Actually it was rather on the dull side, thank God; rather like lunching with a kindly maiden aunt who wants to show you she's interested in all that writing you're doing. John Hayward was there in his wheelchair being paralysed and it was curious, almost macabre, to hear Edith say at the end to him 'Well, give my love to Tom.'[140] Others present included a man called Mister John Pope-Hennessy and an other man called Mister James Pope-Hennessy: as fine and select a brace of turds as you could hope to find anywhere ats shats at short, or even fairly long, notice. Alan Pryce-Jones turned up for a little while and was very oily to the Dame, with whom, it was later revealed, he had recently had a ray of some sort. Then he went away again. I was glad, when he didt tidt did that. An American film director, an Australian pianist and two female cousins of the Dame's completed the rout. I quite enjoyed it, and then it was over, and I was glad.

Have just remembered: there was a horrid moment at the Sitwell lunch when, looking at me, she said: 'Of course, there is just one thing which is absolutely unforgivable. (Pause.) That is to attack someone anonymously.' I felt like an Indian brave whose horse runs away with him at the moment he realises that the white men he is charging have

---

[140]   T.S. Eliot. John Hayward was his flat-mate.

repeating rifles. After another pause, she added: 'That monstrous profile of me in the New Statesman, now.' I fair ped myself in releif. There was a wonderful moment (don't know whether I can describe it adequately) in the pub before the lunch, before I went to the lunch I mean, when Tony Hartley said 'Don't forget to talk to her about texture, now.' John Scott added, 'Oh yes, about the woobwoobwoob' (something inaudible: there was a good deal of noise going on). 'What?' I said loudly. 'Woof' he bawled. A dog in the next bar went into an absolute apoplexy of barking. Funny at the time, you know.

Letter to Philip Larkin, 8 July 1954, in *The Letters of Kingsley Amis*, ed. Z. Leader (2000)

Dylan Thomas (1914–1953) on Sitwell

So you've been reviewing Edith Sitwell's latest piece of virgin dung have you?[141] Isn't she a poisonous thing of a woman, lying, concealing, flipping, plagiarising, misquoting, and being as clever a crooked literary publicist as ever. I do hope you pointed out in your review the real points against the book (you did, I know, but I like being dogmatic)? The majority of the book was cribbed from Herbert Read and Leavis, actually and criminally cribbed. She has misquoted Hopkins at least twenty times, reprinted many poems without the permission of publisher or poet. Yes, that was my poem all right, reproduced without my name, misquoted at the end, and absurdly criticised. I duly sent my protest to Gerald Duckworth and he replied to the effect that so many protests of a similar sort had been received, that he could as yet do nothing about it. It is being hoped that he will have to withdraw the book. I *would* like to see your review of it.[142]

Letter to Glyn Jones, December 1934, in *Dylan Thomas: The Collected Letters*, ed. P. Ferris (1985)

---

[141] *Aspects of Modern Poetry* (1934). Sitwell's book criticized the journal *New Verse*, which had included Thomas's poem 'Our eunuch dreams'.

[142] Later, in January 1936, Sitwell wrote Thomas a surprising letter:

T.S. ELIOT 1888–1965

W.H. Auden (1907–1973) on T.S. Eliot

In writing his verse plays, Mr Eliot took, I believe, the only possible line. Except at a few unusual moments, he kept the style Drab.

Secondary Worlds (1968)

Robert Frost (1874–1963) on T.S. Eliot

We are both poets and we both like to play. That's the similarity. The difference is this: I like to play euchre. He likes to play Eucharist.

In Lawrance Thompson, 'Notes from Conversations with Robert Frost' (unpublished), in *The Cambridge Companion to Robert Frost*, ed. R. Faggen (2001)

Ernest Hemingway (1899–1961) on T.S. Eliot

Ernest was nearly as hard on T. S. Eliot, whom he persisted in calling 'The Major'. He alluded superciliously to the 'heavy uncut pages of Eliot's quarterly', the *Criterion*. When Joseph Conrad died and Ford got together a special Conrad supplement for the *transatlantic*, Ernest

---

Though we have never met, I am unable to resist writing to you to tell you, however inadequately, with what deep admiration and delight I have read your very beautiful poem which begins with the line

'A Grief ago'

and the beautiful and strange poem in this quarter's *Life and Letters* ['Altarwise by owl-light']. It is no exaggeration to say that I do not remember when I have been so moved, profoundly so excited, by the work of any poet of the younger generation, or when I have felt such a deep certainty that here is a poet with all the capabilities and potentialities of greatness. I am completely overcome with this certainty and this admiration.

Thomas replied appreciatively on 17 January 1936, and the two later met. A friendship began, though one interrupted by Thomas's failure to turn up at appointments and other lapses of etiquette. Edith Sitwell was also responsible for many assistances to Thomas, which included chairing a Society of Authors committee that gave £150 to Thomas in 1947 with a recommendation that he go to Italy with it (she thought America would be injurious). Her claim to have 'discovered' Thomas is in some senses a justified one.

went out of his way to remark in print that if he could bring Conrad back to life 'by grinding Mr. Eliot into a fine dry powder and sprinkling that powder over Conrad's grave in Canterbury', he would 'leave for London early tomorrow morning with a sausage-grinder'.

In Carlos Baker: *Ernest Hemingway, A Life Story* (1969)

Christopher Isherwood (1904–1986) on T.S. Eliot

While Auden was up at Oxford he read T. S. Eliot. The discovery of The Waste Land marked a turning-point in his work – for the better, certainly; though the earliest symptoms of Eliot-influence were most alarming. Like a patient who has received an over-powerful inoculation, Auden developed a severe attack of allusions, jargonitis and private jokes. He began to write lines like: 'Inexorable Rembrandt rays that stab . . .' or 'Love mutual has reached its first eutectic . . .' Nearly all the poems of that early Eliot period are now scrapped.

New Verse (1937)

George Orwell (1903–50) on T.S. Eliot

Here is T.S. Eliot on the servant-problem as seen from the Anglo-Catholic standpoint: 'I do not like the situation (i.e. of having only one servant)... I should prefer to employ a large staff of servants, each doing lighter work but profiting by the benefits of the cultured and devout atmosphere of the home in which they lived.' That bit about the cultured and devout atmosphere reminds me, as Samuel Butler said of a cracked church bell he heard somewhere, of the smell of a bug.[143]

Letter to Brenda Salkeld, 7 March 1935, in *The Collected Essays, Journalism and Letters of George Orwell* (1968)

Virginia Woolf (1882–1941) on T.S. Eliot

Tomorrow we are [. . .] going to the Eliots to discuss Tom's new poems; but not only that – to drink cocktails and play jazz into the bargain, Tom thinking one can't do anything simple. He thinks this

---

[143] Orwell is remembering a passage from Samuel Butler's *Notebooks*, in which Butler says: 'Jones was at Gogin's one summer evening and the bells struck up their dingy old burden as usual. The tonic bell on which the tune concluded was the most stuffy and out of tune. Gogin said it was like the smell of a bug.'

makes the occasion modern, chic. He will, no doubt, be sick in the back room; we shall all feel ashamed of our species. He has written some new poems, religious, I'm afraid, and is in doubt about his soul as a writer.

> Letter to Roger Fry, 16 October 1928, in *The Letters of Virginia Woolf*,
> ed. N. Nicolson and J. Trautmann (1975–80)

The rock disappointed me. I couldn't go and see it, having caught the influenza in Ireland; and in reading, without seeing, perhaps one got the horror of that cheap farce and Cockney dialogue and dogmatism too full in the face. Roger Fry, though, went and came out in a rage. But I thought even the choruses tainted; and rather like an old ship swaying in the same track as the Waste Land – a repetition, I mean. But I can't be sure that I wasn't unfairly influenced by my anti-religious bias. He seems to me to be petrifying into a priest – poor old Tom.

> Letter to Stephen Spender, 10 July 1934, in *The Letters of Virginia Woolf*,
> ed. N. Nicolson and J. Trautmann (1975–1980)

KATHERINE MANSFIELD 1888–1923

T.S. Eliot (1888–1965) on Mansfield

I am not running the paper [*The Criterion*] for Binyon any more than for K. Mansfield. Of course I don't mind printing a story by K. Mansfield, though I prefer Binyon and have no use for either. I will however suggest to Lady R[othermere]. that she should secure a story from K. Mansfield. I myself should much prefer to have something from Murry; he is at least in every way preferable to his wife. The latter is not by any means the most intelligent woman Lady R. has ever met. She is simply one of the most persistent and thickskinned toadies and one of the vulgarest women Lady R. has ever met and is also a sentimental crank.

> Letter to Ezra Pound, 7 November 1922, in *The Letters of TS Eliot*, ed. V. Eliot
> (1989)

Philip Larkin (1922–1985) on Mansfield

Katherine Mansfield is a cunt, but I share a hell of a lot of common characteristics with her. [. . .] she luxuriated in emotion [. . .]. Admittedly the head is an evil thing and she's a woman & I'm a tied-up bugger, but anyone who can spew out their dearest and closest thoughts, hopes, and loves to J. M. Murry must be a bit of an anus.

> Letter to James Sutton, 23 June 1941, in *Selected Letters of Philip Larkin, 1940–85*, ed. A. Thwaite (1993)

D.H. Lawrence (1885–1930) on Mansfield

I loathe you, you revolt me stewing in your consumption . . . The Italians were quite right to have nothing to do with you.[144]

> Comments reported by Mansfield in letter to John Middleton Murry, 6 February 1920, in *Katherine Mansfield's Letters to John Middleton Murry, 1913–1922*, ed. J.M. Murry (1951)

Virginia Woolf (1882-1941) on Mansfield

The dinner last night went off: the delicate things were discussed. We could both wish that ones first impression of K.M. was not that she stinks like a – well civet cat that had taken to street walking.[145]

> Diary for 11 October 1917, in *The Diary of Virginia Woolf*, ed. A.O. Bell (1977–84)

---

[144] Mansfield was caught in the crossfire in a dispute between Lawrence and John Middleton Murry. Murry had angered Lawrence by returning some pieces Lawrence had written for Murry's magazine, *The Athenaeum*. Lawrence responded (30 January 1920):

> I have no doubt you 'didn't like them' – just as you didn't like the things you had from Derbyshire. But as a matter of fact, what it amounts to is that you are a dirty little worm, and you take the ways of a dirty little worm. But now let me tell you at last that I know it – not that it's anything new: and let it be plainly understood between you and me, that I consider you a dirty little worm: and so, deposit your dirty bit of venom where you like; at any rate we know what to expect.

Virginia Woolf took Lawrence's side, in 1931 calling Murry a 'bald necked blood dripping vulture [who] kept me off Lawrence with his obscene objurgations.'

Claire Tomalin suggests in her biography of Mansfield that Lawrence may even have passed on his own tuberculosis to her when they lived in adjoining cottages in 1916: Mansfield died of tuberculosis in 1923, Lawrence finally succumbing to the same disease in 1930.

[145] Katherine enjoyed French perfume, which Virginia may have felt a little vulgar. In other diary entries she compares Mansfield to a cat, stressing the olfactory aspect: her cheap scent, she says, 'reeked in one's nostrils'. Nevertheless, there was an uneasy, on-off friendship between them. 'Probably,' Virginia wrote in her diary after Katherine's death, 'we had something in common which I shall never find in anyone else.'

WILFRED OWEN 1893–1918

Henry Newbolt (1862–1938) on Wilfred Owen

Owen and the rest of the broken men rail at the Old Men who sent the young to die: they have suffered cruelly, but in the nerves and not the heart – they haven't the experience or the imagination to know the extreme human agony – 'Who giveth me to die for thee, Absalom my son, my son.' Paternity apart, what Englishman of fifty wouldn't far rather stop the shot himself than see the boys do it for him? I don't think these shell-shocked war poems will move our grandchildren greatly – there's nothing fundamental or final about them – at least they only put one figure into a very big equation, and that's not one of the unknown but one of the very best known quantities.

Letter, 2 August 1924, *The Later Life and Letters of Sir Henry Newbolt* (1942)

W.B. Yeats (1865–1939) on Wilfred Owen

My Anthology continues to sell, and the critics get more and more angry. When I excluded Wilfred Owen, whom I consider unworthy of the poets' corner of a country newspaper, I did not know I was excluding a revered sandwich-board man of the revolution, and that somebody has put his worst and most famous poem in a glass-case in the British Museum – however, if I had known it, I would have excluded him just the same. He is all blood, dirt and sucked sugar stick (look at the selection in Faber's Anthology – he calls poets 'bards,' a girl a 'maid,' and talks about 'Titanic wars'). There is every excuse for him, but none for those who like him.[146]

Letter to Dorothy Wellesley, 21 December 1936, in *W.B. Yeats, The Major Works*, ed. E. Larrissy (2001)

DOROTHY PARKER 1893–1967

Alexander Woollcott (1887–1943) on Dorothy Parker

The outward social manner of Dorothy Parker is one calculated to confuse the unwary and unnerve even those most addicted to the

---

[146] Yeats wrote this in the year of publication of his edition of *The Oxford Book of Modern Verse, 1892–1935*, from which he had excluded not only Owen but all the other First World War poets. Many thought this decision odd. Yeats justified it with tacit reference to Owen's remark that 'Above all I am not concerned

incomparable boon of her company. You see, she is so odd a blend of Little Nell and Lady Macbeth. It is not so much the familiar phenomenon of a hand of steel in a velvet glove as a lacy sleeve with a bottle of vitriol concealed in its folds.

While Rome Burns (1934)

E.E. CUMMINGS 1894–1962

James Dickey (1923–1997) on Cummings

I have often felt that there must be something hiddenly wrong with his cult of spontaneity and individuality, that these attributes have to be insisted upon to the extent to which Cummings insists on them. I feel, also, that 'love' and the other well-known emotions that Cummings tirelessly espouses are being imposed on me categorically, and that I stand in some danger of being shot if I do not, just at that moment, wish to love someone or pick a rose or lean against a tree watching the snowflakes come down. The famous mannerisms too: aren't they, by now, beginning to pall pretty heavily? Were some of them, even when they were new, worth very much?

Babel to Byzantium (1968)

ALDOUS HUXLEY 1894–1963

Ernest Hemingway (1899–1961) on Huxley

To keep my mind off writing sometimes after I had worked I would read writers who were writing then, such as Aldous Huxley, D.H. Lawrence or any who had books published that I could get from Sylvia Beach's library or find along the quais.

'Huxley is a dead man,' Miss Stein said. 'Why do you want to read a dead man? Can't you see he is dead?'

I could not see, then, that he was a dead man and I said that his books amused me and kept me from thinking.

---

with Poetry. My subject is War, and the pity of War. The Poetry is in the pity.' He wrote in his Introduction: 'I have rejected these poems for the same reason that made Arnold withdraw his *Empedocles on Etna* from circulation; passive suffering is not a theme for poetry. In all the great tragedies, tragedy is a joy to the man who dies; in Greece the tragic chorus danced.'

'You should only read what is truly good or what is frankly bad.'

'I've been reading truly good books all winter and all last winter and I'll read them next winter, and I don't like frankly bad books.'

'Why do you read this trash? It is inflated trash, Hemingway. By a dead man.'

A Moveable Feast (1964)

D.H. Lawrence (1885–1930) on Huxley

I have read *Point Counter Point* with my heart sinking through my bootsoles and a rising admiration. I do think you've shown the truth, perhaps the last truth, about you and your generation, with really fine courage. It seems to me it would take ten times the courage to write *P. Counter P.* than it took to write *Lady C.*, and if the public knew *what* it was reading, it would throw a hundred stones at you, to one at me. I do think that art has to reveal the palpitating moment or the state of man as it is. And I think you do that, terribly. But what a moment! And what a state! If you can only palpitate to murder, suicide, and rape, in their various degrees [. . .] – *caro*, however are we going to live through the days? Preparing still another murder, suicide, and rape? But it becomes of a phantasmal boredom and produces ultimately inertia, inertia, inertia and final atrophy of the feelings. Till, I suppose, comes a final super-war, and murder, suicide, rape sweeps away the vast bulk of mankind. It is as you say – intellectual appreciation does not amount to so much, it's what you thrill to. And if murder, suicide, rape is what you thrill to, and nothing else [. . .]. You live by what you thrill to, and there's the end of it. Still for all that it's a *perverse* courage which makes the man accept the slow suicide of inertia and sterility: [. . .] I can't stand murder, suicide, rape – especially rape: and especially being raped. Why do men only thrill to a woman who'll rape them and S– on their face? All I want to do to your Lucy is smack her across the mouth, your Rampion is the most boring character in the book – a gas-bag. Your attempt at intellectual sympathy! – It's all rather disgusting, and I feel like a badger that has its hole on Wimbledon Common and trying not to be caught.[147]

Letter to Aldous Huxley, late October or early November 1928, in *Aldous Huxley: the Critical Heritage*, ed. D. Watt (1975)

---

[147] Lawrence is skirting around his displeasure at the fact that Mark Rampion (Huxley's character in *Point Counter Point*) was a portrait of Lawrence himself. In the poem 'I am in a Novel' he wrote:

George Orwell (1903–1950) on Huxley

You were right about Huxley's book [*Ape and Essence*] – it is awful.
And do you notice that the more holy he gets, the more his books
stink with sex. He cannot get off the subject of flagellating women.
Possibly, if he had the courage to come out & say so, that is the
solution to the problem of war. If we took it out in a little private
sadism, which after all doesn't do much harm, perhaps we wouldn't
want to drop bombs etc.[148]

> Letter to Sir Richard Rees, 3 March 1949, in *Aldous Huxley, the Critical
> Heritage*, ed. D. Watt (1975)

Bertrand Russell (1872–1970) on Huxley

[Of the *Encyclopaedia Britannica*] It was the only book that ever influenced
Huxley. You always could tell by his conversation which volume he'd been
reading. One day it would be Alps, Andes and Apennines, and the next it
would be the Himalayas and the Hippocratic Oath.[149]

> Letter to Ronald W. Clark, July 1965, in *A Bibliography of Bertrand Russell*,
> ed. K. Blackwell and H. Ruja (1994)

I read a novel by a friend of mine
in which one of the characters was me,
the novel it sure was mighty fine
but the funniest thing that could be

was me, or what was supposed for me,
for I had to recognize
a few of the touches, like a low-born jake,
but the rest was a real surprise.

Well damn my eyes! I said to myself
Well damn my little eyes!
If this is what Archibald thinks I am
he sure thinks a lot of lies.

[148] A startlingly diametric point of view to that of Lawrence in the passage
above, who writes to Huxley to say that personal sadistic indulgence will lead to
our ultimate destruction in a 'super-war'.

[149] Huxley unflatteringly portrayed Russell as Scogan in *Crome Yellow*.

EDMUND WILSON 1895–1972

Archibald MacLeish (1892–1982) on Wilson

I'm furious at the critical attitude toward Carl Sandburg! It's largely
the work of Bunny Wilson, who was far from being the critic he's
supposed to be. He was a very small-minded, petty, jealous, mean man
and a stinker of the first order, and if I'm saying those words for all
eternity, I mean them. He hated Carl. He wrote a review of Carl's
enormous *Lincoln* which was contemptuous, demeaning, belittling, and,
as for Carl's being a poet, he disposed of that in a couple of well-
chosen sentences.[150]

> *Archibald MacLeish: Reflections*, ed. B.A. Drabeck, H.E. Ellis,
> and R. Wilbur (1986)

Gore Vidal (1925–) on Wilson

Of a certain Victorian Englishman it was said that no lady's shoe,
unescorted, was safe in his company. It could be said of Edmund
Wilson that, like Cecil B. DeMille, 'he never met a woman's foot he
didn't like.' Is there any reader of Wilson's novel *I Thought of Daisy* who
does not recall Wilson's description of a girl's feet as being like 'moist
cream cheeses'? But Wilson's podophilia did not stop there: he could
have made a fortune in women's footwear. From *The Thirties:* '. . .shoes,
blue with silver straps, that arched her insteps very high . . .,' 'Katy's
little green socks and untied gray moccasins . . .,' 'young Scotch girl
M.P. [with] large feet bulging out of black shoes . . .,' '. . . silver open-
work shoes that disclosed her reddened toenails, such a combination as
only she could wear. . .' In *The Thirties*, I counted twenty-four
references to shoes and feet; each, let me quickly say, belonging to a
woman. When it came to shoes, Wilson was sternly heterosexual – not
for him the stud's boot or the little lad's Ked. But, to be absolutely
precise, there is one very odd reference. Wilson is struck by the
number of Chicago men who wear spats. Reverie: 'Excuse me, sir. But
a hook is loose on your left spat. As chance would have it, I have with

---

[150] Edmund Wilson had remarked: '[T]here are moments when one is tempted
to feel that the cruelest thing that has happened to Lincoln since he was shot by
Booth has been to fall into the hands of Carl Sandburg.'

me a spats-hook. If you'll allow me, sir . . .' Whenever Wilson strikes the
Florsheim note, he is in rut.

'Edmund Wilson: This Critic and This Gin and These Shoes', in the *New York
Review of Books*, 25 September 1980, in *The Essential Gore Vidal*, ed. F. Kaplan
(1999)

F. SCOTT FITZGERALD 1896–1940

Zelda Fitzgerald (1900–1948) on Fitzgerald
It is a wonderful book to have around in case of emergency. No-one
should ever set out in pursuit of unholy excitement without a special
vest pocket edition dangling from a string around his neck.

For this book tells exactly, and with compelling lucidity, just what to
do when cast off by a grandfather or when sitting around a station
platform at 4 a.m., or when spilling champagne in a fashionable
restaurant, or when told that one is too old for the movies. Any of these
things might come into any one's life at any minute.

Just turn the pages of the book slowly at any of the above-mentioned
trying times until your own case strikes your eye and proceed according
to directions. Then for the ladies of the family there are such helpful lines
as: 'I like gray because then you have to wear a lot of paint.' Also what to
do with your husband's old shoes – Gloria takes Anthony's shoes to bed
with her and finds it a very satisfactory way of disposing of them. The
dietary suggestion, 'tomato sandwiches and lemonade for breakfast', will
be found an excellent cure for obesity.

Now, let us turn to the interior decorating part of the book. Therein
can be observed complete directions for remodeling your bathroom along
modern and more interesting lines, with plans for a bookrack by the tub,
and a detailed description of what pictures have been found suitable for
bathroom walls after years of careful research by Mr. Fitzgerald.

The book itself, with its plain green back, is admirably constructed
for being read in a tub – wetting will not spoil the pages; in fact if one
finds it growing dry simply dip the book briskly in warm water. The
bright yellow jacket is particularly adapted to being carried on Fifth
Avenue while wearing a blue or henna colored suit, and the size is
adaptable to being read in hotel lobbies while waiting to keep dates
for luncheon.

It seems to me that on one page I recognized a portion of an old diary of mine which mysteriously disappeared shortly after my marriage, and also scraps of letters which, though considerably edited, sound to me vaguely familiar. In fact, Mr. Fitzgerald – I believe that is how he spells his name – seems to believe that plagiarism begins at home.

[. . .] But don't let that deter you from buying the book. In every other way the book is absolutely perfect.

The other things I didn't like in the book – I mean the unimportant things – were the literary references and the attempt to convey a profound air of erudition. It reminds me in its more soggy moments of the essays I used to get up in school at the last minute by looking up strange names in the Encyclopaedia Britannica.[151]

Review of *The Beautiful and Damned* in *The New York Tribune*, 2 April 1922, in *F. Scott Fitzgerald: The Critical Reception*, ed. J.R. Bryer (1978)

WILLIAM FAULKNER 1897–1962

Conrad Aiken (1889-1973) on Faulkner

The famous remark made to Macaulay – 'Young man, the more I consider the less can I conceive where you picked up that style' – might with advantage have been saved for Mr. William Faulkner. For if one thing is more outstanding than another about Mr. Faulkner – some readers find it so outstanding, indeed, that they never get beyond it – it is the uncompromising and almost hypnotic zeal with which he insists

---

[151] This chaotic anti-review – which both implicitly and explicitly accuses her husband of being boring, pretentious, unoriginal, tasteless and foolish – sprang from a real and justified resentment that Scott had copied parts from Zelda's own writings and was passing them off as his own, a trick he also pulled off in various other works. Zelda returned the compliment in her novel *Save Me the Waltz*, which detailed her life with Scott and made use of events that Scott was simultaneously drawing on for *Tender is the Night*. In the first drafts, the Zelda-figure, the heroine Alabama Beggs, is married to Amory Blaine, who bears the same name as the Scott-figure in *This Side of Paradise*. Scott insisted that she change this name (it became instead David Knight: Knight/Night?) and that she cut and rewrite large chunks of the novel. He also objected to the original title, now lost: Zelda, casting around for a substitute, found a song called 'Save Me the Waltz' in a Victor Records catalogue. He commented: 'my books made her a legend and her single intention in this somewhat thin portrait is to make me a non-entity.'

upon having a style, and, especially of late, the very peculiar style which he insists upon having. Perhaps to that one should add that he insists *when he remembers* – he can write straightforwardly enough when he wants to; he does so often in the best of his short stories (and they are brilliant), often enough, too, in the novels. But that *style* is what he really wants to get back to; and get back to it he invariably does.

And what a style it is, to be sure! The exuberant and tropical luxuriance of sound which Jim Europe's jazz band used to exhale, like a jungle of rank creepers and ferocious blooms taking shape before one's eyes, – magnificently and endlessly intervolved, glisteningly and ophidianly in motion, coil sliding over coil, and leaf and flower forever magically interchanging, – was scarcely more bewildering, in its sheer inexhaustible fecundity, than Mr. Faulkner's style. Small wonder if even the most passionate of Mr. Faulkner's admirers – among whom the present writer honors himself by enlisting – must find, with each new novel, that the first fifty pages are always the hardest, that each time one must learn all over again *how* to read this strangely fluid and slippery and heavily mannered prose, and that one is even, like a kind of Laocoön, sometimes tempted to give it up.

Atlantic Monthly, November 1939, in *William Faulkner: The Critical Heritage*,
ed. J.E.Bassett (1997)

James Gould Cozzens (1903–1978) on Faulkner
Faulkner falsified life for dramatic effect. It's sentimentality disguised by the corncob.

Time, 2 September 1957

Clifton Fadiman[152] (1904–1999) on Faulkner
Apparently the entire population of Jefferson, Mississippi consists of rhetoricians who would blench at the sight of a simple declarative sentence . . . Seriously, I do not know what to say of this book except that it seems to point to the final blowup of what was once a remarkable, if minor, talent.

Review of *Absalom! Absalom!* in *The New Yorker*, 1936, in *Faulkner: A Collection of Critical Essays*, ed. R.P.Warren (1966)

---

[152] American author, pundit, TV personality and publisher.

Ernest Hemingway (1899–1961) on Faulkner

Have you ever heard of anyone who drank while he worked? You're thinking of Faulkner. He does sometimes – and I can tell right in the middle of a page when he's had his first one.

Conversations with Ernest Hemingway, ed. M.J. Bruccoli (1986)

ERNEST HEMINGWAY 1899–1961

Max Eastman (1883–1969) on Hemingway

It is of course a commonplace that Hemingway lacks the serene confidence that he *is* a full-sized man. Most of us too delicately organized babies who grow up to be artists suffer at times from that small inward doubt. But some circumstance seems to have laid upon Hemingway a continual sense of the obligation to put forth evidences of red-blooded masculinity. It must be made obvious not only in the swing of the big shoulders and the clothes he puts on, but in the stride of his prose style and the emotions he permits to come to the surface there. This trait of his character has been strong enough to form the nucleus of a new flavor in English literature, and it has moreover begotten a veritable school of fiction-writers – a literary style, you might say, of wearing false hair on his chest [. . .].[153]

'Bull in the Afternoon', in *The New Republic*, 7 June 1933, in *Ernest Hemingway: The Critical Heritage*, ed. J. Meyers (1997)

---

[153] These remarks rankled with Hemingway, and he had still not forgotten them four years later when he encountered Max Eastman, writer and critic, in the offices of Scribner's. Hemingway took off his shirt to reveal his chest hair, demanding that Eastman tell him whether it was false or not. Eastman was unable to reply; Hemingway then began unbuttoning Eastman's own shirt to see how much hair there was – Eastman's chest was hairless. Eastman tried to laugh the matter off but Hemingway continued to goad him, asking what Eastman had meant by calling him impotent. The exchange led to a fight in which, by some accounts, Hemingway wrestled Eastman to the ground. Hemingway told a reporter that Eastman had 'jumped at me like a woman – clawing, you know, with his open hands'.

Wyndham Lewis (1882–1957) on Hemingway

The sort of First-person-singular that Hemingway invariably invokes is a dull-witted, bovine, monosyllabic simpleton. This lethargic and stuttering dummy he conducts or pushes from behind, through all the scenes that interest him. This burlesque First-person-singular behaves in them like a moronesque version of his brilliant author. He *Steins* up and down the world, with the big lustreless ruminatory orbs of a Picasso doll-woman (of the semi-classic type Picasso patented, with enormous hands and feet). It is, in short, the very dummy that is required for the literary mannerisms of Miss Stein! It is the incarnation of the Stein-stutter – the male incarnation, it is understood.[154]

But this constipated, baffled, 'frustrated' – yes, deeply and Freudianly frustrated – this wooden-headed, leadenwitted, heavy-footed, loutish and oafish marionette – peering dully out into the surrounding universe like a great big bloated five-year-old – pointing at this and pointing at that – uttering simply 'CAT!' – HAT!' – 'FOOD!' – 'SWEETIE' – is, as a companion, infectious. His author has perhaps not been quite immune. Seen for ever through his nursery spectacles, the values of life accommodate themselves, even in the mind of his author, to the limitations and peculiar requirements of this highly idiosyncratic puppet.

So the political aspects of Hemingway's work (if, as I started by saying, one can employ such a word as *political* in connection with a thing that is so divorced from reality as a super-innocent, queerly-sensitive, village-idiot of a few words and fewer ideas) have to be sought, if anywhere, in the personality of this First-person-singular, imposed upon him largely by the Stein-manner.

'The Dumb Ox', *Men Without Art* (1934)

---

[154] Among all the accusations in this passage, this is probably the most cutting, i.e. that of Hemingway's literary debt to Stein (see Stein on Hemingway, page 202, and Hemingway on Stein, page 166). Lewis also says at one point in this essay: 'One might even go so far as to say that this brilliant Jewish lady had made a *clown* of him by teaching Ernest Hemingway her baby-talk. So it is a pity. And it is very difficult to know where Hemingway proper begins and Stein leaves off as an artist.' Hemingway was reportedly so enraged on reading it (in Sylvia Beach's bookshop) that he smashed a vase to the floor. See also Hemingway on Lewis, page 175.

Vladimir Nabokov (1899–1977) on Hemingway

As to Hemingway, I read him for the first time in the early 'forties, something about bells, balls and bulls, and loathed it.[155]

The Contemporary Writer: Interviews with Sixteen Novelists and Poets,
ed. L.S. Dembo and C.N. Pondrom (1972)

Gertrude Stein (1874–1946) on Hemingway

Gertrude Stein and Sherwood Anderson are very funny on the subject of Hemingway.[156] The last time that Sherwood was in Paris they often talked about him. Hemingway had been formed by the two of them and they were both a little proud and a little ashamed of the work of their minds. Hemingway had at one moment, when he had repudiated Sherwood Anderson and all his works,[157] written him a letter in the name of american literature which he, Hemingway, in company with his contemporaries was about to save, telling Sherwood just what he, Hemingway thought about Sherwood's work, and, that thinking, was in no sense complimentary. When Sherwood came to Paris Hemingway naturally was afraid. Sherwood as naturally was not.

As I say he and Gertrude Stein were endlessly amusing on the subject. They admitted that Hemingway was yellow, he is, Gertrude Stein insisted, just like the flat-boat men on the Mississippi river as described by Mark Twain. But what a book, they both agreed, would be the real story of Hemingway, not those he writes but the

---

[155] Nabokov added in the same interview: 'Later I read his admirable "The Killers" and the wonderful fish story which I was asked to translate into Russian but could not for some reason or other.' The phrase 'bells, balls and bulls', so perfect for Hemingway (*For Whom the Bell Tolls*, balls of a non-Austen denotation and *Death in the Afternoon*), seems to have been coined about a century before in *The Finsbury Magazine* (1864), in an anonymous piece to do with the etymology of surnames: 'We have been accustomed to regard the Bells, Balls, and Bulls as comparative nobodies. How many of us thought that they had a pedigree extending back to the ages of Norse Mythology. Yet such is the case, for they can claim descent from Bol, the son of Odin, and these varied forms are all traceable to that one root, only varied by provincial differences in pronunciation [. . .].'

[156] Stein is writing in the voice of Toklas.

[157] Hemingway had begun as a disciple of Anderson, but, perhaps resenting the older man's hold on him, published in 1926 *The Torrents of Spring*, a sustained parody of Anderson.

confessions of the real Ernest Hemingway. It would be for another audience than the audience Hemingway now has but it would be very wonderful. And then they both agreed that they have a weakness for Hemingway because he is such a good pupil. He is a rotten pupil, I protested. You don't understand, they both said, it is so flattering to have a pupil who does it without understanding it, in other words he takes training and anybody who takes training is a favourite pupil. They both admit it to be a weakness. [. . .] But what a story that of the real Hem, and one he should tell himself but alas he never will. After all, as he himself once murmured, there is the career, the career.

The Autobiography of Alice B . Toklas (1933)

Tom Wolfe (1931–) on Hemingway

Take Hemingway. People always think that the reason he's easy to read is that he is concise. He isn't. I hate conciseness – it's too difficult. The reason Hemingway is easy to read is that he repeats himself all the time, using 'and' for padding.

Conversations with Tom Wolfe, ed. D.M. Scura (1990)

LANGSTON HUGHES 1902–1967

James Baldwin (1924–1987) on Hughes

Every time I read Langston Hughes I am amazed all over again by his genuine gifts – and depressed that he has done so little with them. A real discussion of his work demands more space than I have here, but this book contains a great deal which a more disciplined poet would have thrown into the waste-basket (almost all of the last section, for example). There are poems which almost succeed but which do not succeed, poems which take refuge, finally, in a fake simplicity in order to avoid the very difficult simplicity of the experience! [. . .]

Hughes is an American Negro poet and has no choice but to be acutely aware of it. He is not the first American Negro to find the war between his social and artistic responsibilities all but irreconcilable.

Review in *The New York Times*, 29 March 1959, in *Twentieth-century American Literature*, ed. H. Bloom (1988)

JOHN STEINBECK 1902–1968

James Gould Cozzens (1903–78) on Steinbeck

I can't read ten pages of Steinbeck without throwing up. I couldn't read the proletarian crap that came out in the '30s; again you had sentimentalism – the poor oppressed workers.

Time, 2 September 1957

Alfred Kazin (1915–98) on Steinbeck

Nothing in his books is so dim, significantly enough, as the human beings who live in them, and few of them are intensely imagined as human beings at all. It is obvious that his mind moves most happily in realms where he does not have to work in very complex types: the paisanos in *Tortilla Flat*, the ranch hands in *Of Mice and Men*, the Okies in *The Grapes of Wrath*, the strikers in *In Dubious Battle*, the farmers in *The Long Valley*, the symbolic protagonists of democratic struggle and Nazi power in *The Moon Is Down*. But what one sees in his handling of these types is not merely a natural affection for this simplicity, but a failure to interest himself too deeply in them as individuals.

On Native Grounds: An Interpretation of Modern American Prose Literature (1942)

GEORGE ORWELL 1903–1950

Cyril Connolly (1903–74) on Orwell

He would not blow his nose without moralizing on conditions in the handkerchief industry.

The Evening Colonnade, 1973, in John Rodden, *Every Intellectual's Big Brother: George Orwell's Literary Siblings* (2006)

Richard Hoggart (1918–) on Orwell

Whatever the intellectual interest of his ideas and opinions, much the most fruitful and enjoyable way into an understanding of Orwell is through his handling of language. Through the sloppinesses first, since they indicate almost as much about the temper of his mind as do the strengths. He loves extreme adjectives, adverbs and nouns, and does not mind how often he repeats them; redundancy is one of his stylistic tactics. Top of the list is 'dreadful', closely followed by 'frightful'; then 'appalling', 'disgusting', 'hideous'; then 'unspeakably', 'horribly', 'obscenely', and, finally, 'horror'. They are idiomatic and they hammer at you.

So do his demonstrative pointings and jabbings at the reader: 'You see this . . .'; 'You see that . . .'. The 'you's' march on, together with the 'this's', especially in such formulations as: 'You see this business of . . .' It is all very direct, colloquial and arm-grabbing; and mutually involving. Orwell assumes a great range of common knowledge with the reader in such favourite locutions as: 'in that peculiar watchful, loving way that invalids have', or, 'For dinner there were generally those threepenny steak puddings which are sold ready-made in tins'. We are all assumed to have shared such experiences and it all makes for the peculiar intimacy of the writing.

He was a good hater and sometimes his style went melodramatically beyond reason: '. . . all that dreary tribe of high-minded women and sandal-wearers and bearded fruit-juice drinkers who come flocking towards the smell of "progress" like blue-bottles to a dead cat'. Funny but, as he might have said today, 'way over the top'.

For all their force and the irritation they cause at times, these are minor elements in comparison with the virtues of Orwell's prose.

Introduction (1989) to *The Road to Wigan Pier* (1937)

LILLIAN HELLMAN 1905–1984

Mary McCarthy (1912–1989) on Hellman

INTERVIEWER: We don't have the overpraised writer anymore?

MCCARTHY: The only one I can think of is a holdover like Lillian Hellman, who I think is tremendously overrated, a bad writer, and dishonest writer, but she really belongs to the past.

INTERVIEWER: What is dishonest about her?

MCCARTHY: Everything. I said once in some interview that every word she writes is a lie, including 'and' and 'the'.[158]

The Dick Cavett Show, 26 January 1980, in *Literary Feuds*, ed. A. Arthur (2002)

SAMUEL BECKETT 1906–1989

Samuel Beckett (1906–1989) on Beckett

Personally of course I regret everything [. . .] An ordure from beginning to end.

Watt (1953)

Anthony Burgess (1917–1993) on Beckett

Beckett does not believe in God, though he seems to imply that God has committed an unforgivable sin by not existing.

The Novel Now: A Guide to Contemporary Fiction (1967)

---

[158] As a result of this interview, Hellman sued McCarthy for two and a quarter million dollars, mostly for the 'pain and anguish' caused. Hellman was at this time suffering from glaucoma and heart problems, while McCarthy was younger and possibly more ruthless. The suit dragged on for four years, turning chiefly on Hellman's alleged Communist sympathies and on the alleged falsehoods in her memoirs of resistance activities in the Second World War; the feud divided America's literary establishment. It ended when Hellman died of a heart attack in 1984 and the suit was withdrawn. McCarthy died five years later.

W.H. AUDEN 1907–1973

Philip Larkin (1922–1985) on Auden

I have been trying to imagine a discussion of Auden between one man who had read nothing of his after 1940 and another who had read nothing before. After an initial agreement by adjective – 'Versatile,' 'Fluent,' 'Too smart sometimes' – a mystifying gap would open between them, as one spoke of a tremendously exciting English social poet full of energetic, unliterary knock-about and unique lucidity of phrase, and the other of an engaging, bookish, American talent, too verbose to be memorable and too intellectual to be moving. And not only would they differ about his poetic character: there would be a sharp division of opinion about his poetic stature.

'What's Become of Wystan?' *Spectator*, 15 July 1960, in *W.H. Auden: The Critical Heritage*, ed. J. Haffenden (1997)

George Orwell (1903–50) on Auden

But notice the phrase 'necessary murder'.[159] It could only be written by a person to whom murder is at most a word. Personally I would not speak so lightly of murder. It so happens that I have seen the bodies of numbers of murdered men – I don't mean killed in battle, I mean murdered. Therefore I have some conception of what murder means – the terror, the hatred, the howling relatives, the post-mortems, the blood, the smells. To me, murder is something to be avoided. So it is to any ordinary person. The Hitlers and Stalins find murder necessary, but they don't advertise their callousness, and they don't speak of it as murder; it is 'liquidation', 'elimination', or some other soothing phrase. Mr Auden's brand of amoralism is only possible if you are the kind of person who is always somewhere else when the trigger is pulled. So much of left-wing thought is a kind of playing with fire by people who don't even know that fire is hot.

'Inside the Whale' (1940)

[159] Orwell is referring to Auden's poem 'Spain 1937', about the Spanish Civil War, written during the period when Auden was a Communist, and including the line (apparently non-ironic) 'The conscious acceptance of guilt in the necessary murder'. Auden had not fought in the Spanish Civil War (unlike Orwell) and by 1940 (when 'Inside the Whale' was published) had decamped to the USA. Auden later changed the phrase 'necessary murder' to 'fact of murder'.

Edith Sitwell (1887–1964) on Auden

Let us take the example of Mr. Auden. This young poet's rhythms almost invariably produce this sensation of running away, and the rhythms, are, in all cases, the result of outward structure alone. The words lie dead on the page.

Mr. Auden has an able mind, but, unhappily, he writes uninteresting poetry, or, at least, his poetry nearly always lacks interest. When therefore, we are told by an admiring reviewer that, since the publication of his first volume, two or three years ago, 'it has been generally recognized that he is one of the four or five living poets worth quarrelling about' – and that 'Here is something as important as the appearance of Mr. Eliot's poems fifteen years ago' – I can only reply that this is sheer nonsense. [. . .]

What interest, for instance, can this passage, which occurs on page 66 of 'The Orators', arouse in the mind of the reader:

> I'm afraid it sounds more like a fairy story
> There was a family called Do
> There were Do-a, Do-ee, and other Do-s
> And Uncle Dick and Uncle Wiz had come to stay with them
> (Nobody slept that night.)
> Now Do-a loved to bathe before his breakfast
> With Uncle Dick, but Uncle Wiz . . .
> Well?
> As a matter of fact the farm was in Pembrokeshire,
> The week the Labour Cabinet resigned.
> Dick had returned from Germany in love.
> I hate cold water and am very fond of potatoes.
> You're wondering about these scratches?

I am not! I am wondering at the simple credulity of the critics and the public in allowing themselves to be gulled by such unattractive nonsense.

Aspects of Modern Poetry (1934)

STEPHEN SPENDER 1909–1995

Dylan Thomas (1914–1953) on Spender

Do you know anybody in Florence nice to have a drink with? I met Stephen Spender there a few weeks ago. It was very sad. He is on a lecture-tour. It is very sad. He is bringing the European intellectuals together. It is impossible. He said, in a lecture I saw reported: 'All poets speak the same language.' It is a bloody lie: who talks Spender?[160]

Letter to John Davenport, 29 May 1947, in *Dylan Thomas: The Collected Letters*,
ed. P. Ferris (1985)

JOHN BERRYMAN 1914–1972

Clive James (1939–) on Berryman

He took every unattractive aspect of the ambitious artistic psyche and shoved it right up front. In short, he pushed it. In retrospect it turns out that he pushed it to the limit. It's doubtful whether the suicide of an artist should be allowed to lend force to his work, but it's hard to see how one can stop it happening [. . .] At his best Berryman presented the various mental components that are in tension within us all, but at his worst – and sex brought out the worst in him as well as the best – the reader was vouchsafed a revelation of the Superstud, priapic and boring with it.

The Listener, 30 January 1972, in *A Second* Listener *Anthology*,
ed. K. Miller (1973)

Allen Tate (1899–1979) on Berryman

I don't think he was great. He was an original poet and a very interesting one, but he wasn't a great poet . . . He never grew up. That was his whole trouble. And *Dream Songs* is simply paranoid projections of childhood manias and obsessions.

In Thomas Travisano, *Midcentury Quartet: Bishop, Lowell, Jarrell, Berryman* (1999)

---

[160] Thomas was in fact a friend of Spender and frequently solicited his help, asking him to intercede with T.S. Eliot and Kenneth Clark, amongst others, for favours and work.

DYLAN THOMAS 1914–1953

Kingsley Amis (1922–1995) on Thomas

Talking of words, I think I have traced the nastiness of my early words to the influence of Mister Dylan Thos. *Nay*: influences are good if they are good influences, like Auden and you less recently, but if they are SODDING LOUSY influences, like that of Mr. Thos, then they are bad, years, years. I have got to the stage now with mr toss that I have only reached with Chaucer and Dryden, not even with Milton, that of VIOLENTLY WISHING that the man WERE IN FRONT OF ME, so that I could be DEMONICALLY RUDE to him about his GONORRHEIC RUBBISH, and end up by WALKING ON HIS FACE and PUNCHING HIS PRIVY PARTS. I know young chaps sometimes dislike the men they copied because they copied them, but I copied Auden too, and I don't HATT him. I have only to see words like An old man's shank one-marrowed with my bone, or Jack Xt, or man-iron (aooh! aoh! aaoh!!) to groan 8 laid. And if we are gong to call peots bda because of the fefect they have dha on Egnilsh peorty, then he is bad, years, years ('Holders of one position, worng for years, years, years'). These refelctions have been stimulated by reading what mr trees has to say ab8 mr tosz. I think that mr treez is another VERY SILLY MNA, and BDA too, but not SO BDA as mr tozz because he DOESN'T WRITE SO MUCH.[161]

> Letter to Philip Larkin, 9 January 1947, in *The Letters of Kingsley Amis*,
> ed. Z. Leader (2000)

Philip Larkin (1922–1985) on Thomas

Dylan Thos. – yes. I have said all I have to say about him, I think, in an earlier letter. I think there is no man in Ennglad at now who can 'stick words into us like pins' [Ooh! doesn't that sound like a line from an *Auden Sonnet* about a dead wordwriter? You know the kind of thing:

---

[161]   cf. Philip Larkin on Dylan Thomas, below, written the same week in 1947. Several decades later Amis became a trustee of the Dylan Thomas estate and was often called upon to defend Thomas: he later praised his 'impeccable' ear and insisted that correct readings of lines be restored.

Laforgue
You stuck words into us like pins: the great Papa,
Childless with weeping, went on making money;
But the animals were friendly, etc. etc., crip
cropper crup crup, CRAP, CRAP, CRAP

like he can but he doesn't use his words to any advantage. I think a
man ought to use good words to make what he means *impressive*:
Dylan Thos. just makes you wonder what he means, *very hard*. Take a
phrase that comes at the start of a poem in *Deaths & Entrances* –
something about waking up in the 'immortal hospital'. Now that is a
phrase that makes me feel suddenly a sort of *reverent apprehension*, only
I don't know what it *means*. Can't the FOOL see that if I could see
what it *means*, I should admire it *2ce as much*?? But I agree he is a
shocking influence: I had him for a while, but not for very long or
very badly.[162] And as for his imitators – Ah, soles are chip today.[163]

Letter to Kingsley Amis, 11 January 1947, in *Selected Letters of Philip Larkin,
1940–85*, ed. A. Thwaite (1993)

I thought you were pretty charitable about old Dylan, whose letters I
read with almost supernatural boredom, scrounging, apologising,
promising, apologising again, fixing up appointments, apologising for
not keeping them, and all that nonsensical rubbish to P.H.J.[164] in the
first half and Princess whoever she was in the second. And then the

---

[162]   Larkin had encountered Thomas in the flesh six years earlier and been
much impressed. He wrote in a letter to James Sutton (20 November 1941):
'Talking about poetry; Dylan Thomas came to the English Club last week.
Hell of a fine man: little, snubby, hopelessly pissed bloke who made hundreds
of cracks and read parodies of everybody in appropriate voices. He remarked
"I'd like to have talked about a book of poems I've been given to review, a
young poet called Rupert Brooke – it's surprising how he has been influenced
by Stephen Spender. . ." There was a moment of delighted surprise, then a
roar of laughter. Then he read a parody of Spender entitled "The Parachutist"
which had people rolling on the floor. He kept up this all night – parodies of
everyone bar Lawrence – and finally read two of his own poems, which seem
very good.'

[163]   cf. Kingsley Amis on Dylan Thomas, opposite.

[164]   Pamela Hansford Johnson.

letters to Caitlin. You know, what struck me most about them was that he might never have met her before. No cat, no friendliness, nothing to suggest that they had a life they shared and enjoyed. Hardly any (if my memory serves) of 'Do you remember that girl Dilys we met at Ieuan's party, well, she's gone off with that incredible fool Teithryn' – you know the kind of thing? All snivelling and grovelling and adoring and so very impersonal.[165]

Letter to Kingsley Amis, 21 November 1985, in *Selected Letters of Philip Larkin, 1940–85*, ed. A. Thwaite (1993)

Edith Sitwell (1887–1964) on Thomas

The last time we corresponded, it was on the subject of Master Thomas, who is rapidly heading for having his ears boxed.[166] I can feel the tips of my fingers tingling to come into contact with the lobes of his ears. And it would do him a lot of good, for he was evidently insufficiently corrected as a child. *What* a tiresome boy that is, though a very gifted one. Having given us all that trouble, caused me to pester you and to write dozens of letters to busy people who must now curse the name of Sitwell, he has disappeared again, disappeared without leaving a trace. I have received reproachful letters from this person and from that, reproving *me* because *he*, after getting *me* to ask *them* to give *him* an appointment, hasn't kept it. But not a word can we get from him. This disappearance trick seems to be a habit with the younger generation. They ought to join Maskelyne and Davenants,[167] for they'd make the fortune of the place, and we should see a recrudescence of interest in magic.

I'm practically Master Thomas' secretary now, as everybody who can't find him (and nobody can) addresses his letters care of me, and I have to readdress them.

Letter to Richard Jennings, 3 March 1937, in *Selected Letters*, ed. R. Greene (1997)

---

[165] Larkin died eleven days later. This was his last letter to Amis, dictated on to tape and transcribed by his secretary.

[166] Sitwell played an important part in the nourishment of Dylan Thomas's career, though Thomas did not always seem grateful or graceful. See Dylan Thomas's comments about Sitwell, page 187.

[167] Maskelyne and Devant (*sic*) were stage magicians.

ANTHONY BURGESS 1917–1993

Martin Amis (1949–) on Burgess

Burgess's recent prose is characterized by professional haste and a desire to be a stylist. The result is a knotted, cadenced, bogus lustiness: every sentence, every phrase, is sure to contain some virile quirk or other: 'He scribbled something on a message pad, tore, folded, gave' and '"G-Gay?" puzzled Bev' are fair examples of Burgess's gimcrack contortions. And the dialogue is impossible. 'No need to tell me precisely where he sits on his revolving chair and watches the mineral fatness gush,' says Bev chattily of some oil-rich interloper. The workers, by the way, are presented throughout as the usual snarling, snivelling brutes, and Burgess recklessly admits in a postscript that he has been almost as unfair to them as Orwell was. So much for the failure of love. Where does this leave *1985* in relation to *1984*? Hanging on to its 'probability', I imagine, and looking sillier every month.

Review of *1985* in the *New York Times Book Review*, November 1978,
in *The War Against Cliché* (2001)

IRIS MURDOCH 1919–1999

Martin Amis (1949–) on Murdoch

I suspect that Miss Murdoch's huge productivity is, paradoxically, a form of self-defence or self-effacement: 300 pages a year disarm a lot of criticism. She can't, in the nature of things, revise much and probably she never re-reads; she just 'gets on with the next one'. Were she to slow down – were she to allow one of those ominous 'silences' to gather, silences such as more tight-lipped novelists periodically 'break' – she would be accepting a different kind of responsibility to her critics and to her own prodigious talents. She would, in short, begin to find out how good she is, that strange and fearful discovery.

Review of *The Sacred and Profane Love Machine* in the *New Statesman*, March
1974, in *The War Against Cliché* (2001)

J.D. SALINGER 1919–

Norman Mailer (1923–2007) on Salinger

Salinger is everyone's favorite. I seem to be alone in finding him to be the greatest mind ever to stay in prep school. What he can do, he does well, and it is his, but it is finally not very lively to live on a campus where bully-muscle always beats those who feel but feel weak. I cannot see Salinger soon emerging onto the battleground of a major novel.

Of course, this opinion may come from nothing more graceful than envy.

Advertisements for Myself (1959)

Mary McCarthy (1912–1989) on Salinger

I don't like Salinger, not at all. That last thing isn't a novel anyway, whatever it is. I don't like it. Not at all. It suffers from this terrible sort of metropolitan sentimentality and it's so narcissistic. And to me, also, it seemed so false, so calculated. Combining the plain man with an absolutely megalomaniac egotism. I simply can't stand it.

The Paris Review, Winter–Spring 1962

Tom Wolfe (1931–) on Salinger

I think it's really important to stay in journalism. Otherwise you run the danger of getting as completely out of touch as Salinger. What I would have Salinger do is write four pieces of journalism right now because it would force him to get in touch. You can't, by just leading your daily life, really see a goddamn thing. You have to force yourself to get into unfamiliar areas.

Conversations with Tom Wolfe, ed. D.M. Scura (1990)

JAMES JONES 1921–1977

Ernest Hemingway (1899–1961) on Jones

To me he is an enormously skillful fuck-up and his book will do great damage to our country. Probably I should re-read it again to give you a truer answer. But I do not have to eat an entire bowl of scabs to know they are scabs; nor suck a boil to know it is a boil; nor swim through a river of snot to know it is snot. I hope he kills himself as soon as it does not damage his or your sales. If you give him a literary tea you might ask him to drain a bucket of snot and then suck the pus out of a dead nigger's ear ... Best always, Ernest.[168]

Letter to Charles Scribner, 5 March 1951, in P.D. Beidler, *The Good War's Greatest Hits* (1998)

PETER USTINOV 1921–2004

Edith Sitwell (1887–1964) on Ustinov

The other day, at the St. Regis, as we were leaving the restaurant and Natasha was coming in, she introduced a playwright called Peter Ustinov (Osbert knew him already). I *thought* his manner was most odd: he behaved exactly like a blackbeetle that thinks it is going to be killed – tried to crawl into the wall. (Excepting that he was like a fat white slug.) Well, a few days after I arrived here, I found out why. On the 2nd of December, or 3rd, he produced a play of his at the Savoy in London, *written for the purpose of grossly insulting Osbert and me.* There can be no question it was meant for us. We are given the name of *D'Urt*!!!

Miss D'Urt is a famous 'poetess in a turban' (I used to wear these many years ago). Sir Mohammed D'Urt is a famous writer who is a baronet, and they have an eccentric old father. Both of us, apparently, are sex maniacs of an advanced kind. The baronet was described by one paper as 'a lecherous pontiff', and I hunt unwilling gentlemen in and out of bedrooms. The *Daily Express* has said, *in so many words*, that it is meant for us. Can you imagine anything *so foul* as to do this to a poor man who is known, by the whole of London, to have a most terrible disease that is made infinitely worse by any kind of shock or worry?

---

[168] Jones had just produced a best-seller in *From Here to Eternity*, while Hemingway's *Across the River and Into the Trees* of the previous year had done less well. Hemingway later explained: 'I liked the real soldiers only and thought Jones was a phony soldier.' Jones, however, was equally savage with Hemingway after Hemingway's suicide, saying: 'The problem with Papa was he always wanted to suck a cock. But when he found one that fit, it had a double barrel.'

However – the play was booed off. On the first night, every entrance of the actors [...] was booed and yelled at by the gallery. One line of Miss D'Urt's ran, 'We forgive everything' to which a voice replied, 'We don't. We'll never forgive this.' The brave Mr. Ustinov who has insulted a helpless cripple[169] had to hide in his box. The play was withdrawn after nine days ...

Letter to Minnie Astor and James Fosburgh, 29 December 1953, in *Selected Letters*, ed. R. Greene (1997)

KINGSLEY AMIS 1922–1995

Philip Larkin (1922–1985) on Amis

I've been curling up with 'the new Amis' recently – it makes *me* laugh, but if you don't 'happen to like' Kingsley just being Kingsley then I can quite see it must appear a wilful and sordid piece of work. His appearance on Network 3 on jazz (the first of six programmes) has had its obvious effect on me. I am a corpse eaten out with envy, impotence, failure, envy, boredom, sloth, snobbery, envy, incompetence, inefficiency, laziness, lechery, envy, fear, baldness, bad circulation, bitterness, bittiness, envy, sycophancy, deceit, nostalgia, *et cetera*. [...] Have a drink for me – never seem to get any here. Brrr.

Letter to Patsy Murphy, 16 January 1958, in *Selected Letters of Philip Larkin, 1940–85*, ed. A. Thwaite (1993)

Yes, Kingsley's a dysgraphical bastard – last I had was a card in August, saying he would 'write properly' when he returned (from Wales) on September 1. This when he has still to express regret at M.'s[170] illness and my natural gloom at same. The only reason I hope I predecease him is that I'd find it next to impossible to say anything nice about him at his memorial service. What a nasty thing to say, but you know what I mean. He probably thinks the same about me.[171]

Letter to Robert Conquest, 30 October 1983, in *Selected Letters of Philip Larkin, 1940–85*, ed. A. Thwaite (1993)

---

[169] Sitwell was at the time suffering from the early stages of Parkinson's disease.

[170] Monica Jones, Larkin's long-time companion.

[171] In fact Amis gave an address at Larkin's memorial service that revealed the

PHILIP LARKIN 1922-1985

Martin Amis (1949–) on Larkin

The word 'Larkinesque' used to evoke the wistful, the provincial, the crepuscular, the sad, the unloved; now it evokes the scabrous and the supremacist. The word 'Larkinism' used to stand for a certain sort of staid, decent, wary Englishness; now it refers to the articulate far right. In the early Eighties, the common mind imagined Larkin as a reclusive yet twinkly drudge – bald, bespectacled, bicycle-clipped, slumped in a shabby library gaslit against the dusk. In the early Nineties, we see a fuddled Scrooge and bigot, his singlet-clad form barely visible through a mephitis of alcohol, anality, and spank magazines. The reaction against Larkin has been unprecedentedly violent, as well as unprecedentedly hypocritical, tendentious, and smug. Its energy does not – could not – derive from literature: it derives from ideology, or from the vaguer promptings of a new ethos. In a sense, none of this matters, because only the poems matter. But the spectacle holds the attention. [. . .]

What we get at forty or forty-five he had all along. He never did anything about it (you didn't, then); he seemed to nurture this adolescent lassitude; he made it his own patch of melancholy, and tried to write the poetry that belonged there. Humanly, it turned him into an old woman – like his mother. 'I bought a pair of shoes and they

---

depth of his affection for Larkin: 'He could be at his funniest when uttering those same painful truths about life as those he made so devastating in his poetry. And it was all from the heart: he never showed off, never laid claim to feeling what he didn't feel, and it was that honesty, more total in his case than in any other I've known, that gave his poetry such power. He meant every word of it; and so, though he may not have written many poems, he wrote none that were false or unnecessary. His honesty extended to himself; again, nobody was ever more totally or acutely aware of his limitations. He took life seriously, he took poetry seriously, but not himself – nobody who said he looked like a bald salmon could do that. No solemnity about himself as a poet, either; when he'd written a poem he felt pleased, as if he'd laid an egg. But we take seriously what he has left us. We are lucky enough to have known him; thousands who didn't, and more thousands in the future, will be able to share those poems with us. They offer comfort, and not cold comfort either. They are not dismal or pessimistic, but invigorating; they know that for all its shortcomings life must be got on with. And now we must get on with ours, a little better equipped to do so with the help of those fragments of poignancy and humour in everyday things, those moments of illumination and beauty we should never have seen or known but for Philip.'

don't even *try* to keep the water out.' 'I have an insensate prejudice against people who go abroad AT ANY TIME OF THE YEAR, but PARTICULARLY at Easter & Christmas.' Given his opportunities for variety and expansion, he makes Mr Woodhouse, in *Emma*, look like Evel Knievel. 'This is a hell of a week. Must get a haircut. Wanted to get another dark sweater from M and S' – Marks & Spencer – 'but doubt if there'll be time or if they'll have one.' He was so worried about his weight that he took his bathroom scales on holiday.

The New Yorker, July 1993, in *The War Against Cliché* (2001)

Lisa Jardine (1944–) on Larkin

The row over the Larkin letters is in the end about whether we are right to turn our attention to a cultural centre which reflects the diversity and richness of contemporary multi-cultural Britain, and to draw our contemporary values from that rich vein. Or whether to dig in with nostalgic memories of a 'great' Britain that (perhaps) once was, and to spend the fading years of British imperial glory trying to persuade our children that everything of value lies behind us.

The Guardian, December 1992

Tom Paulin (1949–) on Larkin

Larkin's snarl, his populism and his calculated philistinism all speak for Tebbit's England and for that gnarled and angry puritanism which is so deeply ingrained in the culture. Recognising this, Larkin called himself 'one of nature's Orangemen', adopting the mask of an Ulster Protestant, a sort of Belfast Dirk Dogstoerd, in order to ironise his own philistinism. Yet that attitude was itself a strategy because it enabled him to conceal the knowledge that he had created many outstandingly beautiful poems. In that distinctively embarrassed English manner he had to bury his pride in his artistic creations under several sackfuls of ugly prejudices.

Times Literary Supplement, July 1990

NORMAN MAILER 1923–2007

James Baldwin (1924–1987) on Mailer

While I was out of the country, Norman published *Advertisements for*

Myself, which presently crossed the ocean to the apartment of James Jones. Bill Styron[172] was also in Paris at the time, and one evening the three of us sat in Jim's living room, reading aloud, in a kind of drunken, masochistic fascination, Norman's judgement of our personalities and our work. Actually, I came off best, I suppose; there was less about me, and it was less venomous. But the condescension infuriated me; also, to tell the truth, my feelings were hurt. I felt that if that was the way Norman felt about me, he should have told me so. He had said that I was incapable of saying 'Fuck you' to the reader. My first temptation was to send him a cablegram which would disabuse him of that notion, at least insofar as one reader was concerned. But then I thought, No, I would be cool about it, and fail to react as he so clearly wanted me to. Also, I must say, his judgement of myself seemed so wide of the mark and so childish that it was hard to stay angry. I wondered what in the world was going on in his mind. Did he really suppose that he had now become the builder and destroyer of reputations?

And of *my* reputation?

We met in the Actors' Studio one afternoon, after a performance of *The Deer Park* – which I deliberately arrived too late to see, since I really did not know how I was going to react to Norman, and didn't want to betray myself by clobbering his play. When the discussion ended, I stood, again on the edge of the crowd around him, waiting. Over someone's shoulder, our eyes met, and Norman smiled.

'We've got something to talk about,' I told him.

'I figured that,' he said, smiling.

We went to a bar, and sat opposite each other. I was relieved to discover that I was not angry, not even (as far as I could tell) at the bottom of my heart. But, 'Why did you write those things about me?'

'Well, I'll tell you about that,' he said, – Norman has several accents, and I think this was his Texas one – 'I sort of figured you had it coming to you.'

---

[172]   The novelist Wiiliam Styron. Mailer had a famous feud with Styron which began because Mailer suspected Styron was spreading rumours that Mailer's second wife, Adele (the one Mailer later stabbed), was a lesbian. In March 1958 Mailer wrote to Styron: 'So I tell you this, Billy-boy. You have got to learn to keep your mouth shut about my wife, for if you do not, and I hear of it again, I will invite you to a fight in which I expect to stomp out of you a fat amount of your yellow and treacherous shit.'

'Why?'

'Well, if you think there's some truth in it.'

'Well, if you felt that way, why didn't you ever say it to – to me?'

'Well, I figured if this was going to break up our friendship, something else would come along to break it up just as fast.'

I couldn't disagree with that.

Nobody Knows My Name (1961)

Evelyn Waugh (1903–1966) on Mailer

Mrs Kidd's ball was very lavish – nothing remarkable if it had been in Surrey but sensational in Somerset. Two bands, one of niggers & one of buggers, a cabaret, an oyster bar in the harness room, stables flood lit, much to the discomfort of the horses. One bit an American pornographer who tried to give it vodka. [. . .][173]

I had never before met Lady Jean Campbell and was fascinated. She came to us next day bringing the bitten pornographer. He might have stepped straight from your salon – a swarthy gangster just out of a mad house where he had been sent after the attempt to cut his wife's throat.[174] It is his first visit to England. His tour is Janet Kidd, Randolph, Ian Argyll. He will be able to write a revealing pornogram of English life.

Letter to Ann Fleming, 23 September 1961, in *The Letters of Evelyn Waugh*, ed. M. Amory (1980)

ALEXANDER SOLZHENITSYN 1918–2008

Gore Vidal (1925–) on Solzhenitsyn

He is a bad novelist and a fool. The combination usually makes for great popularity in the US.

Views from a Window: Conversations with Gore Vidal, ed. R.J. Stanton (1980)

---

[173] i.e. Mailer.

[174] Mailer had attacked his second wife with a knife.

GORE VIDAL 1925–

Kingsley Amis (1922–1995) on Vidal

Yes, well, it may be laziness, but on the rare occasions when I do pick up Vidal, whose early books I enjoyed before he was as celebrated as he is now, he seems to me to suffer from American cleverness: the fear of being thought stupid, or dull, or behind the times. I think that's a very bad attitude for the novelist to adopt. He must not mind being thought boring and pompous from time to time – let's hope he avoids it, but if he runs too far in the opposite direction, he's heading for disaster.

Paris Review, Winter 1975

Martin Amis (1949–) on Vidal

Having seen 'the picture of him that adorns his latest opus', William Burroughs urgently wanted to know: 'Is Gore Vidal queer or not?'

To which the answer is a strangely qualified yes. Vidal is queer, sort of: but in Vidal's world so is everybody else. There's Capote, Williams, Isherwood, Kerouac, Baldwin, E.M. Forster, and so on. But even the fanatical skirt-chasers – Marlon, Jack, Bobby – betray certain leanings. Greta Garbo had 'an eye for girls'; in Hollywood, so did 'just about every star or star's wife'. Ken Tynan, too, was 'one of nature's innate and unalterable lesbians'. During the war, in Vidal's all-gay army, 'most of the boys' embraced the chance 'to do what they were designed to do with each other'. Earlier, in Vidal's all-gay school, boys 'thought that kissing had been invented by girls . . . it was not always pleasant for us when the increased estrogen flow made their salivas taste unpleasant.' No, unpleasant things are not always pleasant. But I have never before heard a word of complaint about that oestrogen flow, or indeed any mention of it. Maybe the boys I know are differently 'designed'. As elsewhere in his writing, Vidal gives the impression of believing that the entire heterosexual edifice – registry offices, *Romeo and Juliet*, the disposable diaper – is just a sorry story of self-hypnosis and mass hysteria: a hoax, a racket, or sheer propaganda.

Review of *Palimpsest* in *The Sunday Times*, October 1995, in *The War Against Cliché* (2001)

JUDITH KRANTZ 1928–

Clive James (1939–) on Krantz

To be a really lousy writer takes energy. The average novelist remains unread not because he is bad but because he is flat. On the evidence of *Princess Daisy*, Judith Krantz deserves her high place in the best-seller lists. This is the second time she has been up there. The first time was for a book called *Scruples*, which I will probably never get around to reading. But I don't begrudge the time I have put into reading *Princess Daisy*. As a work of art it has the same status as a long conversation between two not very bright drunks, but as best-sellers go it argues for a reassuringly robust connection between fiction and the reading public. If cheap dreams get no worse than this, there will not be much for the cultural analyst to complain about. *Princess Daisy* is a terrible book only in the sense that it is almost totally inept.

Review in *The London Review of Books*, 1980, in *As of this Writing: The Essential Essays, 1968–2002* (2003)

TOM WOLFE 1931–

John Irving (1942–) on Wolfe

INTERVIEWER: You didn't read *The Right Stuff*?

IRVING: Oh please. If I were interested in astronauts I would have tried to be one. Bullshit.

INTERVIEWER: No kidding.

IRVING: He's a journalist, man, he's a journalist. He doesn't know how to write fiction, he can't create a character, he can't create a situation.

INTERVIEWER: He says he's the Dickens, he's the real version of Dickens.

IRVING: It doesn't matter what he says. You see people reading him on airplanes the same people who are reading John Grisham for Christ's sake.

INTERVIEWER: You once said in the magazine, in *Shift* magazine to me, that you don't believe in what you call the McLiterature theory that if it's popular it's shit. I mean he's popular, it doesn't mean he's shitty.

IRVING: I'm not using that argument against him, I'm using the argument against him that he can't write, that his sentences are bad, that it makes you wince. It's like reading a bad newspaper or a bad piece in a magazine. It makes you wince, it makes you wince. You know, if you were a good skater could you watch someone just fall down all the time? Could you do that? I can't do that.[175]

Comments on *Hot Type* (Canadian Broadcasting Corporation TV Show),
17 December, 1999

Norman Mailer (1923–2007) on Wolfe

The book [*A Man in Full*] has gas and runs out of gas, fills up again, goes dry. It is a 742-page work that reads as if it is fifteen hundred pages long. This is, to a degree, a compliment, since it is very rich in material. But, given its high intentions, it is also tiresome, for it takes us down the road of too many overlong and predictable scenes. Electric at best, banal at worst [...] one picks it up each day to read another hundred pages with the sense that the book not only offers pleasure but the strain of encountering prose that disappoints as often as it titillates.

At certain points, reading the work can even be said to resemble the act of making love to a three-hundred-pound woman. Once she gets on top, it's over. Fall in love, or be asphyxiated. So you read and you grab and you even find delight in some of these mounds of material. Yet all the while you resist – how you resist! – letting three hundred pounds take you over.

After a time, I simply began to groan within each time there was a new description. It was not that they were badly written. Taken on its own, the tenth description was as good and certainly as detailed as the first, but quantity, as Engels once remarked, changes quality. Finally, the descriptions became not unequal to a politician declaring: 'I gave my stump speech ten times last night, and the tenth was as good as the first.' Repetition kills the soul, and the narrative élan of Wolfe's novel is

---

[175] Wolfe commented in *The American Spectator* on this interview with Irving: 'Incidentally I have no history with Irving. I had never written about Irving.

injured by the sheer quantity of his descriptions. They convert a stylistic virtue into a vice, then lock us up in an addiction. It is dispiriting to witness. A pall comes over one's happy attention when a brilliant conversationalist turns into a monologuist, only to deaden us further by revealing the true passion – logorrhea.[176]

Review of *A Man in Full* in *The New York Review of Books*, 17 December 1998

JOHN UPDIKE 1932–2009

Gore Vidal (1925–) on Updike

I can't stand him. Nobody will think to ask because I'm supposedly jealous; but I out-sell him. I'm more popular than he is, and I don't take him very seriously. [. . .] He goes grumbling away on those born with silver spoons in their mouths – oh, he comes on like the worker's son, like a modern-day D.H. Lawrence, but he's just another boring little middle-class boy hustling his way to the top if he can do it.

Comment on *Front Row* (UK radio show), 23 May 2008

PHILIP ROTH 1933–

Jacqueline Susann (1918–1974) on Roth

He's a fine writer, but I wouldn't want to shake hands with him.[177]

In Barbara Seaman, *Lovely Me: The Life of Jacqueline Susann* (1996)

He had never written anything about me as far as I know. I had never commented about Irving. But for whatever reason, and I'm not enough of a psychiatrist to tell you why, now when he hears my name, first he will literally start sputtering, then he will try out the naughtiest word he can think of on short notice, and then he'll be incoherent for about 120 seconds, and finally become a rational person again. It is really funny. You should do an experiment: Give him a ring and just say you were interviewing Tom Wolfe and he said you wasted a career as a novelist by not confronting life and should get off your farm, and that'll be enough to get him started.'

[176] Wolfe's comment on this in a letter to writer Anthony Arthur was: 'All I got out of that is the fact that Norman has made love to a lot of three-hundred-pound women.'

[177] Jacqueline Susann repeated the remark on many occasions and it grew to

MICHAEL CRICHTON 1942–2008

Martin Amis (1949–) on Crichton

At his best Crichton is a blend of Stephen Jay Gould and Agatha Christie. He emplaces a series of zoological mysteries which are far more arresting than the conveyor-belt jeopardies of his plot. Animals – especially, if not quite exclusively, velociraptors – are what he is good at. People are what he is bad at. People, and prose.

When you open *The Lost World* you enter a strange terrain of one-page chapters, one-sentence paragraphs and one-word sentences. You will gaze through the thick canopy of authorial padding. It's a jungle out there, and jungles are 'hot', sometimes 'very hot'. 'Malcolm wiped his forehead. "It's hot up here." Levine agrees: "'Yes, it's hot."' Thirty pages later it's still hot. '"Jeez, it's hot up here," Eddie said.' And Levine agrees again: '"Yes," Levine said, shrugging.' Out there, beyond the foliage, you see herds of clichés, roaming free. You will listen in 'stunned silence' to an 'unearthly cry' or a 'deafening roar'. Raptors are 'rapacious'. Reptiles are 'reptilian'. Pain is 'searing'.

Review of *The Lost World* in *The Sunday Times*, October 1995, in *The War Against Cliché* (2001)

SALMAN RUSHDIE 1947–

Martin Amis (1949–) on Rushdie

My mouth talks too much. Only a week earlier[178] my mouth had soured a *New Yorker* dinner at the Caprice in London by indulging in this 'exchange' with Salman Rushdie:

– So you like Beckett's prose, do you? You like Beckett's prose.

---

constitute something of a performance piece for her on TV and in interviews. When asked to elaborate, she said that the reason it had taken so long for Roth to write *Portnoy's Complaint* was that he could only type with one hand. In fact Susann nursed something of a grudge against 'literary' writers, commenting that 'What's literary today is stuff we're not able to understand, books that don't make any kind of real connection with their readers, books that the superior double-domed guys push on the public with pretension.' It must have been particularly gratifying for her when her novel *The Love Machine* was the first to bump Roth's hugely successful *Portnoy's Complaint* into second place on the bestseller lists.

[178] The action takes place in autumn 1994.

Having established earlier that he did like Beckett's prose, Salman neglected to answer.

– Okay. Quote me some. Oh I see. You can't.

No answer: only the extreme hooded-eye treatment. Richard Avedon would need a studio's worth of lights and reflectors to rig up this expression on an unsuspecting Salman. At the moment, though, a passing waiter with an Instamatic could have easily bettered it. Nobody spoke. Not even Christopher Hitchens. And I really do hate Beckett's prose: every sentence is an assault on my ear. So I said,

– Well I'll do it for you. All you need is maximum ugliness and a lot of negatives. 'Nor it the nothing never is.' 'Neither nowhere the nothing is not.' 'Non-nothing the never—'

Feeling my father in me now (as well as the couple of hundred glasses of wine consumed at the party we had all come on from), I settled down for a concerted goad and wheedle. By this stage Salman looked like a falcon staring through a venetian blind.

– 'No neither nor never none not no—'

– Do you want to come outside?

Experience (2000)

Naguib Mahfouz (1911–2006) on Rushdie

INTERVIEWER: Did you read *The Satanic Verses*?

MAHFOUZ: I didn't. By the time it appeared, I could no longer read very well – my eyesight has deteriorated a lot recently. But the American cultural attaché in Alexandria explained the book to me chapter by chapter. I found the insults in it unacceptable. Rushdie insults even the women of the Prophet! Now, I can argue with *ideas*, but what should I do with insults? Insults are the business of the court. At the same time, I consider Khomeini's position equally dangerous. He does not have the right to pass judgment – that is not the Islamic way. According to Islamic principles, when a man is accused of heresy he is given the choice between repentance and punishment. Rushdie was not given that choice. I have always defended Rushdie's right

to write and say what he wants in terms of ideas. But
he does not have the right to insult anything,
especially a prophet or anything considered holy.
Don't you agree?[179]

The Paris Review, Summer 1992

MARTIN AMIS 1949–

Tibor Fischer (1959–) on Amis

Let me go on record here: I've been behind Marty from the start (a long
time before Mr Wylie,[180] I suspect). I own a first edition of *The Rachel
Papers*, Amis's debut, not because I acquired it from a dealer, but because
I got it back in 1973, when it appeared. I was there when Amis read to
six people (including me) in Cambridge in 1980. I enjoyed *The
Information* (OK, it was a rehash of *London Fields*, OK, he was paid too
much, but it made me laugh) and didn't understand the carping. My
friends shook their heads in disbelief when *Night Train* came out, but I
stuck up for Amis, pointing out the remarkable ventriloquism. Amis is
one of the few living writers I can quote from memory.

You could smell the rot with *Experience*, however. Amis's memoir
was beautifully written and clever. Amis is the overlord of the OED.
No one can mobilise the English language like him. No one. But as a
book, *Experience* was a mess, and thin. There was a desperate, largely
unsuccessful, Amisian search for profundity (one of Amis's weaknesses
is that he isn't content to be a good writer, he wants to be profound;
the drawback to profundity is that it's like being funny, either you are
or you aren't, straining doesn't help). This ache for gravitas has led to

---

[179] This segment of the interview was widely regarded as a retraction of Mahfouz's previous position of unconditional support for Rushdie. Mahfouz was
awarded the Nobel Prize for Literature in 1988, the year of the publication of *The
Satanic Verses*: when in 1989 Khomeini issued his *fatwa* against Rushdie, Mahfouz
was thus extremely prominent among the group of Egyptian intellectuals who
had supported Rushdie. Subsequently he received death threats. In 1994 he was
attacked in the street and seriously injured; after that he was forced to live under
police protection.

[180] Andrew Wylie, Amis's literary agent and formerly Fischer's agent.

much of Amis's weaker work: *Time's Arrow* and his writing on nuclear war (it's horrible, isn't it?). [. . .]

Yellow Dog isn't bad as in not very good or slightly disappointing. It's not-knowing-where-to-look bad. I was reading my copy on the Tube and I was terrified someone would look over my shoulder (not only because of the embargo, but because someone might think I was enjoying what was on the page). It's like your favourite uncle being caught in a school playground, masturbating.

The way British publishing works is that you go from not being published no matter how good you are, to being published no matter how bad you are.

Louis de Bernières and I once attended a talk by John Fowles, which was painfully boring and trite (in his defence, Fowles was seriously ill).

Halfway through, Louis reached into his pocket, pulled out a railway ticket, scrawled on it and handed it to me. It was a signed authorisation to shoot him if he ever became an old bullshitter. I think I'll be sending Louis an authorisation to shoot me if I ever produce anything like *Yellow Dog*.

Someone, perhaps his friends, his editors, or even his agent, Andrew Wylie, should have said something to Amis.

Review of *Yellow Dog* in *The Daily Telegraph*, 4 August 2003

A.N. WILSON 1950–

Bevis Hillier (1940–) on Wilson

The man is despicable. When my 2002 volume on Betjeman came out, Wilson wrote in *The Spectator* that Hillier is not really a writer at all. His book is a hopeless mish-mash.[181]

The Sunday Times, 27 August 2006

---

[181] A.N. Wilson had indeed negatively reviewed the second volume of Bevis Hillier's massive biography of Betjeman, a work that had taken Hillier twenty-five years to complete, saying: 'Some reviewers would say it was badly written, but the trouble is, it isn't really written at all. It is hurled together.' Hillier took his revenge by forging a love letter from Betjeman to one Honor Tracy, and forwarded it to Wilson under the name of Eve de Harben (an anagram for 'ever been had'). Wilson was sufficiently impressed to include it in his own biography of Betjeman, published in 2005. The first letters of each sentence (from the second onwards) in the letter spelled out 'AN Wilson is a shit' as can be seen below:

Darling Honor,
I loved yesterday. All day, I've thought of nothing else. No other love I've had means so much. Was it just an aberration on your part, or will you meet me at Mrs Holmes's again – say on Saturday? I won't be able to sleep until I have your answer.
  Love has given me a miss for so long, and now this miracle has happened. Sex is a part of it, of course, but I have a Romaunt of the Rose feeling about it too. On Saturday we could have lunch at Fortt's, then go back to Mrs H.'s. Never mind if you can't make it then. I am free on Sunday too or Sunday week. Signal me tomorrow as to whether and when you can come.
  Anthony Powell has written to me, and mentions you admiringly. Some of his comments about the Army are v funny. He's somebody I'd like to know better when the war is over. I find his letters funnier than his books. Tinkerty-tonk, my darling. I pray I'll hear from you tomorrow. If I don't I'll visit your office in a fake beard.
  All love, JB

J.K. ROWLING 1965–

Harold Bloom (1930–) on Rowling

One can reasonably doubt that 'Harry Potter and the Sorcerer's Stone' is going to prove a classic of children's literature, but Rowling, whatever the aesthetic weaknesses of her work, is at least a millennial index to our popular culture. So huge an audience gives her importance akin to rock stars, movie idols, TV anchors, and successful politicians. Her prose style, heavy on cliché, makes no demands upon her readers. In an arbitrarily chosen single page – page 4 – of the first Harry Potter book, I count seven clichés, all of the 'stretch his legs' variety.

How to read 'Harry Potter and the Sorcerer's Stone'? Why, very quickly, to begin with, perhaps also to make an end. Why read it? Presumably, if you cannot be persuaded to read anything better, Rowling will have to do. Is there any redeeming education use to Rowling? Is there any to Stephen King? Why read, if what you read will not enrich mind or spirit or personality? [...]

Can more than 35 million book buyers, and their offspring, be wrong? Yes, they have been, and will continue to be for as long as they persevere with Potter.

A vast concourse of inadequate works, for adults and for children, crams the dustbins of the ages. At a time when public judgment is no better and no worse than what is proclaimed by the ideological cheerleaders who have so destroyed humanistic study, anything goes. The cultural critics will, soon enough, introduce Harry Potter into their college curriculum, and *The New York Times* will go on celebrating another confirmation of the dumbing-down it leads and exemplifies.[182]

The Wall Street Journal, 7 November 2000

---

[182] It happened that *The New York Times* that Bloom so disparaged was the organ which published a second major attack on Rowling, by A.S. Byatt in 2003.

SOURCES AND ACKNOWLEDGMENTS

Conrad Aiken All quotations by permission of Joseph Killorin and the Estate of Conrad Aiken

Kingsley Amis All quotations © The Estate of Kingsley Amis 2000 and Copyright © Kingsley Amis 1975. Reprinted by kind permission of Jonathan Clowes Ltd., London, on behalf of the Literary Estate of Kingsley Amis

Martin Amis All quotations by permission of Martin Amis and the Wylie Agency

John Berryman Quotation by permission of Kate Donahue

Anthony Burgess Quotation by permission of the Estate of Anthony Burgess

Noël Coward Quotation by permission of NC Aventales AG

James Gould Cozzens All quotations by permission of Gary Snerson

T.S. Eliot All quotations by permission of the T.S. Eliot Estate and Faber & Faber

William Faulkner Quotation by permission of W.W. Norton & Company, Inc./Liveright Publishing Corporation

Tibor Fischer Quotation by permission of Tibor Fischer

E.M. Forster All quotations by permission of The Provost and Scholars of King's College, Cambridge and The Society of Authors as the Literary Representatives of the Estate of E.M. Forster

Bevis Hillier Quotation by permission of Bevis Hillier

Richard Hoggart Quotation by permission of Nicola Beck

H.D. Quotation reproduced by permission of Pollinger Ltd and New Directions Publishing Corporation

Christopher Isherwood Quotation by permission of Don Bachardy

Lisa Jardine Quotation by permission of Lisa Jardine

Philip Larkin All quotations by permission of the Philip Larkin Estate and Faber & Faber

Norman Mailer All quotations © The New Mailer Estate, Norman Mailer Licensing, LLC, All Rights Reserved

Mary McCarthy All quotations by permission of Margo Viscusi

John Middleton Murry Quotation by permission of the Society of Authors

Sean O'Casey Quotation by permission of the Estate of Sean O'Casey

INDEX